D1357348

Personal Relationships and Social Support

Personal Relationships and Social Support

edited by

Steve Duck

with
Roxane Cohen Silver

SAGE Publications
London · Newbury Park · New Delhi

Chapter 1 © Geoff Leatham and Steve Duck, 1990
Chapter 2 © Carolyn E. Cutrona, Julie A. Suhr and Robin MacFarlane, 1990
Chapter 3 © Anita P. Barbee, 1990
Chapter 4 © Brant R. Burleson, 1990
Chapter 5 © John Eckenrode and Elaine Wethington, 1990
Chapter 6 © Daena Goldsmith and Malcolm R. Parks, 1990
Chapter 7 © John J. La Gaipa, 1990
Chapter 8 © John H. Berg and Kelly E. Piner, 1990
Chapter 9 © Stephen Brand and Barton J. Hirsch, 1990
Chapter 10 © Gregory R. Pierce, Barbara R. Sarason and Irwin G. Sarason, 1990
Chapter 11 © David L. Morgan, 1990

First published 1990

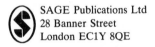

SAGE Publications Ltd
28 Banner Street
London EC1Y 8QE

SAGE Publications Inc
2111 West Hillcrest Drive
Newbury Park, California 91320

SAGE Publications India Pvt Ltd
32, M-Block Market
Greater Kailash - I
New Delhi 110 048

British Library Cataloguing in Publication data
Personal relationships and social support.
1. Interpersonal relationships
I. Duck, Steve, *1946–* II. Silver, Roxane Cohen
302

ISBN 0–8039–8340–9

Library of Congress catalog card number 90–060967

Phototypeset by Input Typesetting Ltd, London

Printed in Great Britain by Billing and Sons Ltd, Worcester

Contents

Contributors   viii
Preface   x
Acknowledgements   xv

1   *Conversations with Friends and the Dynamics of Social Support*
Geoff Leatham and Steve Duck   1

2   *Interpersonal Transactions and the Psychological Sense of Support*
Carolyn E. Cutrona, Julie A. Suhr, and Robin MacFarlane   30

3   *Interactive Coping: The Cheering-up Process in Close Relationships*
Anita P. Barbee   46

4   *Comforting as Social Support: Relational Consequences of Supportive Behaviors*
Brant R. Burleson   66

5   *The Process and Outcome of Mobilizing Social Support*
John Eckenrode and Elaine Wethington   83

6   *Communicative Strategies for Managing the Risks of Seeking Social Support*
Daena Goldsmith and Malcolm R. Parks   104

7   *The Negative Effects of Informal Support Systems*
John J. La Gaipa   122

8   *Social Relationships and the Lack of Social Relationships*
John H. Berg and Kelly E. Piner   140

9   *The Contribution of Social Networks, Work-shift Schedules, and the Family Life Cycle to Women's Well-being*
Stephen Brand and Barton J. Hirsch   159

10   *Integrating Social Support Perspectives: Working Models, Personal Relationships, and Situational Factors*
Gregory R. Pierce, Barbara R. Sarason, and Irwin G. Sarason   173

11   *Combining the Strengths of Social Networks, Social Support, and Personal Relationships*
David L. Morgan   190

References   216
Author Index   245
Subject Index   251

To Joanna, who so adroitly combines skills in personal
relationships and social support

Contributors

Anita P. Barbee, Dept of Psychology, University of Louisville, Louisville, KY 40292, USA

John H. Berg, Dept of Psychology, University of Mississippi, University, MS 38677, USA

Stephen Brand, Dept of Psychology, University of Illinois at Urbana-Champaign, 603 East Daniel St, Champaign, IL 61820, USA

Brant R. Burleson, Dept of Communication, Purdue University, Heavilon Hall, West Lafayette, IN 47907, USA

Carolyn E. Cutrona, Dept of Psychology, Spence Labs, University of Iowa, Iowa City, IA 52242, USA

Steve Duck, Dept of Communication Studies, 151-CSB, University of Iowa, Iowa City, IA 52242, USA

John Eckenrode, Dept of Human Development and Family Studies, Cornell University, Ithaca, NY 14853, USA

Daena Goldsmith, Dept of Speech Communication, University of Maryland, College Park, MD 20742, USA

Barton J. Hirsch, School of Education, Northwestern University, Evanston, IL 60201, USA

John J. La Gaipa, Dept of Psychology, University of Windsor, Windsor, Ontario, N9E 2K9, Canada

Geoff Leatham, Dept of Communication Studies, University of Iowa, Iowa City, IA 52242, USA

Robin MacFarlane, Dept of Psychology, Spence Labs, University of Iowa, Iowa City, IA 52242, USA

David L. Morgan, Institute on Aging, Portland State University, PO Box 751, Portland, OR 97207, USA

Malcolm R. Parks, Dept of Speech Communication, Raitt 205, DL-15, University of Washington, Seattle, WA 98195, USA

Gregory R. Pierce, Dept of Psychology, NI-25, University of Washington, Seattle, WA 98195, USA

Kelly E. Piner, Dept of Psychology, University of Mississippi, University, MS 38677, USA

Barbara R. Sarason, Dept of Psychology, NI-25, University of Washington, Seattle, WA 98195, USA

Irwin G. Sarason, Dept of Psychology, NI-25, University of Washington, Seattle, WA 98195, USA

Julie A. Suhr, Dept of Psychology, Spence Labs, University of Iowa, Iowa City, IA 52242, USA

Elaine Wethington, Dept of Human Development and Family Studies, Cornell University, Ithaca, NY 14853, USA

Preface

This book lays the groundwork for the thesis that the two presently separate literatures on Social Support, on the one hand, and on Personal Relationships, on the other, could learn more from each other and cooperate more than they do at present. I think this is a hypothesis whose time has come, although when I originally proposed it to a leader in the field of social support in 1986, he responded with surprise. 'What on earth,' he asked, as I tried to persuade him to come to talk at the first Iowa Conference on Personal Relationships, 'have those two fields got to say to one another?' At that time I think many would have agreed with him: one field dealt essentially with the consequences of relationships, while the other dealt with the antecedents. Indeed, there are still possibly some readers who have not noted the undercurrents of change and who may approach the conjoining of the two fields with some understandable cautious skepticism. Nonetheless they could be guided by the insight of the above person, who came to the conference and gave a talk, but, having stayed to listen to the rest of the conference, later confided in me that he had completely changed his mind about the relevance of the two fields to each other and now saw clear connections.

What is so persuasive about the conjunction? As will be clear from the chapters in this book, roughly half of which are 'from' each of the fields, there are distinct, common themes. Almost all chapters focus on the transactions that occur between pairs of people in situations where help is needed or desired, or where such offers of help spring naturally from the transactions of daily relationships. A strong emphasis in the personal-relationships field is now on the processes of relationshipping as much as it is on their antecedents (Clark and Reis, 1988; Duck and Sants, 1983). This translates in effect into an emphasis on the real, mundane, day-to-day transactional conduct of social and personal relationships. An equally strong emphasis in the Social Support literature is now on the mechanisms of delivery of social support (Gottlieb, 1985, 1988, 1990; Heller, 1989; Hobfoll and Stokes, 1988). This also translates fairly easily into 'transactions' or processes of daily relating, given the fact implicit in all social-support research that help is delivered by persons whom the target person knows, and thus, by implication,

interacts with fairly often. As the chapters in this book will show, we come to understand both relationshipping and helping if we understand general relational processes, both of day-to-day living and also of specific cases of helping, comforting, sympathizing, and assisting in coping with living. Indeed, such special or crisis-driven activities are rooted in, and contextualized by, the everyday lives of ourselves and our subjects. In a phrase, 'A friend in need is a friend indeed' and we need to understand both 'friendship' and 'need' in order to see exactly how the theory behind the proverb actually works.

I believe that in years to come people will marvel that these two literatures with so much to say to each other could ever coexist without a great deal of cross-referencing for so long. Nevertheless these are early days and a notable feature of the present volume is that chapters are identified with their particular preferred source literature rather easily. Not yet are chapters in social support co-authored with persons having strong connections to the literature on personal relationships, or vice versa, and the occasional wheel is therefore invented in two places at once or parallel evolution of concepts occurs. The process of becoming familiar with each other's literatures and themes is not easy and will take some time, but this book hopes to take the initiative and provide both the leadership and the demonstration that will bring this process about, to the common good.

To emphasize the interconnection, I have arranged the chapters in a way that brings out the similarities between the two literatures' major concepts. In the first chapter Geoff Leatham and I argue for the place of daily routines in our understanding of both relation-ships and social support. We suggest that the language that is used by friends, their talk, and their everyday conversations, are the basis for their relationships and for the sense of attachment that underlies the perception that support is available when needed. Also rooted in the daily talk of friends is the specific reaction to a crisis or special need, and therefore researchers in the future should attend more closely to the conversations of friends.

In the second chapter, Carolyn Cutrona, Julie Suhr, and Robin MacFarlane make an interesting case for analyzing transactions during helping behavior, using the scheme for analyzing interdependence first proposed in the book *Close relationships* by Kelley el al. (1983). This is a quite direct importation of concepts from the personal-relationships literature and a very important and provoca-tive one. Cutrona et al. find that long-standing personal factors influence both interpersonal behaviors and the interpretation of events and that studies of the nonverbal behavioral context for

supportive transactions are needed as well as those focussing on language.

In Chapter 3, Anita Barbee describes and evaluates her intriguing studies of the cheering-up process as actually conducted in existing friendships. This work indicates, in a fresh and innovative research program, that seeking and giving of support is essentially an interactive process, and that characteristics of the helpers, as well as of the targets, are important in the provision of interactive coping. In this respect she draws attention to the fact that interactive coping is difficult to do well, and so she hints at some of the problems studied under the negative effects of social support mentioned in other chapters.

Chapter 4 shows us the extensive program of research that has been conducted over several years by Brant Burleson as he studies the actual dynamics of comforting in face-to-face transactions. As he argues, actions, rather than feelings, convey support. Burleson has done an impressive amount of work aimed at teasing apart the elements of comforting and their influence by language strategies and cognitive structure. His thesis in the present chapter is that certain support behaviors may have profound relational consequences. He reverses the normal routing of studies in social support and asks the important question of how support affects relationships rather than vice versa. For instance, some studies of comforting skills indicate that sophistication of a person's comforting skills affects the degree to which that person is liked by peers. Thus, Burleson's chapter indicates with some force the complex interdependence of the topic of relationships and social support.

In the next chapter, Eckenrode and Wethington, too, focus on the mobilization of support and the consequences for relaters of the attempt to obtain support from the network. They rightly draw attention to the need for much greater research clarity on the question of how people activate their support networks and mobilize the provision of supportive behavior that has so often been supposed to provide comfort in times of stress. As they point out, the social-support literature has only recently begun to address the specific issue of the ways in which support is actually mobilized or delivered. Eckenrode and Wethington review help-seeking as one subset of the support-mobilization concept, but one that precedes its activation. They urge researchers to pay more attention to the routine activity of daily relating and recommend multimethod approaches to the development of research in social support, aided by work on relationship processes.

The next chapter, by Goldsmith and Parks, introduces the difficulties that are often faced by those intending to seek support and

the chapter deals with the communicative strategies that persons use to reduce the risks of seeking social support. They note that the disclosure of problems entails vulnerability and poses social and interpersonal dangers to the individual. The authors consider the ways in which people experience and respond to support dilemmas when they seek help with problems in romantic relationships. The work thus stands squarely at the intersection of social support and personal relationships. In attempting to interrelate the four root terms of interactive dilemmas, social networks, social support, and relationships development, Goldsmith and Parks stress that relationships are created in and experienced through communication. The authors end with a call for the research field to uncover the interactive and communicative dynamics of social-support processes.

The complexity and dynamic force of some of these elements are drawn out further in the chapter by La Gaipa which focusses on the negative side of informal support systems, especially as experienced by the elderly and aging. Using a systems approach, La Gaipa emphasizes the conflicting internal, interpersonal, and social forces that must be negotiated in the delivery of support in an everyday context. He deals with the negative effects of giving support – or of giving it inappropriately – in the pressing circumstances of everyday life. He also draws attention to the conflict between the dependence on necessary resources provided by the support system, on the one hand, and the needs of the individual for autonomy, on the other – a conflict of which the elderly are all too well aware.

Wider questions are tackled by Berg and Piner in their chapter on the matter of the very existence of social and personal relationships. They attempt to relate relationship characteristics to different types of social support and the observed changes in psychological well-being that are consequent upon its receipt. These authors find evidence that, for lonely people, the most important type of support is in the form of companionship and integration. They point out that the existence of certain types of people in one's network and the number of interactions that one has with them become important factors to consider, especially for males. They leave us with the intriguing questions, 'What types of social support and what types of social or personal relationships affect a person's feeling of loneliness?' and 'How do they accomplish this?'

Brand and Hirsch provide some of the answers in their careful analysis of relationships and social support in shiftworkers. They emphasize the complexity of the arrangements of daily living that impact on a person's needs for support and their ability to mobilize

support in that context. Their intriguing work looks at the effects of shiftwork on women's well-being, and makes the case that detailed daily social contexts must be picked apart by careful research if we are to truly understand the mechanisms underlying social support. In particular, their work draws sharp attention to the surrounding contextual networks and the nexus of relationships in which a given relationship exists. Such contexts and networks influence the availability of support in subtle ways that need further exploration.

The final two chapters in this volume have a broad integrative purpose that arises from some of the specific issues covered in other chapters. In the first of these two chapters, Pierce, Sarason, and Sarason argue for the adoption of an interactional framework to guide research on social support. They are clear that social support is a product of interacting influences among persons, their personal relationships, and the situations that they help to create and to which they respond. For Pierce et al., social support is not simply an objective property of social interactions. Instead, it reflects interactive influences among the intrapersonal, interpersonal, and situational contexts in which social efforts take place. This chapter thus offers a challenging and provocative new view of the social-support process based on a greater understanding of the interactions that make up everyday relationships and the broader contexts surrounding them.

This last theme is also drawn out skilfully by Morgan in the final chapter. He widens the focus to include the field of social-network analysis and shows many different ways in which integration of the three areas (personal relationships, social support, and social networks) can be extended to complement the efforts of the others. Morgan argues that these three areas are in fact different perspectives on the broader topic of social relationships. He reviews and presents research-based evidence on the value of combining the three viewpoints this way, rather than just the two of personal relationships and social support.

As such, Morgan closes the book with an implicit challenge to future researchers to use the book as a jumping-off point for the future extension of the concept that it embodies: collaboration in the research community between people with different sorts of background, source material, and expertise. It is to be hoped that the book provides just that impetus for redrawing some of our intellectual maps to include the New World vision that it suggests, and which it demonstrates is not impossible to realize.

Steve Duck

Acknowledgements

As usual, Chris Brenneman has done an excellent, and seemingly untiring, job in dealing with the tremendous amounts of correspondence that are generated by an enterprise like this. She also helped in the compilation of the reference list at the end of the book, which makes the book a useful bibliographic source for workers in the two areas of personal relationships, on the one hand, and social support, on the other.

Finally, I thank Roxy Silver for her invaluable discussions in the formation of the concept of this book, for laying some of the groundwork for incorporation of some of the authors, and for her valuable comments on a number of the chapters. She deserves much of the credit for the working out of the general concepts in the book, even if the final responsibility for the ultimate product rests with me.

Steve Duck

1

Conversations with Friends and the Dynamics of Social Support

Geoff Leatham and Steve Duck

To read the early literature on social support is to be faced with images of human beings and of friends as kindly and competent people who provide the culturally expected close personal relationships. Friends gain support from each other through the mere existence of their relationship, in such an image. Increasingly, recent work has refined this early representation and urged us, in addition, to focus not only on the negative aspects of asking for and providing social support (see La Gaipa, Chapter 7, this volume), but also on the dynamics of giving and receiving support in the context of personal relationships (Gottlieb, 1990; Heller, 1989; Hobfoll and Stokes, 1988).

In addition to their focus on network structure, network density, numbers of available confidants, and personality characteristics of the provider and the needy person, some approaches to social support now emphasize the transactions occurring in personal relationships (Gottlieb, 1988; Hobfoll and Stokes, 1988) – a theme embodied in the nature of this book itself (see especially Cutrona et al., Chapter 2, this volume; Pierce et al., Chapter 10 this volume).

Any emphasis on the transactions of social support aims to tell us *how* social support is offered, how it is received, and what it means to a given person in a relational context. We support those researchers who are studying such transactions, in terms of comforting, giving advice, or supportive interaction between particular individuals (see Cutrona et al., Chapter 2; Burleson, Chapter 4; Eckenrode and Wethington, Chapter 5). The special instances of advice seeking and support giving that occur at dramatic times of crisis certainly advance understanding of social support (for example, Barrera et al., 1981; Cutrona, 1986b; Hirsch, 1979), but we contend that they also arise from the routine, mundane, under-researched interactions of normal daily life. Our argument is that attention needs to be paid not only to the obvious heroic instances of transactions of social support but also to the run-of-the-mill

transactions of friendship that provide the backdrop against which social support is delivered in a crisis or circumstances of special need. As is true of much social science, researchers on social support have tended to focus on the 'figure' of social life's special events and crises, without exploring such 'ground' of routine that provides its everyday context (Duck, 1986).

We realize that without identification of a clear crisis, and the ability to catalog adaptive responses of the target's personal network, the identification of social support is difficult. As Gottlieb (1983, 1990) points out, support is a multidimensional construct. It may well be impossible to draw sharp lines around conduct within personal relationships and say, 'This is social support' and 'This is just normal relationship behavior.' It is our contention, however, that the normal conduct of personal relationships is often supportive, even in the absence of a specific stressor, request for support, or the intention to provide support. Such routine transactions, we argue, are the source of feelings of 'perceived support,' while the dramatic cases may provide both this and 'actual support.'

We will return again to the point that the conduct of social support makes the latter difficult to identify in all facets. For the present, we will take our cue from Albee's (1980; cited in Rook and Dooley, 1985) model of support:

$$\text{Symptoms of disorder} = \frac{\text{vulnerability} \times \text{life stress}}{\text{coping} \times \text{social support}}$$

This model views social support as the interpersonal resources mobilized to deal with the strain inherent in living. This differentiates social support from coping along neat lines. Coping is the mobilization of personal resources, both psychological and tangible, to deal with life stresses. Therefore, any material, psychological, or social resources mobilized to deal with life strain are either support or coping. If the resources are governed by the individual under strain, it is part of the coping process. If the resources are governed by another, social support is occurring.

There are two issues with this conception of social support that must be dealt with. First, the provision and receipt of social support occur within the experience of those in the transaction (Gergen and Gergen, 1983). This makes the 'objective' measure of social support difficult. A mate, large numbers of friends, or close relationships may have some link to actual or enacted support, but the relationship is correlational rather than causal. Second, since so many different stresses and so many different social behaviors can fall within this conception, we hold little present hope that future researchers will be able to make sweeping statements about

all types of social support. We predict that careful researchers will continue to identify and study specific stressors and responses they are interested in within a specific context. We commend efforts like Gottlieb's (1983) to provide broader taxonomies of behaviors that seem supportive in a wide variety of contexts and draw out underlying dimensions. Such approaches seem to offer hope of providing greater generalizability, but the micro-level exploration must be done first.

To lay the ground for such micro-level exploration, our primary focus is on talk, conversations, and the communication which moves the wheels of social interaction. We are also concerned with processes through which memories for these activities are made, since these shape people's beliefs both about social support, on the one hand, and about personal relationships and partners or members of the network, on the other. In both these foci of concern, our interest is in the ways in which people represent to themselves and to others (through the immediacy of the language, the style of talk, the intimacy of the conversation, for example) various aspects of life, including the existence and nature of relationships, the nature of perceived stressors, feeling for the partner and attachment to the network, one's own psychological make-up or ability to cope, and one's availability to help and support the other.

The thesis of this chapter, therefore, is that, while social support is based on social interaction, it is seen to be available, and is actually delivered, through and by reason of the *conduct* of personal relationships through routine conversations, and in the daily encounters of life. Social support springs out of the everyday activity and discourse that characterize any existing relationship and so 'situate' it or give it context. In other words, the bones of our personal relationships – namely, talk and (shared) memories – give form and meaning to instances of support, while the unique rules and rituals enacted within our personal relationships help us to decide how to provide or request support and how to interpret and react to it.

Personal Relationships, Social Support and Communication

Conversation as Medium

Analysis of discourse has been the special province of rhetorical theory and it is instructive to consider the themes that run through such analyses before indicating ways in which they may apply to the present discussion. Rhetorical theory (Hauser, 1988) urges that we regard talk as *situated action* and attend to the situation in which

speaking occurs, including the role of the audience. The situation of speaking, including the perceived needs of the audience members, clearly influences the sentiments that are expressed and the ways in which they are spoken (Montgomery, 1988). Talk is also *symbolic action*, in that symbols are created, used, and understood by the participants, often on the basis of previous interactions. In close relationships such symbols are often personal ones with unique meaning to the partners and can recall past activities, favorite times, or other themes with sentimental value (Baxter, 1987). Talk is also the *transacting* of symbols through the joint interaction of 'audience' and 'speaker,' and the shared meanings that they have achieved through joint history, mutual understandings, and past relationship construction. Thus, relationships are frequently characterized by personal idioms or special words for activities, feelings, people, or parts of the body, and these personal idioms are worked out by the two partners uniquely (Hopper et al., 1981). Talk is *social action* because it involves one person attempting to engage another through interpersonally significant meaning attached to the symbols. In brief, it involves one person influencing another person or another person's views of events through choice of language *style* as well as content (Duck and Pond, 1989; Norton, 1983). Finally, it is *strategic action*, involving the intent, planning, and preparation that go into attempts to influence others, although in some cases the influence is effected at a high level, such as 'I will try to make X feel sympathetic to the plight as I see it,' rather than specific planning about particular words (Berger, 1988).

Although these terms have been used most successfully in the analysis of public address and the construction of speeches, Duck and Pond (1989) have used these concepts to show that conversations in everyday relationships are 'rhetorical' in the sense that they follow the above principles in acting upon an Other person. Everyday communication and memory serve, by means of similar rhetorical methods, to represent relational reality to the Other person and to the self as one attempts to persuade the Other to adopt one's view of reality. A clear example is provided in the present context when a person begins a conversation by saying 'Hey, we're friends, right?' or 'You are the person I feel closest to,' both of which lay the ground for exploration of the rights and obligations that follow from the role. Thus ' . . . and I know I can trust my friends to help me' or ' . . . so naturally you are the person I feel best able to turn to when I get into trouble' would each be unremarkable continuations of the clauses above. Equally, and in everyday life quite predictably, a person's representation of the perceived crisis would follow from such opening remarks. In them

the person would depict daily events, whether hassles or crises, that seemed to him or her to be problematic. These, we argue, are not best viewed as objective reports, but compose a rhetorical representation of the difficulty that suits the speaker, embodies the speaker's approach to the events, and invites the listener to accept the description as 'the way things are and the way they must be faced.' Thus, everyday life conversations create and embody a person's fluctuating hopes and expectations and present them in a way that the partner has to accept, at least at first, as the basis for discussion of them. We can expect that stories about daily life events are somewhat selective in their reporting, may show the speakers up in a good light, might depict the speakers as a victim of another person, or as too self-sacrificing for their own good, or as overwhelmed by insuperable odds (Antaki, 1987). In brief, everyday conversations and explanations serve to present the speaker's views in a rhetorically seductive way rather than to provide an objective report, pure and simple. Conversations, whether in supportive contexts or not, are thus to be seen as active representations of the person's circumstances, rather than as mere media for the transmission of thought, facts, reality, feelings or needs from one mind to another. Conversations depict, embellish, and give an 'angle' on events, rather than simply reporting them. They are significant in representing the person's views of his or her circumstances, because they represent the person's – and to some extent the dyad's – basis for approaching the problem, receiving or seeking social support. It is therefore important for researchers to gain insight into these processes and the ways in which everyday talk can influence the giving and receiving of support.

Whatever else is true of personal relationships, it is undeniable that they are 'situated' and given context through communication. There is increasing evidence that the conversations of everyday life are psychologically important situators for people, even when the substance of the conversations is reported to be of little direct value to the relationship (Duck and Rutt, 1989). Talk with friends is often reported to be insubstantial or trivial in terms of its content, and yet it serves important bonding functions. While conversation has typically been studied through the analysis of discrete, often context-free, messages, an important part of communication is the *memory* for social action that provides the continuing thread of discourse. Duck and Rutt (1989), using the Iowa Communication Record (ICR), a conversational diary method reported in more detail below, have shown that subjects often recall their most meaningful conversations of a given day to have lasted less than ten minutes, to have been low in self-disclosure, and to have had

marginal impact on the future form of the relationship – but nevertheless to be rated as significant for the existence of the relationship
and for feelings about the partner. In short, conversations are
usually recalled as routine and mundane in content, yet important
psychologically and emotionally for the creation and perpetuation
of the person's *sense* of being in a relationship (Duck and Sants,
1983), without truly doing anything to affect the nature of the
relationship or what it *actually* provides. Clearly this sense of being
in a relationship could extend also to a sense of being supported,
a sense of the reliability and helpfulness of the partner, a sense of
being needed by the Other, a sense of despair about the predicament, a sense of one's ability to cope if supported by the Other, a
sense of what needs to be done, and so on. Thus, the content of
conversation may on occasion be less important than the attachment sensed through conversation. In such circumstances the conversation could honestly be reported to a social-support researcher
as one that offered no support and yet paradoxically added to the
sense of being supported.

From these relatively simple points about subjective perception
and phenomenal features of relationships follow some observations
important for the conceptualization of social-support delivery in
everyday life. For one thing, analysis of daily conversations reminds
us of two obvious facts. First, although both parties to a conversation are in some sense in 'the same' interaction, nevertheless,
many scholars have found that each person's recall of the conversation is frequently somewhat different from the other person's
(Duck and Rutt, 1989; Gottman, 1979; Noller and Venardos, 1986).
Second, the essential influence of the conversations upon the person's future behavior is not 'what happened, as viewed or defined
by an outside observer,' but 'what happened as recalled (often
through filtering and editing of memory) by the person being ques-
tioned.' To put this dramatically, all the 'objective support' in the
world is of absolutely no value whatsoever to the individual if the
individual fails to appreciate that it was offered. Once again, we
are led to emphasize the need to clarify a person's experience of a
partner and a relationship through recall of everyday conversation
since such recall provides the basis for understanding that partner's
socially supportive transactional activity.

The Personal Relationship as a Frame for Social Support

Focus on everyday recall of conversation thus faces us with two
intriguing elements of a subject's perceptions about the relationships in which any delivery of social support actually occurs. Yet

both of them show that the continuance of a relationship from which to seek support is, to some degree, a subjective mental representation or belief, and that a key element of this belief focusses on future orientation. By this we mean that the continued existence of a relationship is *perceived by the person* to the extent that the future of the relationship is predictable and definable, and dependent on relationship awareness (that is, relationship mindfulness, or thinking about interaction patterns, comparisons, or contrasts between self and partner in the relationship – Acitelli, 1987; Burnett, 1986). While some scholars interpret continuance of relationships to be based on the relationships' *history*, we, by contrast, will emphasize the implications of partner's beliefs in *the future* of the relationship and we will assume that the thing that makes analysis of relationships relevant here is that they are seen as 'unfinished business.' In other words, from the point of view of the relationship participants, a relationship is a dynamic entity that is incomplete because it has an essentially indeterminate future. Even if today the partners happen to be reasonably confident that the future is pretty well set in its tracks, tomorrow could bring a catastrophe or delight that will influence the form, intimacy, or direction of the relationship.

A second important point about the perception of relationships is the paradox that they change and fluctuate in the minds of participants as a function of their experience of one another day to day, and yet smooth trends of increased intimacy may be reported by participants looking back over their relationships. As Miell (1987) has so interestingly shown, members of relationships are very likely to predict the future of their relationship based on *the last three days* of experience of it rather than on any longer term considerations, even when their relationship has lasted for more than six months. Even if such transformation of memory occurs only in students in certain kinds of relationships (who were the subjects in Miell's study), nonetheless the point is that any person's recall of the trends in their relationship is likely to be affected by recent and regular experiences (cf. Acitelli, 1987). This point should encourage us to explore whether researchers should take for granted, as is usually done, that a relationship is a relationship is a relationship, and is best assessed as a stable feature of the person's life, as the 'mean perception,' as it were, calculated from a range of different perceptions. By contrast, we urge researchers to *verify* that the person's daily experience of his or her relationships is best characterized by the mean, rather than by some measure of variance: to rely only on a person's 'average' experience of a

relationship is to pay no attention to the fluctuations around that average that are experienced day by day.

The above arguments are essentially process oriented: we argue for a vision of social support embedded in the relational, communicative, and, to some extent phenomenal, processes of everyday life. However, it is also important to recognize the paradox that subjective reports of processes do not deal with them as processes, but as states, or as time-bound events (see Duck and Pond, 1989). In essence, human beings are uncomfortable with a process style of language and, as Marcel Proust put it, prefer to describe the continuous flow of experience as a stack of discrete and separated still-photographs rather than movies. To produce such 'photographs' naturally requires subjects (and, let it be noted, other human beings such as experimenters) to make their own particular choices about the best ways to 'chunk' the process into describable units. Thus, although we emphasize process here, we recognize that a first attempt to study the transactive social-support process will require that we begin to understand the ways in which persons (or persons encouraged to do so by researchers) break it down into recognizable segments for description.

Relationships are made up of individuals, and while most relationship work involves the joint construction of dyadic and relational approaches to life and to each other, the individuality of partners is never fully extinguished. Each person has a mind and has views that derive from its operation. Each also can make choices about any aspect of the relationship – even about its continued existence – for while relationships require the activity of two persons to keep them alive, they need only one person to occasion their death (Simmel, 1950). In exploring the nature of relationships and of support, then, we can only benefit if we analyze more closely the individuals' psychological experience in the dyad.

Social Support within Personal Relationships

Just as persons can transform their beliefs about relationships, however, so too the perceived nature of stress is subject to such transformations. One complication here is that the existence of the stressor, as 'objectively determined' by the researcher, has too often been assumed to be the same thing as its phenomenal existence for the person (but see Hobfoll and Stokes, 1988). However, not all people who feel the impact of a stressor experience it as equally forceful at all times and in all circumstances. These seem so remarkable a set of phenomena that workers in this area have begun to devote more attention to it and explore the phenomenal changes

that occur in a subject's perception of, and addressing of, a stressor over a period of time (Lazarus and Folkman, 1984; Vaux, 1988). Not only do we need to know how social support affects a person's reactions to stress, but also we should know how social support and personal relationships, amongst other things, affect a person's *perception* of the force, danger, or stigma of a given stressor at a given time (Hobfoll and Stokes, 1988). In short, all of a person's phenomenal perceptions of the stressor, especially those occasioned by relating to others (Duck, 1988), are important to consider if we are to understand the extent to which the person's own psychological processes act as a buffer of the effects of stress.

Equally, although we have so far emphasized the psychological effects upon a person that are exerted by memory for daily experience of others, so too the context of the relationship urges us to pay closer attention to the dynamics of relationships and support. All communication and all relationships take place in a context, whether provided by a culture, by a social group, by a particular relationship, or by an individual's personal style. Personal relationships between a person and an associate are likely to affect the seeking and the giving of support in a number of critical ways (Gottlieb, 1990). For one thing, even best friends are not immune from dislike of listening to unrelenting painful self-disclosures, complaints, self-pity, and depressed communication for unspecified lengths of time. Thus, the relationship between the person and the would-be supporter could easily be threatened by continual seeking or provision of support. For this and other reasons given above, we need to know more about the precise relational circumstances and the communicative context in which any form of support is sought or offered. Second, although a person may be a good friend, he or she may in the past have been or may now be unwilling, unable, or incompetent to provide specific sorts of support. Such direct, personal, transacted experience of a relational partner's past performance obviously affects one's willingness to seek that person's support or heed that person's advice rather more than does the 'pure existence' of a relationship. In this light, some consideration of a person's experience of a partner's communicative competence seems necessary for a full understanding of social-support provision (Spitzberg and Cupach, 1985). Third, if previous attempts at support have had negative outcomes, a person may blame the partner, devaluing present support attempts. This tension may emerge only during periods of stress. Therefore, we need a close analysis of the relationship between offering/receiving support and the relational and communicative dynamics surrounding the transactions. Fourth, social support is as much an accommodation

to the expectations, demands, or needs of personal relationships as it is a direct accommodation to a present stressor (Gottlieb, 1990). For that reason, provision of social support can do as much to destabilize a relationship as relationships can do to stabilize a person in the face of stress. Given this, we assume that there will be a close connection between support, relationships, and a person's psychological experience of both. Close attention to subjects' recall of everyday life conversations will show us changes in this psychological environment as much as in the social environment.

Thus, while relationships are originally created and maintained socially, the supportive transactions within personal relationships exert their effects psychologically. In this sense, all relationships are processes that are subject to individuals' perceptions and beliefs about them: they can change their character in the future and there are no absolute cast-iron guarantees provided by the past. This fact, we argue, has a psychological effect on the conduct of relationships, especially in the context of social support. When a person needs help, he or she is forced to represent, through talk and behavior, the nature of the relationship as he or she sees it so that the character of the relationship as represented can be used as a basis for presuming upon it.

Likewise, perceptions of support are variable and responsive to current situations, stimuli, or events. Other people have their own lives to get on with and their specific availability to help at a particular time may not reflect their *general* availability, as defined in terms of their perceived usual willingness to help. This fact may have been obscured by use of global questions about the nature of support from others – the kind of support normally assessed in social-support questionnaires such as Sarason et al. (1983) – since subjects are cued, by the wording of the questions, to give global answers that emphasize their own and other people's *dispositional* factors and the persistence of enduring qualities of social support. Thus is research like Norris and Murrell's (1984) study of 1402 older adults focussed on global measures of stress. Multiple regression was used to determine whether six hypothesized functions of resources were supported at the expense of being able to discover the unique ways that the relationships may operate. Indeed, the nature of the social-support network was reduced to either 'strong' or 'weak' resources. Norris and Murrell did find that global measures of network strength generated global, positive results. Strong-resource persons had an advantage over weak-resource persons at all levels of life events using such global measures of persons' dispositions. Researchers should, however, note that in a different context, Schwarz et al. (1988) have shown that

the form of questions strongly guides subjects' responses; for example, the end-points of scales are often seen by subjects as defining the permissible or normal range of responses and this leads them to presume where the 'average' response will be found, if they wish to locate themselves relative to it and appear normal. Since people are often asked to indicate generalized levels of support, those are just what they are likely to report, without reference to the specifics of a particular needy occasion, and where they are asked about specific occasions they may report responses free from all the normal embedding, transactional, fluctuating, daily context.

It is thus self-evident that people are not continually seeking support in any direct way and the likelihood exists that personal reflection and other events in a person's life reassign the need for support to different levels of intensity from time to time. Thus, a person's need for social support either would not be constant or else is constant but would become more or less obtrusive in their thinking as time goes by and events or interactions change the person's focus of attention.

Given the above, it is our contention that the nature of a person's relationships affects the person's perceptions and characterization of the stressor and that we should therefore look at the dynamics of the person's personal networks (Hobfoll and Stokes, 1988). Those who look at social support and stress have amply documented network variables in terms of structure but not dynamics (see, for example, reviews by Bruhn and Philips, 1984; Murawski et al., 1978; or Tardy, 1985). In general, network size and access to strong ties have been used to differentiate subjects who are high or low in social support, however the researchers have defined social support. It is, of course, critical, as has been recognized by several authors (for example, Acock and Hurlbert, 1990; Milardo, 1982), for researchers not to treat these variables in any absolute sense, but to appreciate that in the real world they are subject to fluctuation or moderation by other events or feelings. Researchers quickly recognized the different quality of stress experienced during the weekend or when one's telephone lines are down or the car is out of service or a critical member of the network is away on vacation. From the point of view of the needy person, access to strong ties is a measure of *potential* availability of support when *actual* availability is what is needed on a given occasion of stress or on an occasion when a constant stressor becomes momentarily more urgent, phenomenally. Sudden increases in perceived stress – the only form of stress that really counts for people, after all – can happen in the middle of the night, just as much as at other times, and then access is probably simply illusory, but certainly

problematic and dependent on one's relationship to the sought-for help giver. In brief, then, access to support must be treated as a *variable*, given the dynamics of the real lives as lived by real human beings (Duck, 1986). Clearly, the way in which these dynamics are energized is through conversation and communication with network members and this depends to some degree on a variety of factors. Ease of access is clearly determined in part by the person's feelings about others in the circumstances, and this is what defines 'actual accessibility.' What has been overlooked, we contend, are, first, the stressed person's attitudes to accessing the network; second, the present (perhaps temporary) perceived state of the relationships between the person and others in the network; and third, the perceived availability of the network members relative to the perceived reasonableness of seeking access.

As indicated above and confirmed by diary studies of stress day by day, a person's level of perceived stress fluctuates, depending on what is presently going on in the person's mind, in the rest of life, in his or her daily conversations, and in surrounding circumstances (Cohen and Syme, 1985; Lazarus and Folkman, 1984). The person's way of thinking about stress is likely to be affected by his or her current focus on the stressful issue. This will be affected by the extent to which conversations with friends or supporters DEfocus them from the problem, provide momentary support, and seem to provide new frames for viewing the stressor and the person's ability to cope with it. By contrast, conversations with friends can bring up new dimensions to the problem that were previously unimagined and emphasize hopelessness or fatalism about possible outcomes. (See, for example, the work of Hobfoll and London, 1986, on the 'pressure-cooker effect' and Riley and Eckenrode, 1986, on stress contagion). In brief, conversations with friends about a stressor can reformulate the person's beliefs about the stressor, one's ability to cope with it, and one's perception of oneself as a coper in general. Supporters invite or persuade the stressed individual to adopt an alternative view of the situation, which is in essence a rhetorical process, involving the adjusting of people to ideas and of ideas to people.

In the present context, we argue that consideration of those very day-to-day conversations, and the transactional operations on which they are based, is essential to the understanding of stress, social support, and personal relationships. It is necessary for workers in these areas to refocus their activity away from globalism and onto the minute particulars of the routine daily activities through which all three are experienced.

Methodological Implications

Interestingly, this analysis applies to research as much as to the everyday lives of subjects: researchers prefer to 'chunk' the world into static categories. Thus, although there have been other calls for re-interpretations of the older literature in ways that emphasize process (for example, Hobfoll and Stokes, 1988), such calls have not specified the need to explore daily conversations and have focussed instead on global outcome measures, often in the context of chronic stressors, such as long-term disease (Goldberg, 1981; Grant, 1985), rehabilitation from injury (Smith, 1979), coping with disabled children (Dunst et al., 1986; Ventura, 1986), or facing up to the stresses of war (Hobfoll and London, 1986). Thus, the emphasis on fluctuating perceptions of stress is diminished but so also is any emphasis on process or flow in the perception of relevant factors.

For the social scientist, the study of social support has allowed a rare and possibly meretricious opportunity to use concrete, chunked, 'still photographed' dependent measures such as mortality (Berkman and Syme, 1979), disease (Schaefer et al., 1981), and abuse (Salzinger, Kaplan and Artemyeff, 1983). Nevertheless, such emphases have been criticized, and Heller and Swindle (1983) in particular note the emphasis on predictive validity at the expense of construct validity. A process orientation, by contrast, invites us to focus not on finite influences on social support nor on the finalities of death and disease, but on the continuous parts of life that feed into daily experience of such finalities (or future finalities as they are anticipated). Equally, the independent variables should not be represented as solid-state chunks either. Recent work has focussed on network variables as a part of this orientation but has so far not identified the processual mechanisms by which these factors exert their effects and has not focussed much on the 'massaging' of the networks that occurs to keep them active (Acock and Hurlbert, 1990; Milardo, 1988). Yet networks exist as dynamic entities, not as ossified social structures, and they take their social and symbolic meaning from the ways in which they operate rather than from the ways in which the morphological properties can be schematically depicted by inventive scholars (see Wellman, 1985).

By using a message-based operationalization of social support (Albrecht and Adelman, 1987b), it is possible to code interactions indicating when social support occurs and what it is, from the outsider's point of view, and this has a value. A content coding scheme can easily be created by using categories generated from any of a number of conceptualizations of social support. Messages

can be coded for their function of reducing uncertainty about the situation (instrumental aid), reducing uncertainty about relational issues (socioemotional aid), or being non-supportive. Then within each category, the message can be coded more specifically. Nonetheless, such an approach is incomplete if it does not ask the *subject* to verify the meaning of the message within his or her concept system.

Using a message-based operationalization of social support has strong methodological implications for support researchers, but while we believe that this is important, more important is to record and analyze subjects' *recall* of such conversations, since this is where their phenomenological approach to the interaction has its effects – where, if you like, they create a sense of attachment that is independent of the content of the talk. For too long have messages been thought to be absolute in their effects: rather, we should begin to explore ways in which persons recall and 'editorialize' (Duck and Sants, 1983) their accounts of social experience, since it is through such interpretative activity that a person's response to the impact of a given interaction is to be espied.

In addition to assessing supportive interaction at the message level, we must also assess the relationship that gives meaning to the interaction. Efforts to understand the nature of the subjects' relationships have been limited to labeling the relationships (for example, as spouse, friend, co-worker) or asking for some self-reported estimate of closeness. In addition to being the most easily assessed dimensions of personal relationships, these labels could very well be the most significant dimensions, but could also be misleading. It seems both an unlikely assumption and a naive one, akin to the one made by workers in personal relationships who have constantly assumed that the existence of a certain type of relationship is a sufficient condition for deducing its quality. Thus, some theorists (for example, Kelley, 1983) have assumed that the existence of marriage is sufficient evidence for us to treat it as an intimate relationship or to believe that each partner has an intimate relationship, or that marriage is invariably an intimate relationship (with stressful marriages being a curious exception), and that quality experiences (of some sort) exist in that relationship. Nonetheless, non-intimate, unhappy, distressed, and rocky marriages exist, and most marriages and partnerships experience those features now and again. Therefore, the presumption of intimacy and the ready and satisfactory provision of the needs of individuals from that source are unfounded and cannot be presumed without careful checking. Not only is the very assumption suspect, but its globality and generality are naive. All partners in all relationships go through

periods of ups and downs, both individual and dyadic. Any general statement of the level of satisfaction, intimacy, or provision of support from such relationships should therefore be regarded as tentative and any attempt to provide a smooth curve or a steady defining label for the relationship should be seen in the same light as any mean in any group of subjects. The variance as well as any measure of central tendency can each represent interesting information about a phenomenon.

In the context of research on social support, questions focussing the subject on global answers about present and stable features of social support invite them to present their perceptions of social support in stable and global terms that imply invariance in their experience of particular partners and relationships. Hence, they are cued to focus on their general recall and so may fail to report realistically on their variable moods and the daily tactics of coping. Nonetheless, just as relationships are unfinished business, so, we believe, are perceptions of stress and of social support, and as such are all dynamic processes rather than stable features of a person's social experience.

These observations indicate that 'support as given' (from the supporter's perspective) is not necessarily quantitatively, qualitatively, or emotionally the same as 'support received' (from the person's point of view). Researchers need to move toward assessments of social support that are not only transactional in analytic focus but also person-centered in approach (cf. Hobfoll and Stokes, 1988) and also, in parallel, to do work 'triangulating' these perceptions with the perceptions of outside observers and those of the helper, to find out how each set of perceptions relates to those from the other perspective(s). In short, the nature of support requires an analysis similar to the one offered above for relationships: we researchers cannot assume that the mere claim for existence of support is an adequate basis for presuming anything about its quality, nor that the mere claim is tantamount to establishing agreement between partners about its nature and value. We should, perhaps, instead regard claims made about support as worthy of verification and treat support as a process inasmuch as it occurs in the context of other relationship processes.

Social Support as a Process

Structure
Conceptualization of any topic within the field of social support must create dynamic descriptions of four areas or be considered incomplete. There has been wide study of the *structure of the*

network in which support occurs. Though conflicts exist over the importance of various structural features of social networks, these features have proven significant across many different studies (Asher, 1984; Ell, 1984). In our view, there is a crucial difference between structure as depicted in a diagram and 'structure' as represented psychologically by the person embedded in it, rather as an anatomical depiction of a body in Gray's Anatomy does not tell us how it feels to be in one. 'Structure' – even if it feels static – nevertheless depends on conversational and relational processes and is therefore not truly static, but is liable to minor fluctuations and changes as events unfold. These fluctuations occur in subjects' representations of the network, not in 'real' changes – that is, changing reports of closeness/distance in respect of particular others are *psychologically* meaningful statements about 'the nature of the network.' It is time for researchers to treat such fluctuations not as mere measurement error, that should at all costs be partialed out of hard scientific description of subjects' worlds, but as something real for the subjects that we researchers need to explain and incorporate into theory.

Nature of Relationship

Second, *the nature of the relationships* within the subject's social network has been insufficiently studied in dynamic and processual terms. As Leavy puts it (1983: 5), 'Counting people and computing ratios concerning density and other structural variables does not touch the depth of the concept "support". . . . Social support must therefore be seen as the *availability* of helping relationships and the *quality* of those relationships' (italics added). Both availability and quality are concepts that relate to communication, however, since the person construes both of these concepts in terms of his or her probability estimates about the performance of others, and such estimates, valid or not, are the basis for social action. They are derived perforce from knowledge of the others, which is created, derived, extended, and refined through interactions that involve communication.

In this light it is easier to interpret the regular findings that people prefer to seek help from those to whom they are closest (DePaulo, 1978). Nonetheless, this preference can be seen to have several basic forces behind it as well as a confound, since closeness may be defined partly in terms of preference of access. Preference can indicate (a) personal inclination to approach particular (sorts of) others; (b) ease of access, in terms of proximity or time; (c) availability in terms of psychological closeness; (d) requirements of a role (for example, friends are *supposed* to help); (e) perception

of Other's accessibility, whether accurate or not; or (f) personal importance of the Other to the seeker even though the person is hard to access. For instance, a person may 'prefer' to approach another because of the belief that the Other 'knows me well and could empathize effectively with my predicament' or because 'the Other is my mother and that's what mothers are for.' These represent importantly different psychological sets and underlying beliefs. Clark (1983) lists studies showing that people most often turn to those they are close to, even though the problems differ widely. There seems little doubt that most perceived support comes from our close relationships but the possible dynamics for this remain to be carefully unearthed.

If close relationships are so important to the provision of support, we should know what distinguishes them from other personal relationships. Clark and Mills (1979) make a distinction between exchange relationships and communal relationships. Exchange relationships are governed by the rule of quid pro quo. If person A does something for person B, person B is expected to contribute equivalently to the welfare of person A. But Clark and Mills claim that our close relationships are not governed by this strict rule. Rather, in close relationships, when person A is in need, person B helps, with the understanding that person A would do the same for person B if the situation were reversed. When a communal relationship is established, then mutual or reciprocal support need never actually take place, but both parties just assume that help is available. More commonly, mutual acts of support, both small and significant, take place as a natural part of the relationship. Both parties anticipate support and grow to depend on it. If these acts of support were withheld, the relationship would likely be reevaluated, particularly in voluntary relationships like friendships (Morse, 1983). But like the network variables, there is no evidence that the quality of closeness has been carefully analyzed and more investigation is needed to determine how communal relationships are seen to provide an individual's support.

However, there is reason to believe that the nature of a particular crisis and the nature of a close relationship may interact to determine how effective social support is seen to be. Lieberman (1982) found that when women experience prenatal distress, only the husband's support helped to reduce it: no other relationship had the same effect. Brown and Harris (1978) found that an intimate relationship with a husband or boyfriend protected women from depression after a serious crisis better than an intimate relationship with a mother, sister, or friend. There are some difficulties with this study because of the higher levels of intimacy found with

husbands/boyfriends vis-à-vis other close relationships. These findings tend to support the importance of support from close relationships in buffering the effect of acute stressors, but also raise the possibility that they have effects through the simple reaffirmation of the closeness or attachment on which the support has been presumed to depend.

On the other hand, research on lonely individuals indicates that lack of support leads to higher levels of stress. Loneliness not only denies a person access to others, but also tends to be associated with a suspiciousness and distrust of others (Perlman and Peplau, 1981), with lower ability to cope with crises (Rubenstein and Shaver, 1980), with lesser communicative competence (Spitzberg and Cupach, 1985), and with a tendency to draw fewer distinctions between successful and unsuccessful social experiences (Duck et al., 1989). Lonely persons tend to see the inputs of others as less helpful and less competent also (Spitzberg and Canary, 1985), so that even if they have access to others it is less likely that they will take advantage of it, or will see it as a productive, valuable, or helpful activity. Again, then, the pattern that we argued for above is confirmed in the negative case: part of the importance of support is that it is *seen* by a person to be valuable, desirable, and useful, and in cases where support is absent it could be because it would not be seen by the recipient as supportive even if it were present. Researchers need to explore what it is about a relationship that brings *supportive meaning* to behavior, or precludes such meaning.

Exchange relationships provide significant social support as well. Albrecht and Adelman (1987a: 133) give four functions that these 'weak ties' perform: '(1) extending access to information, goods, and services, (2) promoting social comparison with dissimilar others, (3) facilitating low-risk discussion of high-risk topics, and (4) fostering a sense of community.' The first function seems most likely to have obvious exchange features. Since, as Wentowski (1981) argues, people seeking support from a less intimate relationship often spell out what they expect, support will not be sought unless one has a reason, in the form of a specific stressor that one identifies as the cause for seeking help. This would indicate that support from exchange relationships would be more likely to show a buffering pattern than a direct-effect pattern. Research to date has not passed reliable judgement on this intuition. Two likely reasons come to mind. First, these exchange relationships have not been studied as much as communal relationships like close friendships and family relationships (Cowen, 1982). Second, the other supportive functions of weak ties listed by Albrecht and Adelman seem to be useful with or without a specific acute stressor.

So for communal or exchange relationships, it is difficult to tell how support will affect stress without looking at specific interactions.

Nevertheless, some clues exist as to the value of considering exact conversational interaction and a subject's perception of it. As above, weak ties are approached with a more specific conversational agenda that requires specific action and could be judged successful or not more precisely than in other circumstances. By contrast, Glidewell et al. (1982) have shown that advice is often not asked for directly and is sometimes proffered by means of story telling in a way that contains encapsulations of the problem and its answer without one person having to ask directly, cap in hand, and without the Advisor explicitly having to assume the role of expert. Thus, the social face of the parties is sustained even though the support is given and received. By exploring narrative, conversation, and interactional recall, we would be able to find out more about the person's phenomenal approach to the dynamics of support.

Contents of Interaction
The third critical variable is *the content of the interaction* or the actual talk. Complete understanding of social support is not possible without analysis of the way in which support is discussed, negotiated, or delivered – or offered if not taken (note that we focus not just on delivery of support but on a fuller contextual process). Understanding interaction would help us understand the nature of the supportive relationship, and understanding everyday talk helps us to understand interaction, since interaction does not occur through the mindless collision of disembodied personality traits, but through the communicative activity of individuals. While we can understand something useful about the functioning of support by looking at the way support is requested, offered, given, received, ignored, or declined in a specific context, we also need to explicate the regular context against which it is treated.

Albrecht and Adelman (1987c) list five types of messages which are seen as supportive: (a) perspective shifts on cause–effect contingencies; (b) enhanced control through skill acquisition; (c) enhanced control through tangible assistance; (d) enhanced controls through acceptance or assurance; and (e) enhanced control through ventilation. These five message types seem to be logically divided into two categories. *Instrumental aid or advice* can help one assess contingencies or develop skills. *Socioemotional aid or sympathy* shows acceptance or allows ventilation. Thoits (1982: 147) divides support into the same two categories when she says: 'These needs [for support] may be met by either the provision of socioemotional aid (e.g., affection, sympathy and understanding,

acceptance, and esteem from significant others) or the provision of instrumental aid (e.g., advice, information, help with family or work responsibilities, financial aid).'

Messages that fall into the category of instrumental aid should be relevant when offered in response to some specific stressor-based need of the recipient. Therefore, these types of messages will act to buffer the effect of some stressor. On the other hand, in the absence of a relevant stressor, some types of instrumental aid, such as advice, can be counterproductive or stress-producing (Lehman et al., 1986). With interactions as complex as this, it seems naive to claim that support either always exerts a direct effect on pathology, or that support is best understood as it interacts with stress. Different stressors may produce different effects, and different types of support may do the same as a function of the relationships in which the social-support process occurs and the characteristics of partners in them.

Impact of Support

Finally, *the impact of support* must be analyzed on multiple levels. Support is a complex reciprocal and often open-ended process rather than a simple act: we urge researchers to examine the broader underlying relational processes of gift giving rather than merely the gifts and their packaging! Support affects the individual who receives it (individual level), but also affects the relationship between the giver and the recipient (dyadic level), and the social clique that the giver and recipient share (group level). Lastly, it affects the social sphere or community of the recipient and giver (network level). Effects examined at each level may affect any or all other levels (see Albrecht and Adelman, 1987c). These interactions and dialectics across level have been neglected in the social-support literature although they have been a part of current thinking in the personal-relationships literature since the field first took shape as such (see Hinde, 1979). Looking at these four factors in dynamic terms gives a complete overview of the process of social support, the functions of social support, and the micro and macro contexts in which support is enacted.

The changes in patterns of communication that may occur as a person experiences stress have been the focus of almost no studies, but, unsurprisingly, we argue that they could be illuminating. Remarkably absent from the literatures of both social support and personal relationships is any detailed work showing the patterns of communication that occur in networks as criterial individuals experience stress. As Duck (1985) has pointed out, however, there are good reasons for expecting a person to change the pattern of

interaction and conversations as relational dilemmas and stress arise. Particularly, the occurrence of many life stresses often disrupts the very network that is supposed to provide support against stress. Experience like divorce, a family member leaving home, moving, a death of a close friend are all commonly found on life-stress scales. Yet they may also be interpreted as a change in the potential supportive network. So life stresses, while increasing the need for support, also often reduce those we can turn to for support. In the case of stress in a marriage, Duck (1985) argued that a person will initially seek out less interaction with a spouse and more interaction with advisors and confidantes and that the resultant pattern of communication is one of the signs of change that constitute part of the dynamics of stress, relational dissolution, and social support. As matters come to a head with the partner, and the help of advisors is of lesser value, the partners need to sort out difficulties between them. So the patterns of interaction are again likely to change such that the spouses spend more time with each other (probably arguing) and less with the confidantes. However, the nature of communication is still relevant since the crucial factor here is a change in the style and content of the interactions with the spouse. At this point, advice- and support-seeking are likely to decrease, and ventilation, conflict, complaining, and argumentation are likely to increase over their normal rates. If the partners fail to repair the marriage, communication between the partners would again drop and spouses would return to the remaining members of their network for support over the break-up and attempt to replenish or replace the mundane support previously provided by the former partner.

In covering the aspects of social behavior relevant to social support, we hope to reemphasize the complexity inherent in the support process. Social support is more complex than making a withdrawal from a bank. We do not fill out a check and present it to our social network as though it were a draft on human resources. Support is embedded in the daily processes of social life and efforts to separate it from social life are bound to obscure support processes we should be exploring. For example, daily conversation and events can easily deemphasize the need for social support, either by occupying the person's mind in other ways or by tending to suggest the individual's ability to cope or to enhance his or her self-esteem. When such distraction from a stressor occurs, then the seeking of social support, even in the continued 'objective' presence of the stressor, will obviously be of less concern to a person conducting his or her daily business. Yet if researchers do not attend to such daily distraction, then they will not know why the person

'fails' to seek support even when the stressor has not gone away. In particular, a study of the conversational patterns of a person who is ostensibly under threat from a stressor would help to show whether a person regards coping with stress as 'unfinished business.' Until this phenomenology is explicated, we shall know too little about the ways in which stress and support are experienced and so will have only a partial grasp of what 'support' and 'stress' actually mean to people living their daily lives.

Suggestions for Future Work

A traditional call at the end of most social-scientific papers is for longitudinal work. Yet work does not become good or illuminating or informative merely because it takes longer to complete, and the issue in such work is precisely the same as it is in all other work. Careful analysis of terms and concepts will always be the central issue in social science. In the marrying of the social-support and personal-relationships literatures, we see many more advantages than are obtainable from their continued independent existence, and this is precisely because the issues facing both fields are fundamentally quite similar. Both fields need to pay closer attention to the daily dynamics of relating and also to the talk through which relationships – the basis for support – occur. Both need to address the issue of perspectival dominance and to sort out not whose perspective is more important, but how we incorporate the issue of perspectival differences into our theories about processes. Both need to do more careful scrutiny of everyday life *routines* and regularities as well as daily events and changes that are involved in the phenomena with which they concern themselves. In social support one issue is whether a researcher's view that social support has been delivered counts for more than a subject's claim that it has not. We cannot hope to discover processes unnoticed by the participants if we do not take a different perspective, yet researchers in the field are not attempting to describe the several perspectives at work in social support. Ostensibly objective measures like surveys are not integrated with phenomenological approaches. When phenomenological approaches, like focus interviewing, are used, researchers must guard against the assumption that they have captured the insider's perspective and are transmitting it without distortion. The need is for an addition to methods in this area – one that will allow simultaneous gathering of data about everyday interaction from several persons in a target network and which can be supplemented by longitudinal assessment of the ways in which conversations between persons change in character

and structure as a function of stress to one target person and to those members of the network who offer him or her assistance.

Such work requires the use of an additional sort of methodological style and the Iowa Communication Record (ICR), mentioned above as we developed the case for a phenomenological approach, offers some help here, so we describe it in detail, now that the planks of our argument for its use in refocussing work are in place. The ICR is a structured self-report form on which respondents record their recollection of conversations. Duck and Rutt (1989) outline the ICR in the following way: Subjects are asked to report on such matters as the day of the week, date, time and length of interaction; the nature of the partner with whom it was held (for example, gender, age of partner); type of relationship (stranger, acquaintance, friend, best friend, lover/boyfriend/girlfriend, relative); a variety of measures of the subject's recollection of the conversational content of the interaction; and subjective measures of its quality, purpose, and impact on the relationship. Included in these measures are questions about the conversational context – that is to say, questions concerning the partners' activities immediately preceding conversation, during conversation and after conversation. As can be seen from Figure 1.1, these include such items as watching TV, studying, and eating a meal.

Figure 1.1 *Iowa Communication Record*
Please describe your communication activities. Use one page for each conversation. A conversation is considered to be talk with one other person for 10 minutes or more.

Your I.D.: _____
   Age: _____
   Sex: M or F (circle one)
1. Date of Interaction: _____ _____
                      mo.   day
2. Time of Interaction: _____ AM or PM
                    hour   (circle one)
3. Length of Interaction: _____ _____
                    hour   min
4. Description of Interactional Partner:
   _____ _____ M or F (circle one)
   Initials   Age
5. Length of time you have known partner in years and months: _____ _____
               year   mo.
6. How would you describe the nature of your relationship? (circle one)

1	2	3	4
Stranger	Acquaintance	Friend	Best Friend

5   6
Boyfriend/   Relative   Other:_____
Girlfriend

7. What type of communication? (circle one)

1	2	3
Face-to-face	long distance telephone	local telephone

8. Would you consider the interaction public or private? (circle one and state place)

1	2	_____
Public	Private	Where

9. Were others present? Yes or No

10. What was the role of talk? Indicate the extent to which you agree with the following:
This was talk just for talk's sake.

1	2	3	4	5	6	7	8	9

Strong   Strong
Agreement   Disagreement

Main purpose of talk was to accomplish some task. (Such as gaining information to complete a project, or solve a problem.)

1	2	3	4	5	6	7	8	9

Strong   Strong
Agreement   Disagreement

Main purpose of talk was to facilitate some social objective. (Such as talk surrounding sports activity or party.)

1	2	3	4	5	6	7	8	9

Strong   Strong
Agreement   Disagreement

Main purpose of talk was to facilitate the relationship. (Such as talk to become better acquainted or resolve differences.)

1	2	3	4	5	6	7	8	9

Strong   Strong
Agreement   Disagreement

11. Describe the main topic of talk:

_____

12. Were there other topics? Yes or No
If yes, indicate the number of topics you think were addressed in the talk:

_____

13. What were you doing *right before* the conversation occurred? (circle one or more)

working	eating	driving	study
childcare	housework	watching TV	reading
listening to music	talking to someone else	_____ other	

14. Were you involved in any activities *during* the conversation? Yes or No

    If yes, please indicate which of the above:
    _____

15. What did you do *after* the conversation
    (as above)?_____

16. Was the interaction *planned* or *unplanned?*
    (circle one)

17. If planned, indicate the extent to which you were looking forward to the meeting:

1	2	3	4	5	6	7	8	9

    Looking Forward   Dreading
    to Meeting   Meeting

18. Who initiated the talk (circle one)

You	Partner	Seemed Mutual
Accidental		Not Clear

19. Who seemed to control the conversation; for example who decided topics of talk?

You	Partner	Seemed Mutual
Accidental		Not Clear

20. Who made moves to end the conversation?

You	Partner	Seemed Mutual
Accidental		Not Clear

21. Describe the quality of communication:

1	2	3	4	5	6	7	8	9

    Relaxed   Strained

1	2	3	4	5	6	7	8	9

    Impersonal   Personal

1	2	3	4	5	6	7	8	9

    Attentive   Poor
                         Listening

1	2	3	4	5	6	7	8	9

    Formal   Informal

1	2	3	4	5	6	7	8	9

    In-depth   Superficial

1	2	3	4	5	6	7	8	9

    Smooth   Difficult

1	2	3	4	5	6	7	8	9

    Guarded   Open

1	2	3	4	5	6	7	8	9

Great deal of
Understanding

Great deal of
Misunderstanding

1	2	3	4	5	6	7	8	9

Free of comm.
Breakdowns

Laden with comm.
Breakdowns

1	2	3	4	5	6	7	8	9

Free of
Conflict

Laden with
Conflict

22. Indicate the extent to which you think the talk was interesting:

1	2	3	4	5	6	7	8	9

Interesting

Boring

23. Indicate the extent to which you came away satisfied with the interaction:

1	2	3	4	5	6	7	8	9

Satisfied

Not Satisfied

24. How valuable was this conversation to you for your life *right now*?

1	2	3	4	5	6	7	8	9

Extremely
Important

Not Important
At All

25. How valuable was this conversation for your future?

1	2	3	4	5	6	7	8	9

Extremely
Important

Not Important
At All

26. Indicate the extent to which this talk resulted in a change of your *attitude*:

-3	-2	-1	0	+1	+2	+3

Negative
Change

No
Change

Positive
Change

27. Indicate the extent to which this talk resulted in a change of your *behavior*:

-3	-2	-1	0	+1	+2	+3

Stopped
Behavior

No
Change

Increased
Behavior

Describe behavior change:_____

28. Indicate the extent to which this talk changed your *thinking* or *ideas*?

```
0     1     2     3     4     5     6     7     8     9
```
No   Great
Change   Change

Describe change in thinking/ideas: _____
_____

29. Indicate the extent to which this talk resulted in a change of
your *feelings*:
```
−3         −2         −1         0         +1         +2         +3
```
Negative   No   Positive
                           Change

Describe change in feelings: _____
_____

30. Indicate the extent to which this talk resulted in a change of
your *relationship*:
```
−3         −2         −1         0         +1         +2         +3
```
Much More   No   Much More
Distant   Change   Close

31. Indicate the extent to which this talk changed your *attraction*
toward partner:
```
−3         −2         −1         0         +1         +2         +3
```
Great Decreased   No   Greatly Increased
Attraction   Change   Attraction

32. On an average day how many people do you talk to?

_____

33. Out of the total amount of time you spend conversing per
week, what percentage of that time do you think is spent talking
with this person?
_____%

34. How intimate was the interaction?
```
1     2     3     4     5     6     7     8     9
```
Not Really   Very
Intimate   Intimate

35. How intimate is the relationship, by and large?
```
1     2     3     4     5     6     7     8     9
```
Very   Not Really
Intimate   Intimate

36. How satisfied are you with the relationship as a whole?
```
1     2     3     4     5     6     7     8     9
```
Very   Very
Dissatisfied   Satisfied

THANK YOU!

The ICR thus combines some of the measures of 'quantitative' aspects of interaction, with some direct measures of recollected communication in the interaction, and measures of 'qualitative' perceptions of the interaction. A full copy of the ICR is given in Figure 1.1. The ICR consists of thirty-six questions or rating scales and generally takes about twenty minutes to complete on the first occasion, but is completed much more rapidly after that. Subjects completing the ICR report that it is a meaningful and involving task that they take seriously, a report borne out by checks on the reliability of some of the subjects' responses on 'factual' matters, such as the number of persons spoken with during a week (which typically yield Cronbach alphas above 0.95).

Analysis of the ICR assesses the extent to which the person saw the conversation to have wrought changes in Emotion, Attitudes, Beliefs, or Behavior, the degree to which it affects the subject's perception of the relationship and its likely future, and several other dimensions. It can also be used to assess the 'when, where, and with whom?' questions that would be useful in developing a sense of the means through which subjects conduct their social-support seeking and their everyday relationships with other people. The ICR is based on the basic RIR (Rochester Interaction Record – Wheeler and Nezlek, 1977) that has been used in the context of investigating social support and interaction in the lonely (Reis et al., 1983). The RIR, however, suffers from the absence of any measures of communication during social participation and, while useful for other purposes, would not serve those that we seek to deal with here: namely, the conversational dynamics of transactions between helpers, would-be helpers, friends, and network members.

As agenda for the future, we offer the following foci for research:

1   Work is needed on the precise communicative circumstances where and how support is offered (see Cutrona et al., Chapter 2, this volume). Given this, we should spend more time exploring the conversational dynamics of everyday (supportive) interaction. Methods such as the ICR have already proved useful in assessing such dynamics in other contexts (Duck and Rutt, 1989) and can be readily applied to questions raised above, such as perception of the 'state' of a relationship, the influence or impact of a stressor, and conversational patterns.

2   Analysis is required to 'place' a person's claims about relationships, social support, and stress in the context of others' perceptions of the same things. A major issue in personal relationships and social support is the issue of triangulation and placement of such reports and how we are to deal with discrepancies

between them. The ICR has already been used in a study of this issue in other contexts (Duck et al., in prep.) and could be easily employed in the context of such matters either in chronically stressed groups, or those suffering from acute stress.

3   As part of this central problem, it would be wise for researchers to spend some time explaining systematic influences on the ways in which different persons variously break up their experience and chunk it into elements that seem to relate to each other, and this too can be accomplished by using the ICR in combination with other techniques such as video-recording of events or conversations.

4   Is support always given or sometimes perceived/extracted when not realized as being offered? By investigating the reports of conversations by *both* parties to an interaction, using the ICR, this question also can be embarked upon.

5   A major point made above is that the influence of a subject's present representation of relationships (or beliefs about others and their impact) is critical to furthering our understanding of the processes of social support and this too is measured simultaneously with the other things by the ICR.

6   How does the representation of relationship change as social support unfolds? This key question is one that the ICR precisely addresses.

In concluding our pitch for this new method, based on the arguments we have outlined throughout the chapter, let us summarize the position. Social support work has been too 'objective' and has focussed too much on the views of experimenters imposed on subjects. We urge future workers to heed the frequent advice of George Kelly: if you seek to understand a person('s behavior), you will find that understanding in the way in which the person represents circumstance to himself or herself. We add only that the study of daily conversations is a good way to take this advice.

Note

We are grateful to Stevan Hobfoll and Ben Gottlieb for their comments on an earlier version of this chapter and for their help in clarifying our thinking about the issues in these two areas of social support, on the one hand, and personal relationships, on the other.

2

Interpersonal Transactions and the Psychological Sense of Support

Carolyn E. Cutrona, Julie A. Suhr, and Robin MacFarlane

The belief that others are available to provide emotional and practical support in times of need has been associated with an impressive array of positive outcomes, including good mental health (Wethington and Kessler, 1986), competent immune function (Jemmott and Magliore, 1988), and lower mortality rates (Blazer, 1982). There seems little doubt that this 'psychological sense of support' is an important component of human well-being.

Surprisingly, little is known about the determinants of the sense that one's interpersonal needs for support are adequately met. Associations between frequency of social contact and perceived social support are modest at best (Cutrona, 1986a). Furthermore, correlations between perceived social support and a range of personality characteristics suggest that to some extent, social support may be in the eye of the beholder (Procidano and Heller, 1983; Sarason et al., 1983).

The most frequent sources of social support are individuals with whom we share close relationships (Gourash, 1978). Leatham and Duck (Chapter 1, this volume) argue that social support is most often communicated through ordinary day-to-day interactions between individuals. Yet we know little about the transactions that convey emotional or practical support from one person to another.

In this chapter, a theoretical framework for analyzing the transactions that occur within close relationships (Kelley et al., 1983) will be applied to the study of social support. We will summarize preliminary findings from a series of studies we have conducted on support-related transactions. Using coding schemes designed to capture important events in both the elicitation and provision of social support, we have collected data on different strategies used by married couples and close friends to elicit social support from one another. In an observational study, we obtained data on behavioral acts intended to communicate support and on the effects

of these acts on the subjective support evaluations of the support recipient, the support provider, and uninvolved observers. These data are described only as suggestive beginnings for the study of support-communicating transactions. It is hoped that observational coding schemes such as ours will open the door to significant theoretical advances in the understanding of transactions that communicate a psychological sense of support.

Perceived Social Support

In this chapter, the term 'perceived social support' will be used to refer to the belief that if the need arose, at least one person in the individual's circle of family, friends, and associates would be available to serve one or more specific functions. A high degree of consensus exists in the literature regarding these functions, although they are given a variety of labels. These functions can be classified into those that directly promote problem solving (instrumental support) and those that primarily promote emotional adjustment (emotional support). Included among instrumental support components are tangible aid and informational support. 'Tangible aid' refers to concrete assistance, wherein goods or services are provided (for example, financial assistance, transportation). 'Informational support' involves information, advice, or guidance concerning possible solutions to a problem. Included among emotional-support components are expressions of caring or attachment, network support, and esteem support. 'Attachment' represents verbal and nonverbal expressions of caring, sympathy, and concern. Social integration or 'network support' refers to feeling part of a group where members share common interests and concerns. 'Esteem support' consists of bolstering the person's sense of competence or self-esteem. Providing the individual with positive feedback on skills and abilities or indicating a belief that the person is capable of coping with a stressful event are examples of this type of support.

Transactional Determinants of Perceived Social Support

It is our belief that no single interaction is sufficient to engender a psychological sense of support. Instead, for one person to believe that he or she can rely upon a second person for one or more of the support functions described above, it is necessary for the person to have experienced a *number* of interactions with this individual that communicate support. We hypothesize that certain *regularities* or *recurring interaction patterns,* can be identified that characterize relationships from which individuals derive a psychological sense of support. Research in the literature on marital conflict has demon-

strated recurring interaction patterns in the verbal and nonverbal behavior of distressed couples when they are placed in the context of disagreeing with each other (for example, Gottman, 1979; Raush et al., 1974). Because of the careful research conducted on conflict behavior, we have a good understanding of the conflict behaviors of satisfied versus dissatisfied couples. We hypothesize that recurring interaction patterns can also be identified that characterize couples who derive a psychological sense of social support from one another. To discover these patterns, it will be necessary to observe and encode the interactions of couples in the context of stressful life events. That is, our research agenda for the future should include the systematic analysis of the verbal and nonverbal behavior of couples as they face the major and minor problems of their daily lives to discover behavior sequences that distinguish couples who drive a high versus a low level of perceived social support from one another.

A Theoretical Framework for Analyzing Transactions

In a ground-breaking work on the scientific study of close relationships, Kelley et al. (1983) introduced a number of useful concepts regarding interactions in the context of significant ongoing relationships. One key concept is that the thoughts, emotions, and behaviors of each participant contribute to the ongoing stream of interaction, as well as events and conditions outside of the interaction. Thus, three modes of human experience (cognitive, affective, and behavioral) are included in transactional analyses.

A second key concept is that there are relatively stable causal factors that influence the course of interactions (termed 'causal conditions'), which, because of their stability, account for the *recurrence* of specific interactional patterns. As stated above, we believe that a psychological sense of support results from recurring transaction patterns that communicate the availability of instrumental and/or emotional assistance. Thus, it is of interest to identify the causal conditions that contribute to a psychological sense of support within ongoing relationships.

Three major categories of causal conditions were identified by Kelley et al.: those that are located in the environment, those located in persons, and those located in the relation between persons or between persons and the environment. Causal conditions of the physical environment generate regularities in the physical events that influence interactions between individuals. For example, if both members of a couple work far from their home, the time spent commuting may significantly limit the time available for

discussion of daily problems. The social environment may also affect interactions. For example, the presence of small children in the home may divert the attention of one or both spouses away from each other, decreasing the frequency of personal conversations that communicate support. Personal causal conditions, including the attitudes, beliefs, habits, and personality characteristics of each member of a couple, may significantly affect the course of inter- actions between them. For example, if one spouse believes that it is a sign of weakness to discuss problems with others, the prob- ability of support-communicating transactions is diminished (Eck- enrode, 1983). A variety of personality characteristics has been shown to correlate with perceived social support, including extrav- ersion, neuroticism, self-esteem and assertiveness (Procidano and Heller, 1983; Sarason et al., 1983; Sarason et al., 1986). An individ- ual's personality characteristics may lead to behaviors that encour- age or discourage supportive behaviors from others. For example, a gruff, embarrassed reaction to a kind word may discourage the expression of sympathy in the future. Alternatively, personality characteristics may lead to idiosyncratic interpretations of intended support, for example, the belief that the other is 'trying to get something in return.' This belief may prevent the individual from developing a secure psychological sense of support, even if support- intended behaviors are forthcoming from others.

The final class of causal conditions discussed by Kelley et al. (1983) consists of those that emerge out of the relation between persons or between persons and the environment. Couples may develop regularities in their interactions as a function of particular combinations of attitudes or habits. Some of these relational con- ditions may exist at the beginning of the relationship. For example, if the wife cries easily when discussing personal problems and her husband views tears as manipulative, it may be very difficult for the wife to derive a sense of support from her husband. Other relational conditions may emerge over the course of a relationship. For example, a couple that lost a child to a terminal illness may decide (perhaps implicitly) that it is better not to bring up this painful topic, thus aborting opportunities for shared grief and mutual comfort. Finally, an example of the relation between person and environmental factors as a causal condition might be an insecure young man who works for a corporation that encourages twelve-hour work days and coming to the office on weekends. His compliance with this corporate expectation may not only prevent the opportunity for support-communicating interactions with his wife, but may also sap her sense of his supportiveness by virtue of his apparent choice of work over marriage.

Application of the Kelley et al. Framework to Social Support

The framework provided by Kelley et al. (1983) offers a useful way to organize research on the determinants of a psychological sense of support within ongoing relationships. From the Kelley et al. framework, we derive an approach to ongoing interactions in which not only the behaviors, but also the thoughts and emotions of participants are viewed as relevant events in the course of interpersonal transactions. Thus, methods for tapping all three levels and exploring sequences of events at all three levels are needed.

A second contribution of the Kelley et al. framework is the emphasis placed upon the recurrence of particular interaction sequences. We have argued that no single conversation or act of assistance is sufficient to build a sense of support within a relationship. Instead, recurring interactions form the basis for judgements of whether or not a relationship is 'supportive.' A summation process of some kind occurs, in which past experiences with the other person are the basis for judgements about the future availability of various components of support from that person. The Kelley et al. framework is useful in identifying classes of factors that play a causal role in the repetition and predictability of these sequences. Thus, it is possible to study not only the specific interaction sequences that characterize couples who are high versus those low in the support that they derive from one another, but it should also be possible to identify environmental, personal, and relational causal conditions that contribute to the recurrence of supportive or nonsupportive interactions. This is an ambitious research agenda, but one that seems achievable, given thoughtful conceptualization and instrumentation.

A number of observational coding schemes have been developed to assess the sequences of events that transpire between couples when they interact (for example, Fitzpatrick, 1988; Gottman, 1979; Raush et al., 1974). However, most such coding systems were developed for the purpose of studying marital conflict. A review of such measures revealed that none were sufficient to capture the processes of eliciting or providing the five interpersonal functions that were described earlier as constituting social support. Thus, we have begun to develop such a coding scheme and have conducted a preliminary series of studies on support-related transactions. Although this research is in an early stage of development and does not approach the complexity of the approach described above, our procedures for developing observational coding schemes and preliminary correlational findings using these measures are briefly

summarized to illustrate the feasibility and utility of analyzing support-intended transactions.

Observational Coding Schemes for Support Elicitation and Provision

In most cases, support-communicating behaviors do not materialize automatically without some indication from the stressed individual that he or she is in a state of need. An exception would be situations in which the news of a stressful event is communicated to a potential support-provider by someone other than the stressed individual (for example, an eyewitness to the event). Even if the potential support-provider is aware that the stress victim has experienced a taxing event, he or she may rely on the victim to provide cues regarding the kind of support desired and the times at which support is needed. Thus, we felt that an important component of support-communicating transactions was the behaviors involved in the *elicitation* of support. A code to analyze the interactions that occur when one individual is attempting to elicit support from another is currently under development, and will be described below.

In addition to elicitation strategies, we were interested in the actual behaviors that people emit in their attempts to communicate support to others. Thus, the second part of the coding scheme targets a range of instrumental and emotional help-intended behaviors.

Development of the Coding Schemes

It was our desire to develop codes that would capture a wide range of support elicitation and provision behaviors. Our first step was to conduct a series of questionnaire studies to generate a pool of potential behavior categories. All of the studies were similar in design. Respondents were instructed to imagine themselves in a series of hypothetical stressful situations (for example, 'You have just learned that you are diabetic and must take insulin shots for the rest of your life'). Respondents were then asked to describe very specifically what they would want their spouse to do to help them deal with the stress. In the next question, they were asked to describe very specifically what they would say and do to induce the spouse to provide what they wanted. A follow-up probe enquired, 'If this didn't work, what would you try next?' Each subject was asked to respond to four such hypothetical situations, and then to answer the same questions regarding an actual stressful event in their recent past. For the actual event, subjects were asked to

describe what they had wanted from their spouse at the time and what they actually said or did to elicit this behavior.

We collected data from two samples to generate behavior codes for elicitation strategies. One sample consisted of thirty-one married adults who were recruited by a newspaper ad and a mailing to University Family Housing residents. These individuals ranged in age from 21 to 64. Each individual was also administered a marital satisfaction questionnaire (Spanier, 1976) and the marital version of the Social Provisions Scale (Cutrona and Russell, 1987; Russell and Cutrona, 1984), a multidimensional measure of the degree of perceived social support received from the spouse. The second sample consisted of twenty-three undergraduate students. For each situation presented, the students were asked to think of whom they would most like to assist them in that situation, and to answer the questions with regard to that individual. In most cases, students listed a close friend as their preferred support source. Students were administered the original Social Provisions Scale, which does not ask about any specific source of social support, but rather, the extent to which support is available from all sources.

Elicitation of Social Support   The social-support elicitation behaviors listed by respondents in the two samples were categorized into eighteen separate behavior codes. Table 2.1 shows the number of individuals in each sample who listed each elicitation strategy at least once. Interesting differences emerged between the two samples in respect of the strategies most frequently used to elicit support. For the married individuals, three of the four most frequently reported strategies involved direct requests for a particular type of support. The most frequent behavior was a direct request for tangible assistance (for example, 'I would ask her to learn how to give insulin shots'; 'I would ask him to watch the kids so I could space out for awhile'). Requests for emotional support were also frequent ('I'd say, "I just need you to listen to me"'; 'I'd tell him I needed him to hold me'), as were requests for advice ('I'd ask him what he thought I should do').

Undergraduates, most of whom said they would turn to a friend, requested advice frequently, but did not make many direct requests for assistance or emotional support. Indirect strategies were used more frequently, such as describing their emotional reactions to the stress ('I'd tell her how upset I was') or simply stating the facts of their situation, and hoping that support would be forthcoming ('I'd say, "Guess what! I found out I've got diabetes today!"'). (This latter strategy was also frequently used by the married participants.)

Table 2.1 *Percent of subjects using elicitation strategies at least once*

Elicitation strategy	Raters	
	Married couples (%)	Undergraduates (%)
Describes facts	71.0	0.9
Complains about stressful situation	12.9	17.4
Verbal description of emotions	29.0	69.6
Nonverbal emotion display	2.9	26.1
Expresses doubt over coping capability	9.7	*
Expresses confidence in coping capability	29.0	*
Denigrates self	6.4	30.4
Requests tangible assistance	93.5	4.3
Requests advice, information	51.6	78.3
Requests comfort, affection	67.7	4.3
Appeals to relationship with supporter	19.4	13.0
Appeals to qualifications of supporter	3.2	4.3
Describes consequences of no support	19.4	8.7
Confronts supporter for lack of supportiveness	35.5	13.0
Does nothing – Expects automatic support	32.3	*
Does nothing – Prefers to cope alone	19.4	*
Does nothing – Believes that support is not available	35.5	*

*These behaviors were not included in the coding scheme used in the undergraduate study.

Thus, some differences in elicitation strategies were found as a function of the relationship context in which support was being sought. Married individuals felt free to make direct and specific requests of their spouse. However, the only type of support that

students felt free to request directly from their friends was advice. Other types of support were sought indirectly, through communicating the facts of their dilemma and/or their emotional distress. Closer relationships, in which individuals are more certain of their partner's commitment, appear to allow more freedom for direct support requests.

It was of interest to determine whether certain elicitation strategies characterized individuals who reported high levels of social support. Among married couples, requests for emotional support and stating the consequences of failure to receive support correlated positively with marital satisfaction (both r's = 0.33, $p < 0.05$), and marginally significantly with perceived support from spouse ($p < 0.10$). Expecting support automatically and believing that support efforts would be futile correlated negatively with perceived support from spouse (r's = -0.39 and -0.31 respectively, both p's < 0.05).

Among the undergraduates, the only significant correlation between elicitation strategies and perceived social support was for presentation of feelings, $r = 0.51$, $p < 0.005$. Those who used this strategy more frequently tended to have higher levels of perceived social support. Thus, both direct and indirect efforts to elicit *emotional* support (request for emotional support and description of emotional state) were associated with higher levels of perceived support and relationship satisfaction. Making no effort to elicit support was associated with lower levels of perceived support.

Gender differences were found in the elicitation strategies used by males and females. In both the married and the undergraduate samples, women more frequently described their feelings than men, t (21) = 3.46, $p < 0.005$. Among the undergraduates only, women also more frequently displayed their emotions nonverbally than did men, t (21) = 2.24, $p < 0.05$.

Although we have not yet applied our coding scheme for support elicitation to behavioral interactions, findings based on our questionnaire studies point to the utility of studying this phase of the support process. We plan to pilot the elicitation coding scheme with interacting couples in the near future, which will undoubtedly result in modifications to the coding scheme.

Support-intended Behaviors   Based on the questionnaire data described above, a similar questionnaire administered to an additional undergraduate sample ($N = 40$), and a review of items included in behaviorally focussed social support inventories (for example, Barerra et al., 1981), thirty-three categories of support-intended behaviors were generated. The thirty-three specific

behaviors were then grouped into five larger classes: informational support, esteem support, tangible aid, emotional support, and network or belonging support. The behavior codes are summarized in Table 2.2.

Table 2.2   *Brief definitions of support-behavior codes*

INFORMATION SUPPORT

Suggestion/advice – offers ideas and suggests actions to the receiver.
Referral – refers the recipient to some other source of help.
Clarification – summarizes situation.
Situation appraisal – reassesses or redefines the situation.
Teaching – provides detailed information, facts, or news about the situation or about skills needed to deal with the situation.

ESTEEM SUPPORT

Compliment – says positive things about the recipient or emphasizes the recipient's abilities.
Validation – expresses agreement with the recipient's perspective on the situation.
Relief of blame – tries to alleviate the receiver's feelings of guilt about the situation.
Reassurance – reminds the recipient not to worry about the situation.

TANGIBLE ASSISTANCE

Leave alone – leaves the recipient alone at the recipient's request.
Loan – offers to lend the receiver something (including money).
Direct task – offers to perform a task directly related to the stress.
Indirect task – offers to take over one or more of the recipient's other responsibilities while the recipient is under stress.
Active participation – offers to join the receiver in action that reduces the stress.
Tension reduction – tells jokes or offers to remove the receiver from the situation to distract him or her from stress.

EMOTIONAL SUPPORT

Willingness – expresses willingness to help.
Relationship – stresses the importance of closeness and love in relationship with the receiver.
Physical affection – offers physical contact, including hugs, kisses, hand holding, shoulder patting.
Confidentiality – promises to keep the receiver's problem in confidence.
Sympathy – expresses sorrow or regret for the receiver's situation or distress.
Listening – attentive comments as the receiver speaks.
Understanding/empathy – expresses understanding of the situation or discloses a personal situation that communicates understanding.
Encouragement – provides the receiver with hope and confidence.
Prayer – prays with the receiver.

NETWORK SUPPORT

Presence – offers to spend time with the recipient.
Access – offers to provide the receiver with access to new companions.
Story – tells a story expressing the idea that others have been through similar situations.

Once the list of supportive behaviors was generated and detailed descriptions were written for each, a preliminary study of dyadic interaction was undertaken using the coding scheme. Subjects were thirty-two female undergraduate psychology students who ranged in age from 18 to 20 years. The students were brought into the laboratory in pairs. One subject in each pair was randomly chosen to play the role of the 'helper' while the other subject disclosed a stressful experience that had occurred in her life within the previous six months. The helper was instructed to 'be as helpful as possible' and to try to make the self-discloser feel comfortable and understood. Each interaction lasted ten minutes and was videotaped. Videotapes were later coded by two independent raters, using the thirty-three category supportive behavior code.

Following their interaction, subjects each completed a questionnaire designed to assess their perceptions of the interaction. Items asked for ratings of overall helpfulness as well as the quality of informational, emotional, and esteem-building support provided. Using this questionnaire, the discloser rated the helper (for example, 'She gave me useful information') and the helper rated herself (for example, 'I was sensitive to her feelings'). Using the same qualitative rating scale, the two independent raters also evaluated the performance of each subject in the helper role. Thus, for each interaction, the support-intended behaviors were coded and subjective supportiveness ratings were obtained from four perspectives: recipient, provider, and two independent raters.

Out of the total 258 support behaviors coded, those that fell under the informational support class occurred most frequently (64 per cent). Emotional support behaviors accounted for 21 per cent of the behaviors; and esteem support accounted for 15 per cent. Tangible aid behaviors occurred only once, and network support behaviors did not occur at all. Turning to specific codes, the behaviors that were used most frequently by the undergraduate helpers were suggestion/advice ($n = 69$), clarification ($n = 55$), understanding ($n = 46$), validation ($n = 27$), and opinion ($n = 20$). To summarize, the helpers offered suggestions and opinions to their partner, tried to clarify and express understanding of the situation, and agreed with their partner regarding the seriousness of the situation or the cause for concern. Emotional support was infrequent, as would be expected among strangers. If married couples were observed, it is anticipated that both emotional and instrumental behaviors would occur more often.

Applying the coding scheme to actual interactions revealed the necessity for revision of the behavior categories. For example, the category, 'story,' in which the helper describes an event from his

or her own life or from that of an acquaintance, was originally coded as an instance of informational support. However, it became clear that subjects told stories for a variety of reasons. The stories seemed to serve one of three purposes: (a) conveying that the individual is not the only person to have experienced the stress, and should thus not feel alone; (b) conveying a sense of understanding; and (c) indirectly offering suggestions or advice. Offering advice through stories was also observed in a study of interactions among public-school teachers (Glidewell et al., 1982). This behavior was viewed as a method for communicating helpful information without offending or implying that the storyteller was of higher status than the listener. In light of the different apparent intents behind storytelling, we have modified the code to include three separate storytelling categories.

Of greatest interest was the relation between the coded behavior categories and the quality of perceived social support. As stated previously, it is our belief that certain interaction sequences characterize dyads that perceive one another as supportive, and this study was a first step toward identifying components of those interaction sequences.

Table 2.3 shows correlation coefficients between the frequency with which supportive behaviors occurred (condensed within classes) and perceived supportiveness ratings by each of the four raters. (Only the three classes of behaviors that were observed more than once were included: informational, emotional, and esteem support.) The most striking result was the failure of any support behavior type to significantly affect the support recipient's perceptions. Although the frequency of both informational and esteem support correlated positively with supportiveness ratings made by both the provider and the two observers, neither attained significance for recipient ratings. Thus, it appears that the recipients used different criteria in evaluating the supportiveness of help-intended behaviors. Their evaluations were less closely tied to the frequency of specific behavior classes than were the evaluations of the provider or uninvolved observers. It may be that *nonverbal* aspects of the interaction were most salient to support recipients, or that the behavioral coding system was not sensitive to key behaviors.

Alternatively, the recipients' perceptions of support may have been shaped by 'causal conditions' located outside of the interaction. A key question in the social support literature is the extent to which ratings of perceived social support reflect personality characteristics of the rater rather than actual social resources (Gottlieb, 1985; Sarason et al., 1985). Pierce, Sarason, and Sarason

Table 2.3   *Correlations between frequency of coded support behaviors and perceptions of helper supportiveness*

Support categories	Raters			
	Supporter	Recipient	Coder 1	Coder 2
Informational support	0.30*	0.20	0.53**	0.70**
Esteem support	0.35*	0.04	0.63**	0.44**
Emotional support	−0.13	0.11	0.14	0.15
Tangible aid	−0.05	−0.54**	0.03	0.00
Total number of support behaviors	0.32*	0.20	0.71**	0.79**

*$p<.05$.
**$p<.01$.

(Chapter 10, this volume) have hypothesized that people develop cognitive 'working models' (expectations, beliefs, and attitudes) regarding social support. Thus, a person's evaluations of a given support-intended interaction may be influenced by his or her more general beliefs about the quality, effectiveness, and availability of social support. To further investigate determinants of recipients' supportiveness ratings, a correlation was computed between subjects' reports of the social support available to them in their daily lives (total Social Provisions Scale scores) and their ratings of the helper's supportiveness. A modest but positive correlation was found between recipients' Social Provisions Scale scores and their ratings of helper supportiveness, $r = 0.31$, $p<0.05$. Thus, some evidence was obtained for a general tendency to perceive supportiveness consistently across situations. However, this association between real-life perceived support and supportiveness ratings was not found for the support *providers*, $r = 0.04$, n.s. Apparently, the observed bias in support perceptions applies only to evaluations of support received, and not to evaluations of the support one provides.

An apparent weakness of the support-behavior coding scheme was its lack of sensitivity to behaviors that communicate a sense of emotional support (caring, concern, sympathy). Correlations between frequency of emotionally supportive behaviors and perceived social support failed to attain significance for all four raters. A set of follow-up analyses was conducted to further investigate the failure of the emotional-support behavior categories. An index of emotional support was formed using a subset of items from the perceived supportiveness scale (for example, 'I felt that my partner cared about my situation'). Correlations were then computed between the frequency of individual support behavior codes and perceived emotional support to determine which, if any, contrib-

uted to a sense of caring and concern. Among the behavior codes in the emotional support class, only sympathy correlated significantly with perceived emotional support (independent raters only). Among non-emotional-support behavior codes, two significant correlations with perceived emotional support emerged. Frequency of clarification (summarizing or rephrasing the discloser's situation, feelings, thoughts) correlated positively with perceived emotional support among independent raters and support providers. This finding is reminiscent of Carl Rogers' emphasis on reflection (summarizing the client's thoughts and feelings) as a method for communicating understanding and empathy (Rogers, 1951). The second non-emotional behavior code to correlate significantly with perceived emotional support was criticism. Frequent criticism was associated with lower perceived emotional support among both independent raters and the support recipient.

There are several implications of these findings. First, a sense of emotional support may be linked to variables other than verbal behaviors. These data suggest the need to incorporate measures of nonverbal behavior in studies of support-intended transactions. Second, a sense of caring may be communicated by behaviors that are not direct expressions of affection or concern, such as sensitive clarification statements. Finally, it should be emphasized that a ten-minute interaction between total strangers is far from the ideal context in which to study social support. Emotional support in particular should be studied in the context of close relationships in which individuals genuinely do care about each other. The artificiality of the relationship may also have contributed to the general lack of association between the frequency of specific behaviors and support ratings by the recipients. Recipients were undoubtedly uncomfortable disclosing personal information about themselves to a stranger, and may thus have been focussed more on their own behavior than on that of the support provider. Studies of support-intended communication among marital couples are planned for the near future, and it is anticipated that both the content of the interactions and the behavioral antecedents of perceived supportiveness will be quite different.

Summary and Conclusions

We have hypothesized that a psychological sense of support (that is, confidence that needed emotional or instrumental aid will be available) is not derived from a single conversation or act of assistance, but rather derives from recurring patterns of interactions. Thus, it is anticipated that specific transactional patterns can be

identified that characterize relationships from which individuals derive a sense of support. In the marital interaction literature, recurrent conflict patterns have been identified that discriminate between satisfied and dissatisfied couples, so we are optimistic that recurrent interaction patterns in couples' attempts to deal with stress can be identified that discriminate high- from low-support couples.

Kelley et al. (1983) have proposed a useful framework for conceptualizing factors that contribute to the recurrence of transactional sequences. Using this framework, we believe that it is possible to identify personal, environmental, and relational factors that contribute to the frequency of interactions from which individuals derive a psychological sense of support. Understanding such 'causal conditions' may yield insight into the temporal stability of perceived social support (Sarason et al., 1983), and may suggest methods for interventions designed to increase social support resources.

Thus, a research agenda is proposed in which multiple samples of couples' interactions are collected and analyzed with respect to recurring transactional patterns. Couples should be observed as they face stressful life circumstances to determine sequences of behaviors that yield both an immediate sense of support, and the perception of the relationship as 'supportive.' Couples could be asked to discuss actual stressful events that one or both are currently confronting, or improvisational techniques could be employed. For example, couples could be asked to enact scenes in which one member of the couple has recently experienced an imagined negative event. In this way, the severity and type of stress could be varied by the experimenter. McReynolds and DeVoge (1978) present evidence supporting the realism that can be achieved using improvisational techniques.

Kelley et al. (1983) emphasize the importance of including emotional and cognitive events in analyses of interpersonal transactions. More is known about how to assess behavior than about how to assess ongoing streams of feelings or thoughts. However, a useful technique for obtaining continuous ratings of affect over the course of dyadic interactions was developed by Gottman and Levenson (1985). In this procedure, couples participate in a series of fifteen-minute interactions, which are videotaped. Later, each individual returns separately to the laboratory and views the videotape of the interactions. During this video-replay session, the individual is instructed to use a rating dial (anchored at different orientations by 'very negative,' 'neutral,' and 'very positive') to indicate the emotions they had experienced during the original interaction, adjusting the dial position as frequently as desired to reflect changes in

affect. Affect ratings were synchronized with the videotape so that analyses could link emotion ratings to specific events in the interaction.

Various methods have been devised to investigate individuals' thought processes. A number of 'thought-listing' techniques have been developed (for example, Cacioppo and Petty, 1983), in which individuals are instructed to write or speak their thoughts into a tape-recorder during a specified procedure or time period. This technique could be applied to dyadic interactions in a manner similar to that described above for recording emotions. Individuals could view a videotape of themselves interacting with their spouse, and report the thoughts elicited by the interaction into a tape-recorder. Once again, the videotape and audio could be synchronized to preserve the temporal sequencing of thoughts and actions. As summarized previously, our behavioral codes alone were not sufficient to predict the subjective ratings of support recipients. The combined use of behavioral, affective, and cognitive assessment methods may yield greater insight into determinants of the perceived supportiveness of help-intended behaviors.

Our results highlight the importance of systematic research regarding causal conditions that influence support-intended interactions. In our study of support-elicitation strategies, we found that individuals who believed that support was not available did not report any attempts to elicit support, and perhaps consequently, reported low levels of social support from their spouse. Our study of support-intended behaviors revealed that individuals who perceived high levels of social support in their daily life were more likely to perceive the helper's actions as supportive. Thus, longstanding personal factors appear to influence both interpersonal behavior and the interpretation of events. Such personal causal conditions, as well as environmental and relational causal conditions, should be investigated as predictors of both behavior and perception in support-intended interactions.

To conclude, a psychological sense of support appears to be a powerful determinant of human well-being. To date, we know little about the transactions that engender perceptions of support or about the conditions that perpetuate supportive transactions within a relationship. The methods and findings reported in this chapter are intended as heuristic rather than as final products. Further refinement of the behavioral coding schemes is required, and studies of actual *sequences* of behavior in ongoing relationships must be conducted. However, it is hoped that our preliminary work will motivate others to continue efforts to understand the transactions that communicate social support and the conditions that encourage these transactions to recur.

3

Interactive Coping: The Cheering-up Process in Close Relationships

Anita P. Barbee

The social-support literature provides compelling evidence for the value of gathering with close friends and relations in times of stress (Cohen and Wills, 1985, Gottlieb, 1983). Yet this literature has largely focussed on the retrospective, global perceptions of the recipients of such support. It is clear that people who felt that they had access to social support during times of sadness and trauma tended to do better than others, but we do not know the determinants, or the specific content of the social interactions that were particularly helpful. Conversely, we do not know what individual and relationship dynamics precluded social support from being offered, or from being useful, in cases when it was not (Hobfoll and Stokes, 1988; Shumaker and Brownell, 1984).

The multifaceted and interactive nature of the social-support process can be seen in an example. Imagine that you have had a really bad day. Your water heater at home broke and flooded the basement; your nanny called to tell you that your child has a fever of 101°F, and you received a letter from a journal editor saying that your manuscript needs major revisions and still may not be published. You decide to call your best friend, hoping that she can cheer you up, only to hear that her score on a civil-service exam was too low to justify the promotion she had been hoping for during the past year. Before either you or your friend experience the gentle glow of social support, it seems likely that a complex interplay of mood dynamics, cognitive attributions, and communication behaviors must transpire.

The line of research that I have been pursuing with my colleagues over the past several years has been designed to explore the details of the interactive-coping process as it unfolds between people in close relationships. We want to see what specific behaviors people perform when trying to cheer up a close friend or relation who is depressed or unhappy. We also wish to understand how variables such as the mood of the helper, the nature of the relationship

and the type of problem experienced by the recipient affect this interaction. Finally, we want to understand which behaviors are most effective in making a recipient feel better and in helping a recipient to solve his or her problem.

Our approach to the social-support process has several unique aspects. First, we are examining the many emotional, cognitive, social, interpersonal, and intrapersonal factors which can help or hinder the *helper* in his or her attempt to deal with a close associate's problem, rather than simply focussing on the *perceptions* of the *recipient* of such support. Second, we are interested in how these factors influence the helper's ability to notice that their friend is in need of support, the helper's decision to help, and the helper's decision of what strategies to employ in attempting to cheer up a depressed partner. Third, we are observing the recipient's discussion of a problem with a close friend, in order to carefully record the specific behaviors of the helper in response to his or her friend's distress. In looking at these variables in the context of supportive interchanges between close friends and lovers, we hope not only to enrich our understanding of the interactive-coping process itself, but to expand our knowledge of altruism by exploring the largely uncharted terrain of multiple acts of helping in close relationships. Fourth and finally, we are exploring which specific behaviors are associated with the amelioration of a recipient's negative mood state. Thus, we are documenting the complexity of the social-support process as it occurs in the context of ongoing relationships where the helper has personal ups and downs, as well as the problems of his or her friend to negotiate.

This chapter begins with a presentation of our interactive-coping model and typology, accompanied by a brief review of the literatures on the effects of mood, type of problem, and attributions on the helping process. This is followed by a description of the methods used in four investigations utilizing these variables and a summary of the results obtained to date. Additional questions for future explorations in this domain will be suggested, followed by implications for the study of social support in personal relationships.

Model of Interactive Coping

Our model of interactive coping was designed to integrate insights from three literatures that generally have not been considered simultaneously. *The altruism literature* has given us ideas about which variables may affect an individual's decision to help. *The social-support literature* has illuminated the importance of a person's personal social network in meeting tangible, informational, belonging,

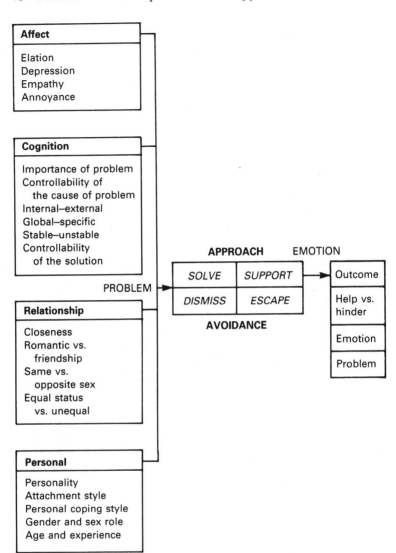

Figure 3.1 *Theoretical model of interactive-coping variables*

and esteem needs during times of stress (for example, Cohen and Hoberman, 1983). Finally, *the coping literature* has emphasized the importance of specific behaviors in alleviating personal distress, and provided a basis for actions to aid others.

The variables included in the present model of interactive coping are presented in Figure 3.1. First, *affective* variables that influence interactive coping include the helper's *mood* state (Carlson and Miller, 1987; Carlson et al., 1988; Shaffer, 1986) and feelings of *empathy*, *distress* (Batson et al., 1983), or *annoyance* towards a depressed friend (Sacco et al., 1985). Second, *cognitive* variables that influence interactive coping include the *nature of the problem* (McCoy and Masters, 1985) and *attributions* made by the helper about the locus of the cause, controllability of the cause, specificity, stability, importance, and focus of the recipient's problem (Weiner, 1980) and the controllability of the solution to the recipient's problem (Brickman et al., 1982). Third, *relationship* variables that influence the process may include the *duration* and *closeness* of the relationship (for example, Clark et al., 1987), and the *type of relationship*, including romantic relationships (Cate and Lloyd, 1988), same and opposite sex friendships (Hays, 1988), parent-child relationships, sibling relationships, intergenerational relationships (Giles, 1989), co-worker or teammate relationships, and relationships of unequal status, such as therapist–client (Winstead et al., 1988) and supervisor–subordinate. Finally, *personal* variables that may influence cheering up dynamics include characteristics of the helper and recipient such as *gender* and *sex-role orientation* (Eagly and Crowley, 1986), *attachment style* (Hazan and Shaver, 1987), *conflict style* (Rahim, 1983), and *personality variables* such as self-monitoring, extraversion, and neuroticism (Eysenck 1981; Snyder, 1979). The interactive-coping typology, and outcome variables, will be discussed below.

Interactive-coping Typology
Although there are many fine measures of personal coping, for helping the self, we found no published measures of interactive coping for helping a friend. We needed a measure that would assess social-support dimensions such as informational, belonging, and esteem support, yet we needed them to be expressed in the form of discrete behaviors that could be observed in overt interactions involving a wide range of problems. Many personal coping measures list discrete behaviors, but such measures generally involve a large number of items and produce scores on a large number of correlated dimensions (cf. Folkman and Lazarus, 1985; McCrae, 1984; Stone and Neale, 1984a, b), which is inappropriate for

behavioral-observation research. To meet this need, we developed a typology which includes the majority of behaviors that researchers of coping and social support have regarded as important (Folkman and Lazarus, 1985; Stone and Neale, 1984a, b), yet incorporates them into a small number of theoretically meaningful dimensions which can be investigated in experimental as well as non-experimental research designs. The typology is detailed enough to reveal the richness of people's behavior when they are cheering someone up, yet is brief enough to complete before an experimental manipulation wears off. Thus, while researchers of coping and social support have focussed on how people work through chronic problems such as the illness or death of a loved one, we are primarily focussing on how people help someone alleviate a transient problem or mood stemming from a difficulty that has some potential for solution or amelioration, such as a depressing academic test failure, sorrowful ruminations after viewing a tragic film, or the loss of a dating relationship.

Folkman and Lazarus (1985) contend that there are two major forms of personal coping undertaken by an individual who is faced with stress. The first type, *problem-focussed* coping, consists of direct action on the problem to remove or alter circumstances appraised as threatening. The second type, *emotion-focussed* coping, consists of actions or thoughts to control the undesirable feelings that result from stressful circumstances. A person who is confronted with a depressed friend may encourage the friend to use a personal coping strategy which that person uses when depressed or troubled (Thoits, 1986). For instance, they may try to problem-solve, as a means of interactive coping, by attempting to plan a solution to the problem with the friend. Less altruistically, the helper may display certain interactive coping behaviors, such as distancing, to control the feelings of anxiety or depression usually created by the demands of providing social support (Gottlieb, 1990).

Thus, interacting with a person who is depressed may involve two levels of coping on the part of the helper. The partner must protect or manage his or her own emotions, as well as help to manage the problems and emotions of the person in distress (Gottlieb, 1990; Lehman et al., 1986). Several ways of coping with a threat to one's own well-being, such as minimizing or escaping, may not be helpful to the other person. Individuals confronted with a friend who needs cheering up, therefore, may react in a negative or maladaptive way, either because of their own patterns of ineffective coping, or because of their present cognitive or emotional state.

1 *SOLVE*: Problem-focussed/approach dimension
  (a) asking friends what's on their mind
  (b) asking questions about the event
  (c) giving suggestions

2 *SUPPORT*: Emotion-focussed/approach dimension
  (a) affirming their ability
  (b) giving them affection
  (c) offering to take them out or give them a gift
  (d) telling them everything is O.K.
  (e) making sympathetic remarks
  (f) telling them a joke to make them laugh
  (g) laughing with recipients
  (h) doing something funny

3 *DISMISS*: Problem-focussed/avoidance dimension
  (a) making fun of friends' problem
  (b) telling them their problem is not serious
  (c) laughing when recipients do not
  (d) talking about their own problems which are bigger

4 *ESCAPE*: Emotion-focussed/avoidance dimension
  (a) talking about something interesting to the helper
  (b) talking about the helper's task
  (c) talking about another topic
  (d) ignoring the person
  (e) reading a magazine
  (f) leaving the room

Figure 3.2 *Interactive-coping circumplex*

Thus, because of the greater complexity associated with interactive compared with personal coping, it may be useful to broaden the Folkman and Lazarus typology into a two-dimensional circumplex model. Roth and Cohen (1986) have presented a case for utilizing the concepts of *approach* and *avoidance* in their analysis of the coping process. In this analysis, helpers may either approach their friend's distress, or try to avoid the situation for the purposes of self-protection. Our two-dimensional circumplex of interactive coping, therefore, incorporates the Folkman and Lazarus dimension of focussing on the problem versus the emotion, which is crossed with the Roth and Cohen (1986) dimension of either approaching or avoiding the problem or emotion.

The resulting interactive-coping typology, displayed in Figure 3.2, includes four types of cheering-up strategies: *Solve*: problem-focussed/approach behaviors such as giving suggestions; *Support*: emotion-focussed/approach behaviors such as giving a hug; *Dismiss*: problem-focussed/avoidance behaviors such as denigrating the

problem; and *Escape*: emotion-focussed/avoidance behaviors such as changing the topic.

Effectiveness of Coping Strategies

Several studies have found that when people are trying to cope with their own problems, the use of planful problem solving and affect regulation was associated with positive outcomes and was inversely correlated with the frequency of negative psychological symptoms. By contrast, emotional forms of coping such as confrontation, emotional discharge, and avoidance have been found to be destructive (for example, Folkman et al., 1986).

Several pioneering studies directly examined the effectiveness of various social-support strategies in helping friends cope with anxiety in the laboratory (Sarason and Sarason, 1986). Winstead and Derlega (1985) found that being with a same-sex friend as opposed to a stranger during a potentially stressful event helped the friend feel less hostility and depression. In a follow-up study, Costanza et al., (1988) examined the effects of conversation topics on coping with stress among same-sex friends. The three major categories of conversational topics assessed were disclosure of feelings, problem-solving talk, and unrelated talk. The stressful event anticipated by the subjects was guiding a tarantula spider through a maze during a 'participant modeling task.' They found that talking about one's feelings had a more negative effect on reported levels of depression and anxiety than problem-solving talk or unrelated talk. In addition, waiting alone was associated with more depression and anxiety than waiting with others. The authors suggested that problem-solving talk could have increased confidence, and unrelated talk could have distracted subjects from the stressor, whereas, sharing feelings before the stressful event could have magnified those negative feelings about the anticipated event.

Winstead and her colleagues may have found negative effects for sharing feelings because *both* people in a dyad were experiencing *anxiety* about a *future* event. Our own research focusses on one member of a pair experiencing depression about a *past* event, and in that context, there is some evidence that expressing feelings can be beneficial (Pennybaker and O'Heeron, 1984). We suggest that if the helper aids the distressed partner in directly assessing the situation and in dealing with the problem, through the use of *Solve* behaviors, or tries to help with the partner's negative feelings, through the use of *Support* behaviors, then the partner is likely to feel better. However, if the helper chooses to avoid the situation or encourages the friend to avoid or minimize the problem, through

the use of *Escape* and *Dismiss* behaviors, then the partner may remain depressed or become worse.

I will now examine how several factors, such as the mood of the potential helper and recipient, attributions of the potential helper about the problem, and type of close relationship, may influence the types of strategies chosen by a potential helper when he or she is confronted by a close associate who is in need of cheering-up.

Emotional and Cognitive Aspects of Interactive Coping

Mood of the Helper in Interactive Coping

The mood or emotional state of the helper may have a significant impact both on the willingness to help a close associate, and on the form of the interactive coping that is provided. Mood states such as elation and depression influence social processes at several levels. A positive mood generally increases helping behavior (Carlson et al., 1988; Shaffer, 1986), whereas, a negative mood may decrease or increase helping behavior, depending on the helper's focus of attention and feelings of personal responsibility to help (Carlson and Miller, 1987).

Cunningham et al. (1980) argued that positive and negative mood states involve different motivational systems. The separate-process model of mood–behavior relations (Cunningham, 1988a, b) states that positive moods often occur when a person experiences propitious personal, social, or ecological circumstances. If life is going well, then a person has less need to be conservative or problem oriented and may place a higher priority on engaging in behaviors which offer a good chance of expanding his or her social network (Isen, 1970) and meeting new challenges. Positive mood is therefore associated with processes that make the individual more optimistic, socially expansive, and self-confident. This expansive motivation causes the person to be more positive in evaluating people (Gouaux, 1971), the self (Alloy et al., 1981), and even personal possessions (Isen et al., 1978). Further, individuals in a positive mood seem to be more interested in social goodwill and are more optimistic about the outcome of their efforts in the social domain (Cunningham, 1988a; Masters and Furman, 1976), and are more likely to respond to a socially oriented charity request (Cunningham et al., 1980) and to help on a task if they witness a model who volunteers to help or who encourages their involvement (Cunningham et al., 1990; Shaffer and Smith, 1985).

A negative mood, by contrast, is associated with events which threaten an individual's personal, social, or environmental adaptation. When someone experiences his or her limitations, or the

trauma of life, it may be adaptive to withdraw somewhat and to engage in self-reflection and ruminative thinking (Greenberg and Pyszczynski, 1986). Thus, negative moods are associated with ego-centric, avoidant motivations which involve an increase in rumi-nations, a decrease in social interest, self-esteem, and optimism, and a socially inhibited rather than an expansive orientation. Nega-tive moods have been found to reduce interest in social interaction and self-disclosure (Cunningham, 1988b), to reduce spontaneous thoughts about donating to charity (Cunningham and Barbee, 1987), and to reduce some forms of helping (Cunningham, 1979). People in a negative mood may be helpful, but only if it offers relief of their own negative state (Cialdini and Kenrick, 1976). Those in negative moods have been found to be influenced by personal rather than altruistic pleas to give to charity (Cunningham et al., 1980), and were more likely to focus on the personal hedonic value of a helping task rather than on social inducements to help (Cunningham et al., 1990; Shaffer and Smith, 1985).

The separate-process model's emphasis on the social versus per-sonal motivations associated with positive and negative moods has direct implications for interactive coping, as will be made evident below. Yet because helping lovers and friends is a dynamic interac-tive process, it can be influenced by the mood and problems of the recipient of helping, as well as by the feelings of the helper.

The Effects of the Mood of the Recipient

The depression of one member of a dyad has been found to cause the partner to feel nurturant and concerned, but also to feel depressed and annoyed toward the originally depressed person. This is especially true when the two are in a close relationship such as one involving a roommate, friend, or spouse (Coyne, 1976a, b; Howes and Hokanson, 1979).

Associating with a depressed person has been found to lead to positive actions such as helping, if help is requested (Sacco et al., 1985), and may increase cooperation, responsibility, and manage-ment on behalf of the depressed partner (Hokanson et al., 1986). Yet frequent interactions with a depressed partner also may lead to negative behaviors, such as poor problem-solving tactics and even destructive behaviors, such as verbal and physical abuse when problems are being discussed (Kahn et al., 1985). The separate-process model suggests that being in a negative mood causes one to become more introspective, pessimistic, and egocentric. Such a disposition may impede the ability of the helper to select effective interactive coping behaviors, and may reduce motivation to persist in giving social support until one's partner is feeling better.

Based on these literatures, it seems plausible to expect a person in a positive mood to be more willing and able than others to cheer up a depressed friend. However, if the negative mood of the friend begins to influence the mood of the potential helper, then the chance for helping may be diminished. On the other hand, individuals who are themselves depressed may be more likely to avoid a depressed partner, or act in an ineffective or hostile fashion if they try to cheer up another person. Alternatively, they may try to overcome their own depressed feelings and help anyway, since a communal versus an exchange relationship is involved (Clark et al., 1987).

Effect of the Reason for the Recipient's Negative Mood on the Interactive-coping Process

The reason for the depressed person's mood may have a major impact on whether a person will help a depressed friend (McCrae, 1984). The cause of the recipient's mood may play a role not only in the emotional reaction of the helper, but in the interactive coping strategy that is employed (McCoy and Masters, 1985). Weiner (1980), for example, reported that subjects responding to scenarios involving a person in need of help were more likely to feel sympathy and pity, and were more likely to render aid, when the cause of a problem was attributed to uncontrollable causes. Such respondents felt anger, however, if the cause was seen as controllable by the afflicted person and were less likely to help. Weiner's attribution–emotion–action model is based on scenarios about strangers. We may find differences in attributions, emotions, and subsequent behaviors when the subject is in a close relationship with the target. For example, even if the cause of the problem was seen as controllable, friends may still try to solve the problem and render as much support as possible because of social norms prescribing that they should try to make their friend feel better (Barbee et al., 1990). Alternatively, pity for a friend may be a function of the perceived importance or seriousness of the problem itself, rather than by the attributions about causality or controllability of the problem (Barbee, 1989a). Yet it remains possible that an attribution of controllability of the cause of the problem will lead to more rejection of the depressed partner in the form of *Escape* and *Dismiss* behaviors and that an attribution of uncontrollability will lead to more sympathy and greater use of *Solve* and *Support* behaviors.

Research on the Interactive-coping Process

A number of studies have examined various facets of the inter-active-coping process. Several of our studies have utilized a scenario format in exploring the effect of mood and attributions on inter-active-coping strategies in different kinds of relationships (Barbee, 1989a; Barbee and Cunningham, 1988; Barbee et al., 1990). The scenario design allowed systematic testing of theoretically impor-tant independent variables in an efficient and minimally intrusive fashion. The scenario approach also allowed responses to be gath-ered on all potential interactive coping behaviors, including those unlikely to be performed in the laboratory.

I also have employed a behavioral-observation design using indi-viduals in existing relationships (Barbee, 1989b). This approach permitted verification of scenario findings, and the determination of whether people in specifically created mood states actually engage in the theoretically predicted interactive-coping behaviors when confronted with a close associate having a particular problem. A description of several specific studies in our program of research will be followed by a summary of how mood and attributions affect the interactive-coping process.

Interactive Coping in Romantic Couples
Barbee and Cunningham (1988) explored the cheering-up process in romantic couples using a scenario format. Ninety subjects were exposed to the Velten (1968) series of fifty statements designed to either put them in a positive, neutral, or negative mood state. The statements were presented on slides, which were accompanied by a musical mood induction which matched the slides in valence (Pignatiello et al., 1986).

Following the mood induction, subjects read two separate scen-arios and were asked a series of questions about their emotional and behavioral responses to their romantic partner in each of these different problem situations. One problem situation involved the partner being sad after viewing a depressing film, and the other had the loved one being unhappy after failing a midterm examination in his or her major. Subjects indicated their emotional reactions to their partners in each scenario, using terms describing feelings of empathy, distress (Batson et al., 1983), and annoyance (Sacco et al., 1985). They also indicated the likelihood that they would engage in any of seventeen interactive coping behaviors later grou-ped into the categories of *Solve*, *Support*, *Dismiss*, and *Escape*.

We found that subjects in an induced positive mood were more likely to use the *Approach* dimension strategy of *Support*, such as

giving a hug, a gift, or just listening to the friend. Induced-negative-mood subjects, by contrast, used the *Avoidant* dimension strategy of *Escape*, reporting that they would either leave the room if the depression was film induced or talk about something of interest to themselves if the depression was failure induced. These results, together with those of the subsequently discussed studies, are summarized in Table 3.1.

Table 3.1 *Effects of mood and attributions on interactive-coping behaviors in four studies*

	Positive mood	Negative mood	Attribution	
			Control.	Uncontrol.
Romantic couples scenario	Support	Escape	Dismiss	Solve
Female friends scenario	Support	Dismiss	Dismiss	Support
	Solve		Escape	Solve
Female friends observation	Support	Dismiss	Dismiss	Support
			Escape	Solve
Male friends scenario	–	–	Dismiss	Support
			Escape	Solve

We found that implicit attributions about the reasons for the problem had an impact on interactive coping as well. When a romantic partner failed a test and helpers regarded the problem as controllable, as evidenced by low reported sympathy and higher annoyance, the helpers were likely to use the *Dismiss* behavior of talking about their own problems that were bigger. When a romantic partner failed a test and the partners felt that the problem was uncontrollable, as evidenced by high reported sympathy, they were more likely to use the *Solve* behavior of offering helpful suggestions. When a partner was depressed after seeing a sad film, helpers said they would use the *Avoidant* strategies of making fun of the partner and making sexual advances. The use of the *Dismiss* behavior was positively correlated with feelings of annoyance and was negatively correlated with feelings of sympathy. Thus, it is plausible that subjects believed being depressed by a film was unimportant and that the friend could control subjects' emotional reaction to the film, causing subjects to minimize the importance of the problem.

Interactive Coping in Female Friends

Barbee (1989a) explored the interactive-coping process among female friends using procedures which replicated the Barbee and Cunningham (1988) study. In addition to the measures of emotional

reactions and behaviors toward the friend, subjects were given an attribution questionnaire concerning each problem situation.

Barbee found that females in induced positive moods were more likely than females in neutral or negative moods to choose the *Approach* dimension strategies of *Solve* and *Support* in order to help their same-sex friends. By contrast, females in induced negative moods were more likely than others to choose the *Avoidant* dimension *Dismiss* strategies of telling their friend the problem was not *really* serious, telling their friend that things could be worse, and making fun of their friend's problem.

We also found that females were more likely to use *Dismiss* and *Escape* behaviors when their friend had seen a sad film than when their friend had failed a test. Analyses of mediating variables again suggested that many helpers viewed their partner's reaction to the sad film as unjustified, and the problem as unimportant. The helper's ratings of the importance of the problem were positively correlated with feelings of empathy, and negatively correlated with feelings of annoyance toward the partner. Feelings of annoyance were also positively correlated with the use of *Dismiss* and *Escape* behaviors, whereas feelings of empathy were negatively correlated with the choice of such actions.

Helpers were more likely to use *Support* behaviors when their friend had failed a test than when their friend had seen a sad film. Their use of such behaviors correlated with their feelings of empathy and distress and with their perceptions that the problem was important and very unpleasant.

Behavioral Observation of Interactive Coping in Female Friends

Barbee (1989b) explored the cheering-up process with ninety pairs of female friends who had been close friends an average of four years. Participants were led to believe that the study concerned how friends communicate their emotions with each other and how talking about an experience affects subsequent feelings and attitudes. They were told that one of them would have an experience and would then relate that experience to their friend to see what effect the conversation would have on each person. The participants were first given personality questionnaires, questions about the nature of their friendship, and a premood measure. Then the experimenter randomly selected each subject to be either the subject needing cheering up (the recipient) or the helper. The pair was separated for the purpose of allowing the recipient to either view a film or take a test, so that afterwards she could tell her partner what happened and her reactions to the event.

The person who was to be the recipient of the cheering-up effort was taken to an adjoining room to receive the mood induction. In the external-focussed negative mood induction the subject viewed a clip from *Gallipoli* depicting the slaughter of young soldiers, followed by a clip from *Sophie's Choice* depicting a mother making a choice to give up either her daughter or son to a Nazi officer. In the internal-focussed negative mood induction, the subject took a psychoneurological and performance test of cognitive ability, and received false negative feedback on it.

In the mean time, elated, neutral, or depressed mood was induced in the helper using a variation of the Velten (1968) mood-induction procedure, ostensibly for a separate experiment (Cunningham et al., 1990). After both mood inductions, a measure of present mood state was given. When both tasks were completed, the partners were brought back together so that the first person could talk about the film or test and her reactions to it. The conversation was videotaped unobtrusively through a one-way mirror for five minutes. Four raters later coded the tapes for the behaviors of the helper as she responded to her partner. After the interaction, each subject pair was separated again in order to give them a chance to anonymously record their perceptions of the encounter.

Barbee (1989b) found that female helpers in a positive mood were seen by the recipients as making more of an *effort* to cheer them up, used more *different types* of cheering-up strategies, and used more *Approach* strategies of *Support* in their cheering-up attempt than helpers in neutral or negative moods. The cheering-up behaviors that were differentially used by the positive mood helpers were rated by the recipients as being among the more effective strategies in cheering them up, which may be why positive mood helpers were perceived to be more *successful* in cheering up their friends than were neutral or negative mood helpers.

Negative mood helpers were perceived by recipients as making *less* of an effort to help cheer them up, used *fewer* cheering-up behaviors than others, and responded to the recipient in a manner which the blind coders of the videotapes rated as not taking the problem seriously, a behavior from the *Dismiss* category.

Helpers were seen as expending more effort to cheer up the friend who had failed a psychoneurological test than the friend who had seen the tragic film. Yet the helpers also engaged in more total *Dismiss* and *Escape* behaviors when their friend failed a test than when their friend saw a depressing film. Further analyses revealed that helpers in the test condition felt higher levels of annoyance and lower levels of empathy than those whose friends had seen the film, and such feelings were correlated with higher levels of *Dismiss*

and *Escape* behaviors. The helpers could be given the benefit of the doubt that their use of *Dismiss* behaviors, such as not taking the problem seriously, was done to make their friends feel better about their poor test performances. Yet since helpers whose friends had done poorly on the test also employed such *Escape* behaviors as changing the topic and talking about their own problem, they may have wished to distance themselves from someone who had failed (Pleban and Tesser, 1981). It also is possible that the helpers felt overwhelmed when trying to help a friend who failed a neuro-psychological test. Interactive coping with a friend who failed an academic test in their major, which was the dilemma posed in the scenario study, may have been seen as an easier chore.

It should be emphasized that the most critical question associated with the variable of type of problem is not whether one or another type of failed test, or a test versus a film, stimulates more interactive coping. More important are the relations of the attributional and affective mediators to the use of the various coping behaviors, and those relations are consistent across studies. Even in the test condition, those subjects who saw their friend's failure as uncontrol-lable, as evidenced by higher levels of empathy and lower levels of annoyance, were more likely to use *Solve* and *Support* behaviors.

The scenario studies found that helpers reported high levels of *Dismiss* and *Escape* behaviors when their friends had seen a sad film, but such responses were not evident in the behavior-obser-vation study. One reason for this apparently inconsistent finding may have been due to the content of the film shown to the recipient. The film clips were based on actual historic events, making the protagonists' plight seem extremely vivid, and making the recipi-ent's reaction seem justified. The reality of the movie could have made the helpers less likely to see their partner's reaction as unim-portant, and unlikely to use *Dismiss* behaviors. Thus, important external-focussed negative events, and internal-focussed negative events that do not annoy or overwhelm the helper, may both stimu-late the use of *Solve* and *Support* behaviors.

Outcome of Interactive-coping Efforts

Barbee (1989b) did not directly manipulate the behaviors used by the subjects during interactive coping, and thus could not serve as a pure test of the effectiveness of various cheering-up strategies. Nonetheless, the behaviors that were seen by the recipient as most successful and indicative that the partner was attempting to cheer them up were all *Approach* behaviors from the *Solve* and *Support* categories.

The behaviors that were seen as least successful were *Escape*

behaviors. These results are largely consistent with those of Lehman et al. (1986) who found that people who had lost a close family member reported supportive acts as effective in remediating their depressed state. Lehman et al.'s respondents also reported that advice giving was an ineffective strategy in helping them get over their family member's death. Yet perhaps when the situation is an extremely serious, externally caused problem such as death, no advice can be sufficient to make the person feel better. Such results further suggest that the use, and effectiveness, of an inter-active-coping strategy may be partially dependent on the helper's perception of the controllability of the recipient's emotion and of the solution to the problem, not just the controllability of the cause of the problem.

Interactive Coping in Male Friends
In Barbee et al. (1990), forty-eight male subjects, who were in neutral moods, were given four parametric variations of four scenario themes based on Weiner's attributional dimensions of controllability and causality, and then asked the same series of questions used in our other scenario studies (Barbee, 1989a) about their cognitive, emotional, and behavioral responses to their best friend. Thus, each subject received scenarios about his or her best friend failing a test, breaking up with a romantic partner, losing a game and having the car break down, which were presented as being controllable or uncontrollable, and internally or externally caused.

We found that male subjects were more likely to report that they would use *Solve* and *Support* behaviors if their friend's problem was either externally caused or uncontrollable. Additionally, these subjects were more likely to use *Dismiss* and *Escape* behaviors if their friend's problem was internally caused *and* controllable. These results are highly congruent with the earlier studies which did not use manipulated attributions.

Summary of Interactive-coping Results

Effects of Mood on the Interactive-coping Process
The foregoing studies indicated that when people are in a positive mood, they are more likely to use *Approach* behaviors, such as actions from the *Support* and *Solve* categories. Conversely, when people are in a negative mood, they are more likely to use *Avoidance* behaviors, such as actions from the *Dismiss* and *Escape* categories. It might be noted that the use of *Avoidance* behaviors on the part of negative-mood helpers is not due to an absence of feeling; negative-mood helpers reported more feelings of empathy

(Barbee, 1989a, b; Barbee and Cunningham, 1988), distress (Barbee and Cunningham, 1988), and sadness (Barbee, 1989b) toward their friend than neutral-mood helpers. Thus, negative-mood helpers appeared to feel concern for their friends, but their negative mood seemed to prevent them from making a determined effort to initiate and sustain *Approach* interactive-coping behaviors. Such ineffective helpfulness may stem, in part, from the preoccupation with the self, and low energy level, which is characteristic of depression (Cunningham, 1988a).

The Attribution–Emotion–Action Link
Our findings generally supported Weiner's (1980) attribution-emotion–action model. We found that if subjects saw a problem as uncontrollable, important, and unpleasant, they were more likely to feel sympathy and empathy and were more likely to use *Solve* and *Support* behaviors. They were also less likely to feel annoyed and less likely to use *Escape* and *Dismiss* behaviors. On the other hand, when subjects saw a problem as controllable, unimportant, and less unpleasant, they were more likely to feel annoyed and were more likely to use *Escape* and *Dismiss* behaviors. Thus, we found that not only is the controllability of a problem important, but the importance, focus, and unpleasantness dimensions of a problem also have an impact on the emotions a person experiences about a friend's plight, and on the subsequent behaviors that are enacted.

Batson et al. (1983) found that emotional reactions of empathy were positively related but emotional reactions of personal distress were negatively related to willingness to offer help. We confirmed the empathy–helping relation in the domain of interactive coping, with the finding that higher levels of reported empathy were associated with greater use of *Solve* and *Support* behaviors. We also found that the emotional reaction of annoyance was associated with a reluctance to help, and the use of ineffective *Dismiss* and *Escape* behaviors.

The Future of Interactive-coping Research

The research described in this chapter provides insight into some of the variables presented in the theoretical model of interactive coping, but many questions remain to be explored. Additional moods in the helper, such as anger and guilt, and different dilemmas for the recipient, such as problems with no obvious solution, may influence the process of interactive coping. What, for example, does a helper do when he or she is the cause of the

problem, such as by carelessly breaking an irreplaceable family heirloom of the recipient: is the recipient even willing to accept *Support* behaviors from that helper? For what types of problems are people more, or less, willing to seek out interactive coping (Barbee et al., 1990), and for what types of problems are each of the *Solve, Support, Dismiss,* and *Escape* behaviors likely to be most effective? A longitudinal study currently being conducted with the support of the Computer Assisted Panel project of the University of North Carolina may provide some answers to these questions.

Interactive coping is a form of problem solving, and we are curious about the decision steps which a helper must execute while engaged in this process. The helper must confront the question of whether to focus first on the problem or the emotion of the recipient. The helper must also decide whether or not to persist with a behavior if it does not seem effective, or move on to another category of coping. We do not yet know whether there is a progression of action from *Solve* to *Support* to *Dismiss* to *Escape* in unsuccessful interactive-coping efforts, yet such a cycle seems possible.

The actions of the recipient which encourage persistence by the helper in a specific category of interactive coping are largely unknown. Informal observation suggests that some recipients initially decline to cheer up to see how long their partner will persist in his or her *Approach* behaviors, as a test of the helper's commitment to the relationship. The duration, closeness, and investment in the relationship, and the gender, temperament, and personality of both the helper and recipient, may all play a role in selection and persistence in an interactive-coping behavior.

Conclusions and Implications

I will raise four main points in conclusion. First, I believe that recent work from several laboratories, including my own, has demonstrated that the seeking and giving of social support is an interactive process. Researchers in the field must recognize and account for this complexity in future investigations. There are support-seeking behaviors that the recipient enacts which either elicit the type of support needed, or implicitly discourage the giving of such support by the helper. Conversely, *Dismiss* or *Escape* behaviors enacted by the helper early in the encounter may dishearten the recipient from pursuing the interaction. Consequently, we need further information on the microdynamics of this process: the recipient's initial behaviors, the helper's responses, the recipient's

reactions to those efforts, and so on through the cycle of the interaction (Kenny, 1986).

The second implication of this research concerns our understanding of those low in perceived social support. People obtaining low scores in measures of perceived social support (PSS) are rated lower in physical attractiveness, have poorer social skills, (Sarason et al., 1985), are more lonely (Jones, 1985), more introverted, neurotic, and low in self-esteem (Sarason et al., 1983), and actually receive less social support than their counterparts (Cutrona, 1986a). All of these traits imply that the person who does not receive support is not able to establish and maintain supportive relationships or communicate his or her needs when they arise. However, our data suggest that characteristics of the *helpers* also may contribute to a lack of social support. It may be the case that people low in PSS are seeking support from close associates who themselves are under a great deal of stress, since individuals tend to affiliate with those from their own academic and socioeconomic level. Thus, the people in the networks of those low in PSS may be incapable of providing enthusiastic, sustained interactive coping because of their own negative moods. Future investigations on perceived social support should obtain information from the members of a person's social-support network, as well as from the recipient, in order to test this hypothesis more directly.

Third, this research suggests that the providing of support may be more difficult than the previous literature suggested; interactive coping is difficult to do well. It requires a great deal of cognitive work to adequately interpret and respond to the friend's problem. Providing interactive-coping behaviors that are effective requires sensitivity, creativity, energy, and persistence, often in the face of repeated failure to ameliorate the friend's unhappiness. Not only do factors such as negative mood and biased interpretations of the friend's problem undermine the interactive-coping process, but cultural myths about how to cheer someone up may also hinder a person from effectively dealing with a friend's plight. As we study the process in detail, we will be better equipped to teach people how to bolster their friend's emotions with sympathy, affection, laughter, and affirmation and to persist even when feeling defeated, to forego *Dismiss* and *Escape* in favor of *Solve* and *Support*.

Finally, while we remain deeply interested in the dynamics of social support in close relationships, the interactive-coping circumplex is not limited to friends and lovers. We have found the same categories of *Solve*, *Support*, *Dismiss*, and *Escape* employed by athletic coaches in their half-time and post-game pep talks (Gibson et al., 1990). Similar behaviors may be observed in clinical counse-

ling, academic advising, parent–child instruction, and supervisor–subordinate interaction. Further investigation of the specific dimensions and fine-grain behaviors of interactive coping, and their attributional and emotional mediators, may provide greater insight into the general dynamics of human social interaction.

Note

Thanks are expressed to Michael R. Cunningham and Steve Duck for their helpful comments on an earlier draft of this chapter.

4

Comforting as Social Support: Relational Consequences of Supportive Behaviors

Brant R. Burleson

Most discussions of social relationships and social support emphasize the supportive nature of relationships. For example, some theorists (for example, Cobb, 1976) suggest that the presence or existence of social relationships is itself supportive. Quite a bit of evidence relevant to this position has accumulated.

Recently, however, the notion that relationships per se are supportive has been subjected to both criticism and amplification. One criticism of 'relationships-are-supportive' doctrine is that it ignores the fact that all relationships (or interactions within relationships) are *not* supportive. Indeed, researchers (for example, Rook, 1984) have reported data showing that some relationships (or interactions) are destructive and harmful.

Other theorists (for example, Kessler et al., 1985) have pointed out that relationships themselves are not directly supportive (or unsupportive). That is, although remembering relational ties may be comforting at times, it is usually not the simple existence of a relationship per se that provides support. Rather, it is specific actions that one relational partner carries out on behalf of the other partner that provide support: actions, rather than relationships, convey support. Relationships are important because we expect that certain relational partners (for example, friends) will engage in appropriate support acts either spontaneously or when called upon during stressful times. From this perspective, then, it is the specific acts of informing, advising, empathizing, or giving of material aid that actually provide support. This recognition has led to more microscopic analyses of support behaviors. For example, some research (for example, Cutrona, 1986b) has focussed on understanding how various interactions within a relationship serve support functions.

The recent interest in how specific features of relationships provide (or fail to provide) support holds considerable promise. However, most of this work continues to center on the question of how

relationships provide support: in such work, the causal path flows rather clearly from relationships to support.

In the current chapter, I want to pursue implications of a somewhat different thesis, namely that certain support behaviors may have profound relational consequences. That is, I examine a complementary causal path to the one implied by most research on social support, a causal path that extends *from* support behaviors *to* features of interpersonal relationships.

It does not take long to develop reasons for thinking that support behaviors might influence the character of people's interpersonal relationships. For example, support behaviors may help relieve suffering or distress, and people are inclined to like those that make them feel better – especially when it appears that the supporter was acting with the intention of making the distressed other feel better. On the other hand, clumsy or inept support attempts, even if well intentioned, may hurt the distressed other and thus foster dislike of the supporter. Further, people expect certain relational partners (for example, friends, family members) to provide support in times of need. Acting in accord with this expectation may reinforce the relationship between helper and helpee. In contrast, failure of relational partner to fulfill support expectations may result in feelings of disappointment, doubt, and betrayal. Moreover, since the helpee is already in a distressed state, failure of a relational partner to provide support (or the right kind of support) may exacerbate the stressful situation.

Although there are thus ample reasons for thinking that the provision of social support – and the skill with which it is given – may have substantial relational consequences, these are not matters that have received much attention in the social-support literature. Most social-support researchers have, quite understandably, focussed on such matters as which members of the social network provide support, the forms of support provided by network members, and how supportive actions relieve or buffer the effects of environmental stresses. In contrast, communication researchers have recently exhibited considerable interest in the relational effects of different message forms. In particular, studies have examined the effects of different persuasive or compliance-gaining messages on variables such as interpersonal liking (for example, O'Keefe and McCornack, 1987). Of course, persuasion and compliance gaining are not paradigm instances of social support, so the results of these investigations may not tell us much about how social support influences the conduct of relationships. However, comforting communication is a much clearer instance of social support. Examining how *comforting* behavior affects the quality of interpersonal

relationships may thus provide some general insight about the relational consequences of social support.

The present chapter thus explores whether and how the routine comforting that goes on among ordinary people in everyday life is a significant form of social behavior, especially with respect to its consequences for the formation and maintenance of interpersonal relationships. My colleagues and I recently initiated a series of studies directed at determining the social significance of comforting in several distinct populations (for example, children, adolescents, young adults). This chapter summarizes the findings of those and related studies. These findings provide some backing for the claim that comforting is a consequential behavior. The verbal comfort people receive from peers appears to improve the quality of their lives and otherwise affect social relationships, at least in some instances. Before discussing these findings, however, I provide a context for this recent work by briefly reviewing previous research on the production and effects of comforting messages.

Comforting Communication Skills

Much of our initial research on comforting communication was motivated primarily by theoretical interests. Certainly, we believed that comforting was an important process in everyday life. However, most of our early research on this form of communication stemmed from an interest in how developmentally based individual differences in social-cognitive abilities contributed to skill in the production of messages addressing difficult communicative tasks. Comforting someone who had experienced a recent loss or upset clearly appeared to be a difficult communication task.

In this research, comforting behaviors were defined as those messages having the goal of alleviating or lessening the emotional distresses experienced by others (Burleson, 1985). The research was restricted to comforting activity addressing the mild-to-moderate feelings of disappointment, hurt, or sadness arising from a variety of everyday events. For example, among children we examined such situations as a friend not receiving an invitation to another child's party or not doing well on a test in school. Among young adults we examined such common situations as a roommate being dropped by his or her dating partner or a friend failing to receive a prestigious scholarship. We did not deal with extreme feelings of depression or grief, the situations producing these feelings (for example, the loss of one's spouse), or the strategies used to manage these extreme feelings. Some research (for example, Lindemann, 1965) suggests that these more intense emotional experiences call

for responses quite different from those used to manage everyday emotional upsets, and may sometimes require the intervention of professionals. Given our interest in issues related to the development and social-cognitive correlates of communication skills used by ordinary people in everyday life, we focussed on the moderate hurts and upsets people routinely experience since virtually everyone encounters and has to manage them. Although there are no hard data on how often people engage in routine comforting acts, informal observation suggests that the occasions calling for the provision of comfort are common, if not constant.

During the early phases of our research program, we examined aspects of comforting behavior such as the development and antecedents of comforting skills (for example, Burleson, 1982; Delia et al., 1979). These studies documented that comforting skills developed in a progressive manner over the course of childhood and adolescence and were influenced by parents' behaviours. More important, several studies (for example, Applegate, 1980; Burleson, 1984a) found that, in both children and adults, the ability to produce sensitive and sophisticated comforting messages was related to individual differences in social cognition, particularly differences in interpersonal cognitive complexity, a variable indexing the degree of differentiation and integration in the cognitive structures used to represent the social world. From a theoretical point of view, these findings were especially significant because they showed that the structure of persons' communicative behaviors reflected underlying features of their cognitive schemes for interpreting and representing the world.

Other studies during this period motivated by theoretical concerns examined (a) dispositions affecting the use of comforting skills (for example, Samter and Burleson, 1984), (b) situational factors influencing the exercise of comforting skills (for example, Burleson, 1982), and (c) sociological factors related to the development and distribution of comforting abilities (for example, Applegate et al., 1985). (For reviews on the developmental, cognitive, motivational, and sociological correlates of comforting skills, see Burleson, 1984b, 1985.)

One assumption of this research was that because comforting messages produced by people with high levels of cognitive complexity exhibited more concern for the recipient's feelings, perspective, and situation, these strategies would generally be more effective at relieving the distressed states of others. We examined this assumption in a series of studies assessing (a) the perceived sensitivity and effectiveness of different comforting strategies (for example, Burleson and Samter, 1985a, b), (b) how exposure to different

comforting messages affected both the recipient and producer of these messages (for example, Samter et al., 1987, 1989) and (c) the effects of individual differences in comforting skill on the quality of persons' social relationships (for example, Burleson and Waltman, 1987; Burleson et al., 1986).

In this research, 'sophisticated comforting strategies' were operationalized as messages explicitly acknowledging, elaborating, and legitimizing the feelings of a distressed other (see Applegate, 1980; Burleson, 1984b). This model of comforting skill was built by fusing aspects of Bernstein's (1975) analysis of 'person-centered' speech, Werner's (1957) structural-developmental theory, and Rogers' (1961) client-centered psychotherapy. To code the 'sophistication' or 'sensitivity' of comforting messages, a nine-level hierarchy was developed (Applegate, 1980; Burleson, 1984a). Messages coded in the lower levels of this hierarchy tend to deny the perspective and feelings of the distressed other; those coded in the middle levels provide some implicit appreciation and support for the other and his or her feelings; and those coded in the highest levels explicitly acknowledge and elaborate the other's feelings. More specifically, within this scheme 'sophisticated' comforting strategies, compared to less sophisticated messages, project a greater degree of involvement with the distressed other, are more neutral evaluatively, are more feeling centered, are more accepting of the other, and contain more cognitively oriented explanations of the feelings experienced by the other.

As anticipated, we usually found that 'sophisticated' comforting strategies (those typically produced by persons with high levels of interpersonal cognitive complexity) were perceived as doing a better job of both improving the affect state of the recipient and serving subsidiary objectives such as relationship maintenance (for a detailed summary of these results and further analysis of 'sophisticated' comforting strategies, see Burleson, in press). In particular, we found that messages acknowledging, elaborating, and legitimizing the feelings of distressed others were perceived as the most effective means for relieving distressed states and were most likely to result in positive evaluations of the comforter. These findings are consistent with research detailing the forms of verbal behavior generally most effective in counselling contexts (see, for example, Elliott, 1985), as well as with research identifying strategies that bereaved individuals find particularly helpful (see Lehman et al., 1986).

In sum, our research, in conjunction with the efforts of other scholars, has articulated some message types that seem generally effective in the management of moderate levels of emotional dis-

tress. We thus gained some appreciation of how 'good' comforting messages differ from 'poor' ones. However, as we neared the completion of these studies, it occurred to us that we could not say whether this newly acquired knowledge was socially significant – whether it had meaningful practical implications. Certainly, the effective relief of emotional distress (even moderate forms of distress) is worthwhile, so knowing which messages generally do a better job of providing such relief has some social value. But how much value? To answer this question, we needed to understand more about the distresses typically addressed in comforting messages and the effects of providing comfort on a variety of fundamental social processes.

More specifically, our previous research had not asked whether the activity of comforting itself played a prominent role in the social world. Thus, although we could say which comforting messages were generally 'good,' we could not say whether the benefits of training people in the use of 'good' comforting messages would outweigh the costs. Nor could we explain the role, if any, of comforting behavior in social processes such as relationship formation and maintenance. We thus undertook a series of studies directed at ascertaining the significance of comforting behaviour in everyday life, with particular attention on relational consequences of comforting behavior.

The Social Significance of Comforting Behavior

Reducing the degree of emotional distress experienced by others would appear intuitively to be quite important (especially if *we* are the 'others' whose distress is being reduced!). Obviously, people want to feel good about themselves and their lives, so they should value efforts that help them overcome unpleasant emotions and like those who seem adept at improving their emotional states. Thus, it would certainly seem that comforting ought to be a socially significant form of behavior with potent relational consequences. However, some reflection suggests several reasons why comforting might not be all that important in everyday life.

First, hurts and disappointments come in all sizes, ranging from minor upsets experienced somewhat regularly to infrequent, but emotionally shattering life crises. As noted above, the focus in our comforting research has been on the management of emotional pain arising from a variety of everyday defeats and disappointments. Perhaps these relatively minor hurts have little impact on people's lives. Thus, behavior directed at managing these hurts may not be very important.

Second, some observational studies suggest that comforting may be a relatively rare form of behavior. In part, this may be due to social pressures motivating the maintenance of a positive public 'face,' which make it unlikely that scientists would have access to many real-world acts of comforting by adults. However, observational studies of children, who are more accessible to researchers and less conscious of face-maintenance pressures, have reported few instances of comforting behavior. For example, Iannotti (1981) observed fifty-two children over a five month period and recorded numerous prosocial events, but classified only one of these as an instance of comforting behavior (also see, for example, Strayer, 1981). Thus, it is possible that not much comforting takes place in the everyday world.

Third, some of our data (for example, Samter and Burleson, 1984), as well as data reported by other researchers (for example, Notarius and Herrick, 1988), show that many, even most, responses to distressed others are relatively insensitive. Although this might be because many people are unskilled in comforting others, it also could reflect the belief – a belief grounded in reality – that mild to moderate instances of emotional distress are not significant and should thus be dismissed or ignored.

These considerations provoke several questions about the social significance of comforting behavior. (a) Are the minor 'everyday' or 'mundane' upsets people routinely face important? That is, do ordinary emotional upsets and distresses exert a major impact on mental, emotional, and physical health? (b) Does verbal comfort from peers provide relief from ordinary distresses and the effects of these distresses? In other words, is the moderation of ordinary emotional distress associated with a meaningful improvement in the quality of people's lives? (c) Do people value the activity of comforting? Do they appreciate those who are particularly skilled at this activity? (d) Does the activity of comforting, or skill in comforting, play an important role in social processes such as the development, maintenance, and dissolution of friendships and other interpersonal relationships? These four sets of questions provide a framework for assessing the social significance of comforting.

Significance of the Upsets Addressed in Comforting Messages

Researchers concerned with stress and its management (for example, Lazarus and Cohen, 1977) distinguish between three types of stressors. *Major events* are acute, extremely intense, but rare situations (for example, death of a spouse, loss of a job). *Chronic conditions* are more permanent features of a living situation (for

example, having few friends, living in a bad neighborhood, poverty). *Daily hassles and disappointments* are acute, minor events that create temporary emotional upsets and problems (for example, getting yelled at by the boss, being rejected by an acquaintance).

A growing body of evidence shows that the minor hassles, disappointments, and hurts people routinely experience are major determinants of moods and psychological well-being. Several studies (for example, Stone, 1981) have reported significant associations between depression or negative mood states and the frequency with which unpleasant events are experienced.

Although these results are not surprising, two other studies (Eckenrode, 1984; Kanner et al., 1981) found that stress resulting from everyday hassles and disappointments was a much better predictor of mood and psychological well-being than stress resulting from major life events or chronic conditions. Indeed, the results of these latter studies suggest that major life events and chronic conditions affect psychological variables such as depression primarily through disrupting established patterns of daily living and increasing the number and range of minor hurts and hassles experienced (see Eckenrode, 1984). Related research (for example, DeLongis et al., 1982) shows that the stress resulting from daily upsets is a better predictor of physical health than the stress resulting from major life events.

In sum, it appears that the ordinary distresses and upsets addressed by peers in comforting messages are significant. These emotional conditions appear to be major determinants of mood, psychological well-being, and even physical health.

Significance of the Relief Provided by Comforting Behavior

Does the emotional support provided in comforting messages help people manage the upset and stress associated with everyday hurts and disappointments? Does the relief obtained through the comforting efforts of others result in a meaningfully improved quality of life?

People may readily turn to those in their social network during times of emotional need, but as suggested above, not all social interactions should be assumed to serve supportive functions. Some research (for example, Rook, 1984) indicates that social interaction can lead to undesirable mental-health outcomes; indeed, unpleasant interactions may do more harm than pleasant interactions do good. This is worrisome since instances of insensitive comforting appear to be abundant. Studies of the bereaved (for example, Lehman et al., 1986) report that they often are targets of

comforting attempts which they regard as insensitive and unhelpful. Research on the messages that college students say they would use to help friends work through emotional problems (for example, Reisman and Yamokoski, 1974) indicates that few individuals use messages reflecting high levels of empathy and support. Further, Notarius and Herrick (1988) found that over half of the subjects in their study responded unsupportively to a confederate feigning moderate depression.

Fortunately, an increasing volume of research suggests that messages expressing concern and solidarity, prompting the articulation of feelings, displaying sympathy and understanding, and providing new information or alternative perspectives on a distressful situation, significantly contribute to feelings of well-being, acceptance, and control over events (for example, Elliott, 1985). These feelings, in turn, are important predictors of functional modes of coping with stress and several indices of physical and emotional health (see Albrecht and Adelman, 1987a; Thoits, 1985).

The effects of supportive messages on the management of stress are nicely illustrated in a recent study by Cutrona (1986b). This researcher employed a diary method, having her participants record for fourteen days all stressful events experienced, various types of messages and behaviors received from friends, mood states, and overall perceived levels of social support. Cutrona found that many more help-intended messages were received following stressful events than in the absence of such events. Moreover, persons receiving the greatest number of helping behaviors following a stressful event reported experiencing the highest overall levels of social support. In addition, the perceived *quality* of help received was associated with overall level of perceived social support. Finally, Cutrona found that persons receiving more helping behaviors were less depressed following stressful events and had better attitudes toward life.

Cutrona's results indicate that the support received from peers in times of stress is experienced as significant and materially helps with both the resolution of problems and the maintenance of positive moods. These findings suggest that relief obtained through the comforting efforts of peers is an important determinant of the quality of life.

Given the mental and emotional harms potentially resulting from everyday upsets, it might be inferred that the relief of these upsets through sensitive comforting would yield appreciable benefits in people's lives. The findings reviewed here are consistent with this inference. However, with the exception of Cutrona's study, little research has examined changes in quality of life or health directly

attributable to the comforting efforts of peers. Existing data thus warrant only tentative conclusions about the effects of peer comforting on a distressed other's coping and life quality. Future research should attempt to determine more directly the multiple ways in which peer-provided comfort affects people.

The Perceived Value of Comforting Skill in Everyday Life

People may have some intuitive understanding and appreciation of how others' communication skills help them cope with negative events. That is, because the relief received from sensitive comforting efforts may improve the quality of their lives, ordinary people may come to view comforting as a significant activity and value comforting skill in those close to them.

Research on the friendship expectations of adolescents and adults (see reviews by Serafica, 1982; Tesch, 1983) is consistent with this hypothesis. Many studies have found that older adolescents and adults look to friends as primary providers of emotional support in times of need (Davis and Todd, 1985). In particular, friends are expected to provide comfort, understanding, encouragement, and related forms of verbal support (Adelman et al., 1987). Moreover, although females place somewhat greater emphasis on the emotional support function of friends than males, most males still look to their friends as sources of support during troubled times (for example, Lewis, 1978). This suggests that the comforting skills of friends should be highly valued.

In an effort to learn the relative value placed on comforting skill, my colleagues and I recently undertook a series of studies in which samples of college students evaluated how important it would be for friends to have each of eight communication skills. The skills included: comforting ability, ego-support skill, referential ability, narrative ability, conversational skill, regulative skill, conflict-management ability, and persuasive skill. To assess perceptions of the importance of these skills, we developed an instrument called the 'Communicative Functions Questionnaire' (CFQ). The CFQ is composed of both rating and ranking tasks: subjects first rate the importance of forty items reflecting outcomes typically achieved through the exercise of the skills. For example, items tapping ego support include 'Makes me feel like a good person,' and 'Makes me believe in myself,' while items tapping comforting skill include 'Can really help me work through my emotions when I'm feeling upset or depressed,' and 'Helps me understand why some things hurt or depress me so much.' Subjects then rank order the skills

for their importance in same-sex friends. Table 4.1 gives definitions of the eight skills and displays the ranking task used in these studies.

Table 4.1   *Skill ranking task of the Communicative Functions Questionnaire* (CFQ)

Instructions: Listed below are eight definitions of general types of communication ability. Please read through the entire list and decide which skill is the *single most important* communication ability for same-sex peers to possess. Place a '1' in the space across from that skill. Next, decide which of the remaining skills is the *second most important* communication ability for same-sex peers to possess and place a '2' in the space across from that skill. Repeat this process for all eight skills, ultimately placing an '8' in the space across from the skill you think represents the *least important* communication ability for same-sex peers to possess. Please make certain to read and rank each communication ability.

Conversational skill
   The ability to initiate, maintain, and terminate casual   _____
   conversations that are enjoyable for all parties.

Comforting skill
   The ability to make people feel better when they are down,   _____
   upset, or depressed about something.

Referential skill
   The ability to convey information to others in a way that can be _____
   easily understood.

Conflict-management skill
   The ability to reach a solution that is mutually satisfying to the _____
   people involved in a personal conflict or dispute.

Persuasive skill
   The ability to get people to believe or do things they probably   _____
   wouldn't otherwise believe or do.

Ego-supportive skill
   The ability of one person to make another feel good about   _____
   him/herself.

Narrative skill
   The ability to entertain people through stories, jokes, and/or   _____
   gossip.

Regulative skill
   The ability to help someone who has broken a commonly held   _____
   rule, norm, or regulation understand why his/her action was wrong
   and how to fix his/her mistake.

Burleson et al. (1988) analyzed the responses of 383 college students to the rating task of the CFQ. The most valued communication skill was ego support (the ability to make others feel important or good about themselves). However, the second most valued

communication skill was comforting (defined in this study as the ability to make others feel better when depressed, sad, or upset).

Two other studies have replicated and extended the findings of Burleson et al. (1988). Burleson and Samter (1988) examined the responses of college students ($N = 410$) to both the rating and ranking tasks of the CFQ. These researchers also assessed the extent to which valuings of the communication skills varied as a function of interpersonal cognitive complexity, a variable indexing level of social-cognitive development. On the rating task, ego support once more emerged as the top-rated skill, followed immediately by comforting skill. However, when subjects rank ordered the formally defined skills, comforting was ranked as the most important of the eight skills for friends to possess. Both ratings and rankings of the communication skills were qualified by interactions with cognitive complexity. In particular, persons with high levels of cognitive complexity placed greater value on friends' comforting skills than those of lower complexity levels. Still, even those low in cognitive complexity rated and ranked comforting as one of the more important communication skills that friends should possess.

Werking et al. (1989) examined gender differences in the value placed on friends' communication skills. These researchers report two studies employing the CFQ; in both studies females rated the comforting skills of friends as significantly more important than did males. These results are consistent with research showing that females are more inclined than males to discuss feelings with their friends (for example, Winstead, 1986). However, the gender differences observed by Werking et al., though statistically reliable, were not large. Moreover, men rated comforting among the more important communication skills, suggesting that even males place a relatively high premium on the comforting skills of their friends.

Overall, the results of studies using the CFQ suggest that college students have a strong appreciation for the significance of comforting activity. The results are also consistent with the fact that people view friends as a primary source of emotional support during times of stress (Adelman et al., 1987). Future research should examine the value other populations (for example, children, older adults) place on the comforting skills of friends and other intimates.

Although most comfort is probably received in private settings from friends and family, comforting may also occur in the workplace, especially when the work environment is stressful and institutional norms encourage displays of emotional support to co-workers. One such work environment is the hospice. Zimmermann (1989) examined the value members of interdisciplinary hospice teams placed on comforting received from co-workers. Significant

correlations were found between the frequency with which respondents received comfort from fellow team members when distressed and their general satisfaction with team communication, overall satisfaction with the team, desire to stay with the team, and overall job satisfaction. Satisfaction with the quality of comfort received from team members was also significantly associated with all these variables. Thus, comforting is perceived as a significant social behavior in at least some work settings.

In sum, the available evidence indicates that people value the comforting they receive from friends, family, and co-workers. These findings raise the possibility that persons with poor comforting skills may be susceptible to difficulties in their interpersonal relationships.

Relational Consequences of Individual Differences in Comforting Skill

If sensitive comfort from peers in times of trouble improves the quality of people's lives, and if people place high value on the conforting skills of their friends, then it might be anticipated that persons with good comforting skills enjoy satisfying interpersonal relationships with peers while those with poor comforting skills have more problematic peer relationships. We have examined this hypothesis in several recent studies.

Our initial studies addressing the relational consequences of comforting skill showed that persons displaying sophisticated comforting abilities were perceived as nicer and more likeable people than those exhibiting less sophisticated comforting skills. For example, in one study (Burleson and Samter, 1985a, Study 1) we had female college students interact with a confederate who feigned distress about having been 'dumped' by her boyfriend. Evaluative ratings of the subjects made by both confederates and observers were substantially associated with the sensitivity and sophistication of the subjects' comforting messages. A subsequent study (Samter et al., 1987) found that participants reading conversations containing sophisticated comforting strategies rated the fictional source of the messages more positively than subjects reading conversations containing less sophisticated strategies.

Another series of studies has explored the effects of individual differences in comforting skill on acceptance by the peer group. Burleson et al. (1986) had seventy-five grade-school children complete tasks yielding assessments of six different communication skills, including the ability to produce sophisticated comforting strategies. Sociometric methods were employed to classify the participants into groups of 'popular,' 'average,' 'neglected,' and 'rejected'

children. Popular children were those liked by nearly all their peers, rejected children were disliked by nearly all their peers, neglected children were rarely mentioned by peers as either being liked or disliked, and average children received both some positive and negative mention from peers. Of the six communication abilities assessed in this study, comforting skill best discriminated among the groups of children, with those in the rejected group having significantly poorer comforting skills than children in any of the other groups.

Although the correlational data of this study will not support strong causal inferences, much other research has found differences in children's social and communicative skills causally related to acceptance by peers (see the reviews by Burleson, 1986; Renshaw and Asher, 1982). Thus, it is reasonable to suggest that one factor contributing to the poor peer relationships experienced by rejected children is the inferiority of their comforting skills. A child with poor comforting skills, even if well motivated, may make a distressed peer feel worse rather than better. Many children have sharp memories for emotional hurts inflicted by peers.

Burleson and Waltman (1987) attempted to replicate the results of Burleson et al. (1986) with a group of preadolescents. Unfortunately, the task used to assess comforting skill in this particular study failed to yield a meaningful range of scores (virtually all participants responded to the comforting situations with stereotypic strategies); thus, no relationship was found between comforting skill and peer acceptance. However, Burleson and Waltman did find that both peer- and teacher-based measures of the emotional support children offered to classmates were positively associated with interpersonal cognitive complexity, a known correlate of comforting skill. These latter results are consistent with several studies (Kurdek and Krile, 1982) finding acceptance by peers positively related to children's affective and social role-taking abilities – abilities instrumental in the production of sophisticated comforting strategies (for example, Burleson, 1984a).

The relationship between comforting skill and peer acceptance in adult populations is currently being addressed by Samter in dissertation research (Samter, 1989). Samter had the members of fraternities and sororities living in chapter houses complete a variety of measures, including several communication-skill assessments (among them a measure of comforting skill), the Communication Functions Questionnaire, and sociometric questionnaires which yielded measures of peer acceptance and rejection. The data from this study are still being analyzed and the results appear to be complex. Preliminary analyses, however, suggest that although

there is no correlation between individuals' comforting skills and the number of positive peer nominations received, there is a small but significant negative correlation between comforting skill and the number of *negative* peer nominations received. That is, house members with poor comforting skills were more disliked by peers than those with good comforting skills. This pattern of results is similar to that obtained by Burleson et al. (1986): in both studies, comforting skills were found to predict rejection, but not acceptance, by peers. Thus, for both children and adults, it appears that although good comforting skills will not necessarily lead to popularity or acceptance by peers, poor comforting skills increase the likelihood of being rejected by peers.

Several other results from Samter's study are worth noting. For example, people who rated comforting on the CFQ as an important skill for their friends to possess had more sophisticated comforting skills themselves. This result takes on added importance in the light of findings that people rating comforting as important on the CFQ (a) reported lower levels of loneliness on the UCLA loneliness scale, and (b) were nominated more often by house members as a sensitive individual with whom to discuss personal problems. In sum, Samter's study suggests that both skill in comforting and the valuing of comforting skill in intimates are related to several indices of interpersonal success with peers.

The studies reviewed above indicate that individuals' comforting skills may influence the quality of their interpersonal relationships. Interestingly, two recent studies suggest that the comforting skills that parents exhibit with their children may influence their children's social competence and acceptance by peers. Roberts and Strayer (1987) found that teachers' ratings of children's competence were substantially related to the extent to which parents encouraged their children to express feelings when upset. Somewhat similarly, Burleson et al. (1990) found that individual differences in mothers' comforting skills were inversely correlated with their children's rejection by peers: mothers with poor comforting skills had children more likely to be rejected by their grade-school classmates.

Although the findings of these two studies are intriguing, they do not provide many clues about the empirical links between parental comforting and children's social competence and acceptance. It is tempting to speculate that parental comforting models appropriate behaviors for children to use when addressing the emotional upsets of peers. It is also possible that the strategies parents use when responding to their children's emotions may have broad effects on children's social-cognitive abilities and social competencies (see

Hart et al., in press; Pettit et al., 1988). Additional research is needed to evaluate these possibilities.

The literature reviewed here provides limited support for the hypothesis that comforting skills affect the quality of people's interpersonal relationships. Although laboratory studies find that people evaluate the users of sensitive comforting messages favorably, there is no indication that good comforting skills cause people to be liked by peers. However, there is some evidence suggesting that those with poor comforting skills have a greater risk of being rejected by peers than those with good comforting skills. People with poor comforting skills may generally be insensitive to the feelings of others and, even when trying to support distressed others, may make them feel worse rather than better.

Conclusion

This chapter has explored the possibility that the social support people provide to others affects the quality of their interpersonal relationships. In particular, I have considered whether everyday comforting, as a form of social support, addresses problems of consequence, provides significant relief from these problems, and enhances the development of stable interpersonal relationships.

A growing body of evidence supports the claim that routine comforting efforts constitute a socially significant form of behavior. The events prompting comforting efforts, though less intense than life crises, may have serious implications for mental, emotional, and physical well-being. Fortunately, sensitive comforting strategies appear to aid recipients in functionally coping with stressful events, and thus help improve the quality of people's lives. Consistent with these findings, people view comforting as a significant activity and place high value on the comforting skills of their friends. Some research even suggests that the sophistication of persons' comforting skills affects how well they are liked by peers.

Comforting thus appears to be an important form of behavior with significant relational consequences. There are, however, risks inherent in efforts intended to relieve another's distress, and these risks should be considered. As suggested above, well intentioned but unsophisticated comforters may harm rather than help distressed others, and may thereby contribute to their own social rejection. Moreover, Notarius and Herrick (1988) review evidence indicating that interacting with upset or depressed individuals may be a stressful, unpleasant experience for the provider of support. Although Notarius and Herrick found that users of sophisticated comforting strategies were less inclined to experience such stress

than the users of unsophisticated strategies, potential providers should still be aware that efforts to comfort distressed others may prove harmful to their own emotional health.

In spite of the risks associated with it, peer-delivered comfort has the potential to accomplish much good. Beyond relieving emotional distress in an immediate situation, sensitive comfort may aid the recipient in managing future distressful incidents, may facilitate the social-cognitive development of recipients, and may foster the development of deeper, more meaningful relationships with others (see Burleson, in press). Moreover, the troubles and upsets addressed in routine comforting efforts do have significant effects on the quality of people's lives. Consequently, the moderation of these upsets can yield improvements in people's outlook on and experiences of life. Comforting is a primary way in which people provide support to those in their social network, and people appear to value it as such. The comforting that occurs among ordinary people in everyday situations warrants our continued examination. Students of social support might profitably consider how other supportive behaviors affect the formation and maintenance of inter-personal relationships.

5

The Process and Outcome of Mobilizing Social Support

John Eckenrode and Elaine Wethington

Commensurate with a growth over the last decade in the number of studies that have examined the health-promoting effects of social support has come a reexamination of the strengths and weaknesses of that literature. Several insightful reviews of the social-support literature have come to the conclusion that this literature has failed to attend to the process by which social ties become mobilized (Gottlieb, 1983; Heller and Swindle, 1983; Shinn et al., 1984; Vaux, 1988). Most attention has been paid to social support defined as the number of ties a person possesses, the psychological sense of support a person feels, or the self-reported end-product of a support-mobilization process following a stressful event such as the number of people who helped and what they did. What such studies have not revealed are the personal and situational contingencies surrounding the activation of potentially supportive social ties, the patterning of supportive transactions over the course of adjustment, and how these factors may in turn be related to the efficacy of support mobilization as a part of the process of coping with stressful experiences (Gore, 1985; Jacobson, 1986; Pearlin 1985). In this chapter, we will address some of these issues in an attempt to draw attention to the special problems faced by researchers concerned with the support-mobilization process itself, as well as its impact on the psychological and physical health of the support recipient.

The Concept of Social-Support Mobilization

Support mobilization is the process of marshaling social-support resources in anticipation of or in response to a perceived threat. Through this process social ties forming the person's potential support network are selectively activated to form a smaller subset of actual supporters. The challenges of research on support mobilization are to define the basic parameters of mobilization, to isolate the steps in the mobilization process, to study situational contin-

gencies that influence the course of that process, and to identify mobilization processes that appear to promote rather than impair well-being.

The social-support literature has only recently begun to even discuss the support-mobilization process itself (Pearlin and McCall, 1990; Vaux, 1988). However, related research literatures which have focussed on help giving and receiving as well as coping suggest a plausible model of support mobilization. For example, Gross and McMullen (1983) have summarized a three-stage model of help seeking based on their review of that literature:

1   perception of the situation, including its importance and severity, as well as the degree to which it is amenable to outside aid;
2   the decision to seek or not seek help, which involves an assessment of resources available and the costs and benefits associated with seeking help from these resources;
3   the strategies and tactics of seeking help.

These authors point out that the help seeking process may be cut short at any of these stages. For example, the person may perceive the problem as one that is not sufficiently serious to warrant the help of others. Even in the face of problems perceived to be serious, the person may judge helpers as unavailable or too costly (psychologically, socially, or monetarily). The person might also lack the skills to find and utilize help that is available. An attractive feature of the analysis of help seeking provided by Gross and McMullen (1983) is that they explicitly consider help seeking within the context of personal resources available to the person in need. Within this model, the decision essentially reduces to one involving helping oneself versus asking for the help of others.

This type of model bears a clear resemblance to Lazarus and Folkman's (1984) conceptualization of the coping process as one involving the cognitive appraisal of problem severity or degree of threat (primary appraisal), appraisal of coping resources (secondary appraisal), and coping behaviors or strategies. Coping behaviors, in turn, include the seeking of help from others as well as individually centered cognitive and behavioral strategies. Both the help seeking and coping conceptualizations also explicitly recognize that these stages often temporally overlap or occur in an order different from that outlined above (for example, persons providing aid may do so by helping the person in need define the nature of the problem). They also acknowledge the role of individual differences in these processes that may be socially and culturally determined (for example, gender differences in symptom definition and help seeking behavior). For the purpose of developing a model of support mobi-

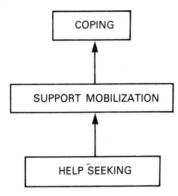

Figure 5.1 *The conceptual relationship of support mobilization to help seeking and coping*

lization it is useful to think of coping as being a more general set of processes within which support mobilization forms one component (see Figure 5.1). Help seeking itself is one aspect of support mobilization which forms a mid-level construct. As we discuss in more detail below, the reason we view help seeking as a subset of support mobilization is that there are many instances when support mobilization occurs in the absence of overt attempts at help seeking on the part of the person in need.

In discussing the seeking and receiving of support in marital couples around the issue of work-related stress, Pearlin and McCall (1990) have recently outlined a conceptualization of the support-mobilization process similar to the stages of help seeking discussed by Gross and McMullen (1983). These are (a) revelation and recognition of the problem; (b) appraisal, particularly with regard to the issue of legitimization of the stressor and the partner's distress; (c) the forms of support mobilized; and (d) the consequences or outcomes of support. Within each of the stages discussed by Gross and McMullen (1983) and Pearlin and McCall (1990), psychological and social processes can be isolated which contribute to the overall outcome of that and subsequent stages. Social comparison and attributional processes are important at the early stages of problem definition (Wills, 1983). There are motivational factors that may influence this definitional process as well. For example, Wills (1983), in reviewing the literature on social-comparison processes, has concluded that self-enhancement (vs. self-evaluative) motives increase as the level of stress increases, leading to the use of downward social comparison as an appraisal process. Some researchers have indeed argued that self-esteem maintenance is the primary

psychological process that either facilitates or inhibits the help-seeking process (cf. Fisher et al., 1988).

In addition to cognitive processes that influence problem perception and appraisal of resources, social behaviors that have received a great deal of attention in the research literature also form the components of support mobilization at later stages, after the problem is defined and resources appraised. Self-disclosure, for example, (Jourard, 1964) is an obvious and important pathway by which problems become known to potential supporters. Research has shown that self-disclosure processes are influenced by the topic being disclosed, characteristics of the discloser or the target person (for example, gender), characteristics of the relationship (for example, degree of intimacy), as well as other situational constraints such as the setting in which the disclosure occurs (Cozby, 1973).

When considering support mobilization as a process (vs. a stable set of social ties, for example) temporal issues also will determine its effectiveness as a coping response. Although it is important to explore the forms of support that are mobilized, it is also important to learn *when* this occurs. A basic parameter here is the speed with which support is forthcoming following a direct request for help or following the onset of the occurrence of a stressor. Delays in a supporter's response may decrease the effectiveness of the support or may change its meaning for the recipient. It may signal, for example, that the supporter is reluctant or unwilling to help, leading in turn to feelings of disappointment on the part of the recipient and hence to negative feelings about the relationship.

But temporal concerns cover more complex issues than the issue of how quickly support is offered. In the social-support literature, it has been hypothesized that social support is most effective when its content is matched to the demands of the stressor (Cohen and Wills, 1985). However, the adjustment to a given stressor may well demand the person to cope with a series of demands that change over time. In that case, another type of matching must be considered: whether the content of the support mobilized at a given time fits the needs of the support recipient at that time. A given functional type of support may markedly vary in its effectiveness to improve coping and reduce distress as a result of the point when it occurs in the stress process. Jacobson (1986) has recently discussed these temporal issues in some detail, using the stages of coping with loss to illustrate the importance of the timing as well as the content of support when evaluating its effectiveness. For example, an offer of advice about establishing new relationships may be perceived as unhelpful in the early stages of the bereavement process, while such support may be welcome at a later stage

when the person is seeking to reorganize his or her life. Weiss (1990) and Pearlin and McCall (1990) also point out the detrimental effect that advice giving can have as a form of support when one spouse seeks to offer support to the other. This is particularly the case when advice giving occurs early in the support process, before emotional support has bolstered the distressed spouse's self-esteem and reinforced a sense of control over the stressful situation.

In summary, in an attempt to adapt concepts such as coping and help seeking to the study of social-support mobilization, we must explore ways in which support mobilization may entail processes different from those discussed in the help-seeking or coping literatures. As suggested above, support mobilization as a construct falls between the narrower concept of help seeking and the broader concept of coping. We will argue below that the primary set of processes that need to be added to the help-seeking model when considering support mobilization involve unsolicited assistance given to the person under stress.

The Status of Support Mobilization in the Social-support Literature

In the social-support literature, little attention has been paid to the actual social transactions that make up the process by which potential support is transformed into actual support (cf. Cutrona et al., Chapter 2, this volume). The primary way in which support mobilization has been represented is captured in the distinction made in the literature between 'perceived' support and 'received' support. Some authors have used the term 'enacted' support in place of received support (Barrera, 1986; Tardy, 1985). Perceived support most generally refers to the psychological sense of support derived from feeling loved, valued, and part of a network of reliable and trusted social relationships (Gottlieb, 1985). It is not context dependent, and hence is more stable over time.

Received support, on the other hand, represents concrete instances of helping derived from one's social network, with this help (or 'provisions') usually being categorized as emotional support, instrumental support, appraisal support, and informational support (House and Kahn, 1985). Received support is most often assessed by having subjects recall help they received following a specific stressful experience or the frequency of helping aggregated over time and situations. One of the more popular measures of received support is the Inventory of Socially Supportive Behavior (ISSB; Barrera et al., 1981). Such measures may yield data regarding who helped, what they did, and whether the recipient was

satisfied with the help, but the research employing them provides little in the way of explicating the process by which potential supporters were mobilized to begin with, the factors that influence the success or failure of this process, or whether variations in the way in which support was mobilized or the context in which it occurs lead to more positive outcomes. However, studies exploring received support represent a useful starting point for the field in examining the role of support mobilization in the general process of coping with stress.

The empirical literature examining the health-promoting or stress-buffering qualities of social support has generally focussed on the concept of perceived support, with only a few studies including measures of received support (Barrera, 1986). There are several reasons for this imbalance. Coyne and DeLongis (1986) have discussed this in terms of a general tendency in the social-support literature toward the 'cognitization' of social relationships, while Lieberman (1986) refers to the 'psychologizing' of this literature. Generally, in the field of social psychology the study of social cognition has often taken precedence over the study of actual social relationships and social transactions (cf. Leatham and Duck, Chapter 1, and Morgan, Chapter 11, both in this volume). Such a bias would partly account for the preference for studying perceived support over received support.

There are methodological reasons for this imbalance in emphasis as well. Most researchers have been concerned with testing the stress-buffering qualities of social support, typically defined as the presence of an interaction between a stressor variable and a support variable when predicting psychological or physical well-being. Estimating such effects is best accomplished when the proposed stress buffer is not correlated with the stressor – that is, social support is a resource in place prior to the onset of the stressor, does not affect the occurrence of the stressor, nor is affected by the stressful event. Indeed, finding correlations between stress and support variables has been viewed as problematic in the literature (for example, Cohen and Wills, 1985). The requirements of such stress-buffering models have in turn favored the use of perceived-support measures that reflect feelings of being supported or support availability outside of the context of specific stressful experiences. Other relationships between stressors, support, and well-being, including those reflective of support mobilization, have therefore been relatively neglected in the research literature.

Recently, however, renewed attention has been given to other ways of representing the effects of social support within the stress process (Barrera, 1986; Gore, 1985; Vaux, 1988; Wheaton, 1985)

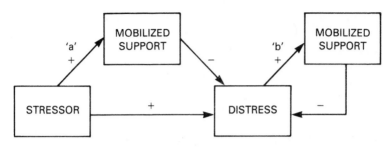

Figure 5.2 *A model of support mobilization as a response to a stressor and to subsequent distress*

that view the interrelationship between stress and support variables as an important object of study, as opposed to 'controlling' for it or eliminating it (Eckenrode and Gore, 1981). Viewing social support as a mediating as well as moderating variable within a stress-buffering model also serves to focus attention on social support as an outcome variable in itself. For example, Eckenrode (1983) has presented data showing that the level of support mobilization is related not only to the size of the potential support network, but also personal characteristics such as level of education, locus of control, and beliefs about the efficacy of help seeking.

Figure 5.2 presents a simple model showing two possible points in the stress process where a positive relationship between a stressor or distress variable and a measure of mobilized (received) support may be observed. We distinguish between path 'a' where the trigger to mobilization is the stressor itself and occurs prior to elevated levels of distress. This type of mobilization may take place early in the stress process where the stressor is highly visible to potential supporters, facilitating a quick offer of help, or where the person experiencing the stressor quickly responds to the potential threat of the stressor by seeking help. In path 'b' mobilization is occurring somewhat later in the process after signs of distress are already evident. The trigger to mobilization is now as much the distress caused by the stressor as it is the stressor itself. Later in this chapter we discuss possible differences between these two routes to mobilization. These pathways are also distinguished from a situation where stressors or distress show a negative relationship to support mobilization, a topic which we will also raise below.

A model characterizing relationships between stress and support variables, such as shown in path 'a' of Figure 5.2, represents what Wheaton (1985) has termed a 'stress-suppressing' model, what Lin (1986) has labeled a 'stress-counteracting' model, and what Barrera

(1986) calls an 'effective support mobilization model.' As Wheaton (1985) has demonstrated, such a model is a form of stress buffering since the total effect of the stressor is reduced in the presence of support mobilization. This model represents those situations where a stressor serves to activate formerly latent support resources (the positive relationship between stressor and mobilized support) and where the mobilized support in turn leads to a subsequent decrease in stress proportional to the amount or quality of support mobilized (the negative relationship between mobilized support and distress).

Only a few studies have reported data relevant to this type of model. Three cross-sectional studies using the ISSB as a measure of received support have reported positive associations between stress events and mobilized support together with negative relationships between received support and psychological well-being (Barrera, 1981; Cohen and Hoberman, 1983; Sandler and Barrera, 1984). Aneshensel and Frerichs (1982) also report longitudinal data consistent with this model, although their measure of support was not restricted to mobilized support, but included number of friends and relatives as well.

Other studies have reported data that are not supportive of such a mobilization model. Wethington and Kessler (1986), for example, in analyses of cross-sectional data from married respondents in a large national survey, failed to find strong evidence that mobilized support (when compared to perceived support) buffered stress. Mobilized support from one's spouse did reduce psychological symptoms, whereas support received from other sources did not. These authors conclude that perceptions of support availability have a more generalized buffering function (through appraisal processes) than mobilized support which they argue is relevant only to a portion of stressful experiences where individual coping efforts fail. It is undoubtedly true that for some people, mobilizing support is the end-point of ineffective individual attempts at coping with the stressor. For such situations, support mobilization may occur late in the coping process when distress levels are already high. Data reported by Pearlin and Schooler (1978) show that help seeking in their community sample was related to higher levels of distress and this is consistent with our present line of reasoning. Some individuals may also overutilize their support resources or use them ineffectively in lieu of individual coping efforts. For example, Billings et al. (1983) reported that a sample of depressives engaged in more information seeking from their networks (and less problem solving) in response to stress than non-depressives, even though the latter group reported larger networks. Support that is mobilized

may also be experienced as unhelpful (for example, Lehman et al., 1986). Finally, as discussed below, help seeking often entails psychological costs in terms of feelings of embarrassment, vulnerability, weakness, or indebtedness. For each of these reasons it is not surprising that aggregate measures of received support which simply reflect the amount of 'help' received may not strongly or consistently show stress-buffering effects.

The benefits of mobilized support are therefore likely to vary as a function of the characteristics of the recipient (for example, personality, individual coping resources), characteristics of the relationship between the support recipient and support provider (for example, degree of intimacy), characteristics of the recipient's social network (for example, its density), when in the stress process it occurs, as well as situational constraints (for example, type of stressor encountered). Although few studies have explored such contingencies, Riley and Eckenrode (1986), in a study of women who were users of a health clinic, demonstrated that mobilized support was related to lowered level of negative affect only among those women who had higher levels of socioeconomic resources (for example, higher education-levels) or generally beneficial person dispositions (for example, internal locus of control). For women with fewer socioeconomic or personal resources, mobilized support actually seemed to increase distress. Averaging both groups together resulted in a nonsignificant overall relationship between mobilized support and distress. It therefore becomes crucial to study the situational constraints on the mobilization process and individual differences in the use of social support before we can draw firm conclusions about when and how mobilized support is effective as a stress buffer. In the remainder of this chapter we will discuss some conceptual distinctions that we feel will lead to a better understanding of support mobilization as part of the stress process.

Support Mobilization and Help Seeking

Planful attempts to mobilize support as part of the coping process, such as verbal requests for help, clearly fall within the domain of the help-seeking behavior. We distinguish these behaviors, however, from unsolicited offers of support. Together, solicited and unsolicited support comprise the domain of support mobilization.

Such a distinction is important for several reasons. First, solicited and unsolicited support are likely to occur through somewhat different processes and there are likely to be different social and psychological contingencies leading up to each. Solicited support will often

be preceded by verbal self-disclosures of problems and explicit requests for help. Verbal disclosures of problems will also occur when unsolicited support is mobilized. In that case, however, the pathway to help is much more likely to involve the supporter responding to signs of distress communicated by the person in need or to information obtained through common social relationships which signals the nature of the stressor being experienced.

Third, solicited support differs from unsolicited support in terms of its implications for self-esteem. Seeking help from others often carries psychological costs in terms of feelings of vulnerability, weakness, or failure (Nadler, 1983) and is more threatening to one's self-concept than accepting help that is offered without asking (Gross et al., 1979). In addition to potentially generating feelings of embarassment or weakness, help seeking can be interpreted as a sign of poor coping (for example, running short of money) or an inability to handle stress (for example, upset over a relatively minor event). Such barriers to help seeking may result in 'disguised' attempts at help seeking whereby help is sought through indirect means that protect the recipient from public admissions of inadequacy (Rosen, 1983). Glidewell et al. (1982), for example, describe the use of 'experience swapping' by teachers as an informal means of obtaining advice and information from fellow teachers without explicit requests for such support.

Fourth, the nature of the stressor will in part determine whether support will be offered unsolicited or must be sought. Stressors that are visible to one's social network and are non-stigmatizing (for example, a car accident, a spouse's sudden death) are more likely to result in unsolicited support from the social network that comes at an earlier point in the coping process than are stressors that are not as visible or which are stigmatizing, such as contracting AIDS or a teenage pregnancy (Fisher et al., 1988),

Fifth, the type of relationship between the supporter and the person under stress will in part set conditions for the way in which support is mobilized. Support from professionals will almost always be preceded by a request for help (except where outreach efforts are in place to locate persons in need and offer assistance). Relationships which are more intimate and long lasting, however, are characterized by more indirect forms of help seeking and more unsolicited support giving (Clark, 1983). Intimacy, by the nature of everyday shared experiences, increases the visibility of problems that each person in the relationship encounters, but also sets the stage for one person to detect early 'distress signals' which may generate the support that is needed to cope with stressors at an early stage or allow a person to acknowledge stressors unknown to

his or her intimate which were threatening to self-esteem. Weiss (1990) has recently discussed such a process among married couples where the husbands held managerial-level jobs often involving a great deal of stress. These generally successful, middle-class men mostly hesitated to disclose problems at work to their wives (cf. McMullen and Gross, 1983) but were nonetheless often in need of their wives' emotional support. The process by which such support was mobilized only infrequently involved overt requests for help; rather, the wives would respond to signs of distress, and in happy and satisfied couples would gauge their support giving in such a way that their husband's work stressors would be disclosed without either a threat to his self-esteem or any feelings of a loss of control.

An implication of the help seeking literature is that a good, perhaps even the best, social network may be the one that is responsive without being asked for help (Fisher et al., 1988). The necessity to ask for help from one's intimates may in fact be the sign of a poorly functioning support network (Moos and Mitchell, 1982). The best sort of support may be that which you do not have to ask for. It does not require the kind of conscious efforts in help seeking that bring uncomfortable feelings about the self to the surface. It does not tax one's resources, or expose deficiencies that were heretofore undetected. This is a case where two different mechanisms of support mobilization may produce different levels of perceived satisfaction with the outcome of support, even though the actual type and amount of received support looks objectively the same. An example concerns everyday expressions of love in intimate relationships. A spontaneous and unsolicited expression of love ('I love you!') may be much more appreciated and reassuring than the same declaration coming as an answer to the question 'Do you love me?'

Another example might be solicitous attention to another's physical or mental health (Perlman and Rook, 1987). Household members often provide services and assistance almost automatically, without either party in the transaction being fully aware of its 'support' function. Well organized and low-conflict households probably function very smoothly in this regard. These smooth transactions include rapid reaction to the demands that household members are under from outside institutions and environments, such as work. Two recent studies which collected day-to-day data from married couples illustrate this process. In one study, Bolger et al. (1989) observed that spouses 'compensated' for the heavy work load of the other spouse by doing more work at home in the evening when the other had experienced a bad day at work. In another recent study, Repetti (1989) related the workload of air-traffic con-

trollers to marital interaction patterns at home. The results showed that social withdrawal is a common coping strategy used by these workers to reduce job-related stress. Furthermore, when wife support was rated as high, this coping strategy was not accompanied by feelings of anger or hostility. This study not only demonstrates the link between social support and coping behaviors, but also suggests that coping behaviors that could lead to increased levels of conflict in couples with low levels of mutual support (such as withdrawal) take on a more positive meaning in high-support couples. These are just two examples of the types of unsolicited support processes that occur in social networks. The commonality of such experiences is such that unsolicited support is more likely to occur in the context of an established relationship, which is distinguished by its comfortable, habituated, and therefore well regulated interaction pattern.

We have concentrated our attention on unsolicited forms of support because we believe that social-support researchers have failed to appreciate the importance of such social transactions. We do not advocate, however, that unsolicited support will always be superior (in terms of its health-promoting and stress-buffering qualities) to support that is actively sought. Unsolicited support may at times be unwanted or misguided support, as the research of Wortman and her colleagues has pointed out (for example, Wortman and Dunkel-Schetter, 1979). It may also reflect overinvolvement, which among family members has been shown to be associated with psychological problems (Coyne et al., 1988).

Even though we characterize unsolicited support as favored, we also do not wish to imply that it is rare. It is common, not only in terms of adult relationships, but across the life course of individuals. Small children, save those that are neglected or abused, are not routinely in the position to actively seek help. Perhaps such experiences of unconditional care are translated into the desire for such relationships in adulthood (as theories of attachment imply; cf. Hazan and Shaver, 1987).

Although unsolicited support may not be rare, it is also clear that such experiences are not equally distributed across the population. The middle- and upper-status individual is more likely to be so favored, and the married are likely to have such relationships, particularly the stably married (Gove et al., 1983). In summary, we believe that the mobilization processes surrounding unsolicited support have not been the focus of systematic attention by support researchers. The inclusion of these types of social-interactional processes within the domain of support mobilization raises an interesting set of questions.

First, how did support of this sort get there to begin with? The answer, we think, lies in the maintenance of relationships that have the expectation for emotional and instrumental support already built in, relationships such as marriage and close friendships. Second, given the existence of an individual social network and the social-support functions that the network provides, to what sorts of situations or cues given out by the focal person do network members respond? Henderson (1974: 172) has labeled these as 'care-eliciting' behaviors, and defined them as 'a pattern of activity on the part of one individual which evokes from another responses that give comfort.' In infants this may take the form of crying or arm raising, while in adults nonverbal cues such as facial expressions or body postures are common cues that occur alongside more direct requests for support. To date, social-support researchers have not seriously examined the cues to which supporters had responded, nor have they asked recipients of support to assess the ways in which they received support. The literature on 'pathways to help' has dealt with finding professional help only.

Third, how conscious is this process of cuing and response from the points of view of both the recipient and the supporter? To the extent that support-eliciting behaviors and supportive responses have long phylogenetic origins and are socialized early in life, they may become so expected and ordinary that respondents to many surveys and questionnaires do not label them as 'support.' The dilemma posed here for researchers is that such spontaneous support exchanges in the context of intimate relationships may not even be recognized as 'support' by the recipient (see Leatham and Duck, Chapter 1, this volume), making the task of measuring such supportive transactions difficult and opening up the possibility that support researchers have overlooked important types of support transactions (Pearlin and McCall, 1990). Perhaps it is the unusual circumstance when a major unexpected life event occurs that the support process is brought into high relief and the support previously taken for granted becomes suddenly very salient. But we believe that, even here, in the midst of coping with a stressful event, supportive behaviors, particularly from intimates, may not be accurately recalled.

Fourth, are the people receiving support the best reporters of the sorts of support they actually receive? For example, many women may not necessarily experience the financial support their husbands provide or typical male gestures of help (such as walking the dog or washing the car) as 'love,' although men report that they offer these types of services as tokens of love (Cancian, 1987).

Fifth, does the recipient necessarily agree with the supporter

about what functions of support are provided in a relationship? To this question, the answer seems to be no, according to research on the perception of social-support functions conducted by Antonucci and Israel (1986) which shows that agreement between two members of a network on the functions provided by each member to the other averages 50 percent.

Stressor Characteristics and the Mobilization of Support

The characteristics of the stressor itself are likely to form an important part of the context influencing the process and outcome of support mobilization. Although stressors may vary along a number of dimensions we will discuss a few that we believe may be particularly relevant to support mobilization.

We had mentioned above the potential importance of the stressor's visibility for support mobilization. Problems that are unknown to one's social network are unlikely to elicit unsolicited offers of help, necessitating help-seeking behavior or postponing support mobilization until a point in the stress episode when distress levels (or associated coping behaviors such as excessive drinking) increase and serve as the cue for the network's response (path 'b' of Figure 5.2). Degree of visibility is in part a function of the stressor itself so that, for example, psychological problems are inherently less visible than more environmentally based stressors (for example, a house fire). Visibility, however, is also likely to vary as a function of contextual factors including the network's structure. A dense (that is, highly interconnected) network facilitates the flow of information and would thus increase the speed or likelihood of a stressor becoming known to potential supporters (Hall and Wellman, 1985). Well integrated networks may therefore serve to increase the visibility of stressors within the network, facilitating a supportive response without the need for explicit calls for help. At the same time, for stigmatizing stressors that are likely to be unacceptable to network members, a dense network may in fact lead the person to seek help from outside sources such as professional care givers.

Chronic stressors differ from acute stressors in ways that also are likely to influence the course of support mobilization. Chronic problems may lead to a degree of cognitive accommodation that inhibits help-seeking behaviors. As Pearlin (1983) has pointed out, the mere existence of chronic stressors may be interpreted by the affected person as evidence for their inability to cope, which will only reinforce feelings of inadequacy and lack of control that should inhibit help seeking. Acute stressors, on the other hand, may be less likely to lead to such self-blaming attributions.

The perceptions and responses of potential supporters are also likely to vary as a function of the stressor's chronicity. Since chronic stressors represent relatively unchanging problems, network members are more likely to be responding to changes in the distress levels of the potential support recipient, rather than to a recognition of environmental changes in the life of the affected person. Distress as a cue to mobilization has a different meaning for potential supporters than environmental changes, as noted above. Heightened distress levels may indeed signal that the person is not coping adequately. Persons viewed as not coping well with stressors may in turn be seen as unattractive and avoided (Coates et al., 1979). The likelihood of support being offered, as well as its form and timing, may therefore vary from a situation where the person is identified as needing support because of exposure to some acute life change and where the successful resolution of the stressor is still a distinct possibility.

Chronic stressors may also require supportive responses that differ from effective support for acute stressors. For many acute stressors, the most effective support may be emotional support that bolsters the person's self-esteem and sense of mastery, encouraging them to persist in adaptive individual coping efforts (Cohen and Wills, 1985). Chronic stressors, such as poverty, often reflect stable personal dispositions or intractable environmental conditions. The type of support needed to create a change in such conditions (for example, material support) may not be readily available to the person's informal network (Jacobson, 1986).

Finally, chronic stressors represent long-term problems that may result in supporters being repeatedly mobilized. Short-term and episodic mobilization of the support network may have the beneficial effect of meeting the needs of the recipients of support and in strengthening the bonds between network members (assuming some reciprocity over time). Within the context of intimate relationships, the balance of giving and receiving that occurs over time may be an important ingredient for the relationship's stability (Walster et al., 1978). Couples also must learn the most effective ways to elicit as well as give support, and this takes practice. In this case support mobilization becomes a mechanism for the maintenance of informal social ties.

Chronic stress, on the other hand, may lead to a depletion of the support available to the person experiencing such a long-term stressor (Vaux, 1988). Brickman et al. (1983) have suggested that an extended process of helping leads to a decrease in the supporter's sense of effectiveness over time, akin to the burnout observed among helping professionals. This is particularly likely to occur

when the help giving is one way. Lack of reciprocity over long periods, such as when family members provide caregiving to persons with chronic physical or mental disabilities, may have negative psychological effects on both the caregiver and the care recipient (Shumaker and Brownell, 1984). Coyne (1976a, b) has also discussed the difficulties that chronically depressed persons have in maintaining the integrity of a support network. There is an obvious long-term cost to the distressed person in having his or her support network become less responsive over time. There may well be long-term costs to the support providers as well. Kessler and McLeod (1984), in a study which examined data from several large-scale surveys, found that the characteristically higher levels of depression found among women can be linked to their greater involvement in caring for the needs of persons in their social networks. Although these researchers were not explicitly concerned with the chronicity of the stressors women and men responded to, their data do suggest that recurrent mobilization of social support may entail costs for support providers occupying certain social statuses.

The above discussion of chronic, in contrast to acute, stressors also implies that stressors may be related to changes in the size or responsiveness of a person's support network over time. Acute stressors may also represent a loss of support, as is common in the case of life events such as divorce, death, job changes, and residential moves. Barrera (1986) has summarized the evidence from studies which have reported data consistent with the notion that stressful events may lead to a decline in levels of perceived support. Thoits (1982) has also discussed methodological issues with regard to estimating the buffering effects of social support when the stressor in question involves a loss of support.

Our concern here is with the effects of social-loss events on the support mobilization process. First, the person suffering a social loss is faced with the immediate task of coping with that event. In addition to coping with the emotional distress and instrumental needs caused by the loss, salient coping tasks may involve replenishing the social-support network (for example, making a new set of friends), redefining existing relationships (as when divorce results in the redefinition of friendships jointly shared with the spouse), or adjusting to a life with fewer intimates or a smaller social network. Research has not yet defined how the support-mobilization process differs for life events involving losses to the person's support network compared to those which do not, although detailed accounts of coping with social losses such as the death of a spouse are available (for example, Parkes and Weiss, 1983).

In summary, we have sought to suggest that characteristics of

the stressor must be considered when considering the process by which social support becomes mobilized, the efficacy of that mobilization for adjustment, and the long-term implications for the social network. These issues go beyond the question of whether stress and support measures are correlated and the implication of such correlations for the estimation of stress-buffering effects. Researchers should explore the relationship between stressors and support mobilization as an important substantive issue in its own right.

The Social Context of Support Mobilization

Finally, we must consider how the mobilization of social support is determined not only by characteristics of the stressor, characteristics of the recipient, the potential supporter, and their relationship, but also by the broader social context. These contextual effects are evident at the level of the social network, but also at the level of position in the social structure: gender, age, life-cycle stage, ethnicity, and social status (House et al., 1988). Social-structure position and social-group memberships of this sort shape barriers and opportunities for social-support mobilization. These factors, we argue, have an impact not only on the mobilization of close others (so-called 'strong ties'), but also on the mobilization of more loosely connected individuals ('weak ties'; cf. Granovetter, 1973).

Social position and social-group membership affect the capacity of close network affiliates to provide adequate support in times of stress. Our argument is that membership in less socially advantaged groups increases the probability that close others will be too overburdened to provide support when asked. Most of the research relevant to this observation has focussed on either gender or poverty.

There is some evidence to suggest that network 'overburden' will particularly affect help seeking among women. Wethington et al. (1987) report that in one national study of help seeking after crisis, women were 30 percent more likely than men to have been reported as helpers. This means that the average woman is more likely to be asked for help than the average man. In a related analysis, Kessler and McLeod (1984) demonstrated that women report more psychological distress than men for events that happened to network members. One obvious explanation for this finding is that women experience network events as more distressing because they experience more frequent demands for help. This explanation is congruent with what is known about day-to-day demands for care-

giving that women face in their roles as spouses and parents (Hochs-child, 1989) and as children to aging parents (Brody, 1981). Thoits (1986) and others have noted that women also appear to reap fewer social-network benefits from employment than do men, presumably because they are limited by demands from other social roles. There is a plethora of evidence, moreover, that women are disadvantaged in male-dominated work organizations because of their lack of integration into powerful informal networks (for example, Kanter, 1977).

Belle (1983) has found that poverty imposes other constraints on social networks. The stresses of poverty affect marital continuity and family functioning, reducing the capacity of marital and parent-ing relationships to serve as 'buffers' under stress. The networks of the poor, moreover, are often emotionally costly in that they expose their members to more frequent stresses and interpersonal conflicts. This burden of stress is associated with disruptions in family relationships (Unger and Powell, 1980; Wahler, 1980).

Network overburdens such as those documented among women and the poor impose three sorts of constraints on support mobiliz-ation. The first would be that a woman asking another woman for help might find mobilization more difficult, stemming from the reluctance of the potential provider to take on any more demands of this sort (Belle, 1983). The second constraint would be the reluctance of the victim to ask for help from an already overbur-dened network. A third constraint, suggested by Belle (1983), is that some individuals might choose to isolate themselves from their families and communities in order to avoid experiencing the stresses in them. Self-imposed isolation is a risk factor for depression, par-ticularly among the poor (Brown et al., 1975).

Social position and social-group membership, moreover, affect the likelihood of eliciting support from less-close ties. Men, individ-uals at their 'prime' of life, the married, whites, and economically advantaged are more integrated into networks that connect them to a wider society. In modern Western society, labor-force partici-pation is the primary means of social integration outside the immediate family. Labor-force participation is thought to have posi-tive effects on well-being, not only through its economic benefits, but also through its provision of additional social relationships (Gove and Tudor, 1973; Thoits, 1986; Verbrugge, 1983). Women, the very young and old, minorities, and the poor have less access to this important role.

Chronological age and stage in the life cycle also affect access to the wider social world. Degree of participation in occupations, service and religious organizations, and public life in general is

graded by age and sometimes even developmental stage (married vs. unmarried; childrearing vs. not; cf. Clausen, 1986). Discriminatory practices limit the access of ethnic minorities to employment, social organizations, and informal networks (Wilson, 1987). Low socioeconomic status limits access as well (Belle, 1982b). Such limits to mobilization may have life-threatening effects, as when a response to the early signs of serious health problems is delayed due to a lack of integration into a network of health providers. Wilson (1987) has argued that social isolation exacerbates and intensifies the economic disadvantages of the underclass, primarily by excluding it from job-seeking networks. It is not difficult to imagine that support-mobilization processes and outcomes for a stressor such as unemployment could vary considerably according to the social status of the unemployed individual.

Although we have only briefly touched on how support mobilization may be sensitive to social forces larger than the individual and his or her immediate set of intimate ties, we believe that it is imperative for researchers to consider such processes when designing research on the health effects of social support.

Conclusion

The study of the process by which social support becomes mobilized and the differential effects on health-related outcomes of alternative pathways to support mobilization have not been topics that have received a great deal of attention from social-support researchers. We believe that increased attention to such process issues may help address certain paradoxes present in the social-support literature.

One concerns research findings apparently showing that help seeking is an ineffective coping strategy when compared to more individualized coping behaviors (for example, Pearlin and Schooler, 1978). An explicit consideration of the placement of help-seeking behaviors within the total context of coping with particular stressors would perhaps clarify why such an empirical relationship has been found. One possibility is that help seeking occurs later in the coping process, after other attempts at problem solving have failed and distress levels have increased (Gore, 1979). The distinction between help seeking and unsolicited support mobilization may also clarify why certain individuals who tend to mobilize their social networks when under stress do not show long-term benefits in terms of mental health (for example, Billings et al., 1983). It is apparent that support mobilization, by itself, is not necessarily an effective coping

strategy. Our discussion in this chapter has tried to point out the costs associated with support mobilization, as well as the benefits.

Explicating the circumstances under which support mobilization leads to better, as opposed to worse, adjustment to stressors may also explain why measures of received support generally have failed to show stress-buffering effects when compared to measures of perceived support. In addition to the relative absence of studies designed to adequately test a support-mobilization model, our discussion has attempted to make clear that there is no reason to believe that support mobilization will have uniformly positive effects. The research question of most relevance to the literature at this point is not *if* mobilized support buffers the effects of stress, but *when* and *for whom* mobilized support buffers stress. Although we would argue that a direct comparison of the size of the stress-buffering effects obtained when using a measure of perceived or received support represents only a mildly interesting analysis, analyses which attempt to relate perceived support and mobilized support to each other, as well as to outcome measures, are quite relevant to uncovering important dynamics within the stress and coping process. Equally important, however, will be studies that seek to test interactions between mobilized support and contextual variables thought to moderate its effectiveness as a coping strategy (for example, Riley and Eckenrode, 1986). We suspect that for certain groups of people and under circumstances that limit the psychological or social costs of support mobilization, strong stress-buffering effects of mobilized support will be found.

Our foregoing discussion also implies certain challenges for social-support researchers that may demand newer methodological approaches than those used in literature to date. For example, the fact that many of the supportive exchanges that occur in close relationships are so routinized within the context of day-to-day lives as to render them somewhat invisible to the participants in such exchanges poses obvious problems for researchers attempting to measure social support (see Leatham and Duck, Chapter 1, this volume). Knowing beforehand which subtle as well as highly visible behaviors constitute 'support' from the points of view of the partici-pants of such exchanges is clearly a difficult task. Ironically, we may obtain the least reliable self-report data from support recipients embedded in the most smoothly and effectively functioning social networks since the support is more likely to flow to the recipients in an unsolicited and 'disguised' manner. On the other hand, for social support to have any usefulness as a concept in the social sciences, we must be able to define its parameters and distinguish

it from other interpersonal behaviors. If all behaviors become defined as support, the concept loses its meaning.

Multimethod approaches to research are critically necessary at this point in the history of social-support research. Broad community-based surveys should be supplemented with intensive micro-analytic studies that include data collection from more than one party in the support transaction and utilize data collection methods that facilitate recall (for example, daily diaries), do not rely on entirely self-reports (for example, videotapes) or directly manipulate support transactions, whether in the laboratory or in the field (see the chapters by Burleson, Leatham and Duck, and Morgan, this volume). Of course, longitudinal investigations which secure information on support transactions over the course of the adjustment process are also most valuable to the field. As the complexity and sensitivity of our research strategies begin to approximate the complexity of the social phenomena that encompass the concept of social support, significant new insights will be realized from the next generation of social-support studies.

6

Communicative Strategies for Managing the Risks of Seeking Social Support

Daena Goldsmith and Malcolm R. Parks

Disclosing a personal problem can be risky. Researchers have focussed more on the benefits than on the risks of seeking social support, but those in distress are often acutely aware of the dangers. Almost all of the cancer patients interviewed by Dunkel-Schetter (1984), for instance, said that at one time or another their fear of others' reactions had prevented them from seeking social support. Such fears are not limited to those facing a life-threatening illness, but also occur in comparatively more mundane situations such as when men and women seek help with problems in their romantic relationships (for example, Goldsmith, 1988). Indeed, we believe the support process is almost universally experienced in terms of conflicting desires to reveal and withhold personal information. In this chapter we report research on how people experience and respond to these 'support dilemmas' (Albrecht and Adelman, 1987c).

We have chosen to focus on the support dilemmas surrounding romantic relationships because they appear to be extremely common (Goldsmith, 1988) and because work in this area can contribute to our understanding of both personal relationships and the social support process. Recent studies have shown that the development and deterioration of both romantic relationships and friendships is closely associated with the participants' generalized perceptions of support for their relationship from members of their surrounding social networks (for example, Milardo and Lewis, 1985; Parks and Eggert, in press). Because of this, it is vital to understand what occurs when romantic partners discuss their relationship problems with others. Learning how people go about discussing personal problems with others also contributes directly to the literature on social support. As several researchers have noted, far too little attention has been devoted to understanding how support is actually provided and how support seekers manage the possibility that their efforts may yield both positive and negative

outcomes (for example, Albrecht and Adelman, 1987a; Fiore et al., 1983; Rook, 1984; Silver et al., in press; Winstead and Derlega, in press).

Our goals were therefore to extend research on personal relationships by explicating the dynamics of network influences on development in greater detail and to extend research on support by focussing on the communicative episodes that truly constitute the social support process. We explored these issues in a study of ninety-seven university students who had discussed a romantic problem with someone besides their romantic partner. Participants were drawn on a voluntary basis from classes at the University of Washington. They ranged in age from 17 to 67, though most were between 18 and 24. Most were female (71 percent). The individuals with whom the participants discussed their relational problems were quite similar to the participants themselves. A similar proportion was female (72 percent) and their age range (17–68) paralleled that of the participants. Participants most often sought support from same-sex close friends (74 percent), friends (14 percent), and family members (7 percent). After selecting a support encounter that had occurred in the last week, participants responded to closed- and open-ended questions about the initial psychological and situational context of the encounter, the topics discussed and the strategies used to discuss them, and the outcomes. This chapter will summarize the findings, beginning with the dilemmas that support seekers experienced and then turning to a discussion of the ways respondents managed them. Finally, we identify factors that influence the ways in which people responded to the cross-pressures of seeking support and the outcomes they obtained.

Risks and Benefits of Seeking Social Support

Our respondents sought help with a great variety of problems ranging from simple boredom, bad manners, and chronic lateness to more serious problems like basic incompatibilities in personal characteristics and attitudes, infidelity, and disagreements over where the relationship was heading. Regardless of the particular type of problem in their romantic relationships, however, our respondents experienced rather similar cross-tensions about seeking support from an outside party.

The fact that support seekers experienced conflicting motivations to disclose and withhold information is consistent with our belief that support episodes, indeed all communicative transactions, are the product of dialectical tensions. On the one hand, people are motivated to disclose their problems by a desire to obtain infor-

mation and advice, emotional validation, direct assistance, and perhaps even by a desire to build a closer relationship with the support provider or to exchange mutual aid (for example, Clark, 1983; Thoits, 1985). Of course, not all the motivations to share a problem are so positive. We may disclose because we think others expect it or because we do not want them to hear about our problems from someone else (Goldsmith, 1988).

We must also add to this mix a series of potential risks of disclosure, of motivations to withhold problems and avoid support. The most obvious is stigma (for example, Chesler and Barbarin, 1984; Dunkel-Schetter and Wortman, 1982). Disclosing relationship problems can lead not only to negative evaluations of oneself, but also of one's romantic partner, and of the overall relationship.

Violation of confidentiality is another major risk. Not only does the support seeker risk that others may be told damaging information, but the very act of disclosing a relationship problem to an outsider may be viewed as a violation of the sanctity of the romantic relationship.

Support seekers may be reluctant to burden someone else with their problems. Some feel that discussing a relationship problem with outsiders is simply ineffective or inappropriate (Goldsmith, 1988). Beyond this, trying to help may cause the support provider to feel more vulnerable to the same problems (for example, Wortman, 1983), overwhelmed, and unable to help (Silver et al., in press), or emotionally or physically drained by actually giving help (for example, Rook and Pietromonaco, 1987). These reactions may circle back to make the support seeker feel less competent, especially if he or she feels overly indebted or unable to reciprocate (for example, DePaulo, 1982; DiMatteo and Hays, 1981; Wills, 1983).

We wrote survey items corresponding to these and other benefits and risks. Based on a series of factor analyses and our own conceptual efforts, we pose five broad categories of benefits and four types of risks our respondents perceived in seeking support (see Table 6.1).

Strategies and Tactics for Managing Support Dilemmas

The risks and benefits inherent in the support process imply that people seeking help are more or less constantly facing a dilemma. Unfortunately only a smattering of the strategies and tactics that might be used to cope with these cross-tensions have been identified

Table 6.1 *Benefits and risks of seeking support for relationship problems*

Benefits	Sample questionnaire items
Cognitive and affective support	'I felt that discussing the problem with this person would help me understand it better.'
	'I thought just talking about the problem would make me feel better.'
Supporter intervention	'I wanted this person to step in and talk to someone, get someone to do something, or give me or my partner something.'
Closer relationship with supporter	'I hoped that sharing the problem with this person would bring us closer together.'
Help other by discussing problem	'I thought telling this person about my problems would help them.'
Relational obligation	'Given the kind of relationship I have with this person, I thought his/her feelings would be hurt if I did not talk about the problem.'

Risks	
Negative impressions	'I was concerned this person would get a negative impression of me if I discussed the problem.'
Confidentiality	'I was worried that this person might tell others about the problem.'
Burden to supporter/indebtedness	'I did not want to burden this person with my problems.'
	'I was hesitant to talk about the problem because I did not want to feel dependent on this person.'
Disclosure ineffective/inappropriate	'I worried that it was wrong to share this problem with someone besides my partner.'
	'I doubted whether talking about the problem would do any good.'

(for example, Dovidio and Gaertner, 1983; Glidewell et al., 1982; Rosen, 1983; Silver et al., in press; Wills, 1983; Wortman and Dunkel-Schetter, 1979). Until now no theoretical perspective has been able to recognize and organize the various options open to support seekers.

Our own theoretical approach to the problem began by noting the underlying theoretical parallel between support dilemmas and broader dialectical perspectives on personal relationships (for example, Altman et al., 1981; Baxter, 1988, 1989; Bochner, 1984;

Goldsmith, 1988; Parks, 1982). Both conceptualize interaction against a backdrop of necessarily conflicting motivations. These motivations include simultaneous desires for intimacy and privacy as well as for autonomy and dependence. Our next step was to elaborate on the ways in which people cope with contradictory motivations by linking work by these theorists with work on how communicators reconcile conflicting interactive goals (for example, Bavelas, 1985; Baxter, 1988; O'Keefe and Delia, 1982).

The result of our theoretical work was a set of eight strategies and tactics which we grouped into three larger categories (see Table 6.2). The most straightforward way to resolve communicative dilemmas is by *selection* – in this case, choosing to be completely open about one's problems in spite of the risks. This was the most frequently used strategy, perhaps because most respondents reported having deliberately chosen a person whom they felt would be receptive, sympathetic, and knowledgeable. Another general strategy for resolving communicative dilemmas is *separation* – sending messages that attend to both sides of the conflict but at different times (temporal separation), or with different listeners (network separation), or with different verbal and nonverbal messages at the same time (behavioral separation). Temporal separation was the most commonly used of these tactics and was used as often as simple selection. Indeed, selection and temporal separation were used significantly more often than any of the remaining six strategies. Verbal openness with nonverbal denial (behavioral separation I) was used more than either network separation or the form of behavioral separation that involved nonverbal openness coupled with verbal denial. A final general strategy for resolving communicative dilemmas is an *integration* in which all one's conflicting motives are serviced. This can be accomplished by attenuating their expression (integrative moderation), by expressing them equivocally (integrative disqualification), or by somehow synthesizing the conflicting desires so that they no longer conflict and each is fulfilled (integrative reframing) (see Bavelas, 1985; Baxter, 1988). Our results showed that integrative moderation and reframing were used with moderate frequency and significantly more often than integrative disqualification.

Patterns of Strategy Use

Most people used more than one strategy to manage changing currents of their support episode. A series of cluster analyses convinced us that support seekers could be divided into four categories according to the mix of communicative strategies they selected.

Table 6.2 *Strategies and tactics for managing support dilemmas*

Strategy or tactic	Sample questionnaire items
Selection	'I decided to come right out and tell as much as I could about the problem even though there were risks to being that open.'
Temporal separation	'I go back and forth between talking about relationship problems and keeping them to myself.'
Network separation	'I talked to this person because I wanted to talk to someone different than I had been talking to.' 'Next time I'll go to someone else so I don't talk too much to this person about this problem.'
Behavioral separation I	'I told this person there was a problem, but did things that made it seem like it was not a problem.'
Behavioral separation II	'I told this person that there was no problem, but I also did things to let them know there really was.'
Integrative disqualification	'I was vague about whose problem this actually was.' 'I was vague when it came to telling this person what the problem really was.'
Integrative moderation	'I compromised so that I could say some things about this problem and yet hold other things back.' 'I hinted that there was a problem and hoped that the person would figure it out without me having to say it directly.'
Integrative reframing	'I had some concerns about discussing this problem, but I figured out a way to discuss it like I wanted without anything negative happening from discussing it.'

The most common type was the *Cautious Discloser* (43 percent of sample). These people recognized the risks of being open about relational problems and used a combination of temporal separation, selection, and behavioral separation to cope with them. That is, while they alternated between talking about relational problems and keeping them to themselves, they had decided to be open in the current encounter. Even so, most of these people reported hedging their openness in some way – usually by using behavioral separation to admit the problem verbally at the same time as down-

playing it nonverbally. This is illustrated by the following description provided by a 20-year-old female: 'Every time I tell her of my feelings, I end up having to stick up for my boyfriend. She almost becomes irrational towards him. . . . And all I can do is make light of the situation, act like it didn't bother me . . . ' In other cases the problem was signaled nonverbally and the support provider had to probe rather actively. Consider, for instance, the caution displayed by this 19-year-old female:

L.K. and I were just talking about our weekends and what we'd done. L.K. could tell something was bugging me or that I was kind of preoccupied. She asked, 'Is something wrong; are you and – in a fight or something?' I answered, 'Yeah, we got in a fight on the way home.' She just said, 'Oh.' This was kind of a chance for me to either drop it or continue. I said, 'It was really stupid – I blew up at him . . . '

The second most common type (29 percent of sample) was the *Strategist* – so named because they used the greatest number of strategies to avoid the negative consequences. The great majority (79 percent) used integrative reframing to achieve this goal. And for most of these people, the belief that they had recognized risks and reframed the discussion so as to both express and protect themselves represented a summary judgement. That is, they achieved integrative reframing through the use of other strategies. Notice, for example, the disqualified way in which this 24-year-old male comes to the problem:

I told my friend that I had a problem and needed to talk to him. As we began to talk, I asked him his view on premarital sex. He stated that it depends on the nature of the relationship and what the partners wanted. I told him that conflicting views can often destroy relationships. He agreed but said 'Are you having that problem?' I replied, 'Yes!'

Or consider the infrequent and indirect way in which this 19-year-old female discusses her problems: 'I seldom talk to anyone about my romantic problems. If I do, I normally do not refer directly to the person I am talking about. I only discuss problems such as lack of understanding between the two of us [with] my closest friend whom I can trust.'

Overall the Strategists used moderation, disqualification, and both forms of behavioral separation to a greater extent than any other group. Members of this group also utilized selection and temporal separation strategies; although they, unlike members of other groups who used these strategies, did not rely on them alone. So aside from the summary belief that some sort of integrative reframing had been achieved, the Strategists showed little consistency in their strategy choices. One possible explanation for this is

that the Strategists adapt flexibly to local conversational conditions rather than pursuing goals with a fixed strategy set.

Opposite the Strategists were those in the third group (15 percent of the sample), the *Expressives*. These people seemed to be aware of the risks of openness, but simply decided to be as open as they could anyway. Having selected openness, they did not use any other strategy within the encounter. Moreover, because none of them reported switching off between support providers over time and only a few (13 percent) reported alternating cycles of openness and privacy over time, we concluded that such openness in the face of risk was a more or less consistent strategy choice for them. The directness characteristic of the Expressives is illustrated in this young man's approach to telling a friend about his relational problems:

> Well, I just called him up and said that I needed to talk to him about something important. . . . I went up to his room and I told him everything I was feeling at the time. I was really angry and I opened by saying 'She is such a bitch. I can't handle her any more. She makes me sick.' He told me to calm down and just tell him what was wrong. So I explained the problem. Anger was running through my body as I described the problem.

We called those in the final group (13 percent of the sample) the *Gatekeepers*. They were notable both for what they did and did not do. What they did was temporal separation. Nearly two-thirds (64 percent) reported alternating back and forth between being open and closed about relational problems. But they did not do anything else. Only one subject scored above the midpoint on the scales for any of the seven remaining strategy measures. The Gatekeepers saw little risk in the current encounter, perhaps because of the person they had chosen, and therefore did little to adapt to risk. This differentiated them from the Cautious Disclosers and the Strategists, who saw risk and decided to adapt to it, and from the Expressives, who saw risk and decided to ignore it.

Correlates of Strategy Use
Once we were able to identify types of strategies and strategy users we began to explore the factors that might be associated with strategy choices. We considered both the number of strategies people used and their larger patterns of strategy use.

Although most respondents reported relying on between one and three strategies, the number and mix of strategies used varied widely. We thought that the initial situational and relational conditions surrounding the encounter might account for this variation. So we used a series of seventeen predictors in a stepwise regression

in which the dependent variable was the number of frequently used strategies. The predictors covered a variety of contextual factors including the prior relationships among the parties, how much the problem had been discussed previously and in the current interaction, how important the problem was, and, of course, the risks and benefits perceived to accompany seeking support.

Of the seventeen predictors, four entered significantly into the stepwise regression equation. The strongest of these was an impression-management concern. More strategies were used when there was a greater fear that disclosing the problem would result in negative impressions of the self, the romantic partner, or of the overall romantic relationship. Subjects also reported that they used a greater number of strategies when they had a closer relationship to the support provider and when they felt the relational problem was more important. Curiously, we found a negative association between number of strategies used and the length of the support encounter. We suspect this reflects how people cope when they perceive negative reactions. First, in an effort to produce positive reactions or to manage interactional difficulties, they increase the number of strategies they use. If this is not successful, then they cut the encounter short. Naturally, the results also reflected complex associations among the predictors. As a case in point, those who had higher initial concerns about confidentiality also tended both to have shorter encounters and to use more strategies.

Our next step was to determine if differences in the initial context of the support encounter were associated with whether respondents chose the role of Expressive, Strategist, Cautious Discloser, or Gatekeeper. A MANOVA indicated that there was indeed a significant multivariate effect linking the four types of strategy users to variations in the initial conditions, so we went on to explore it with a series of multivariate and univariate analyses.

One of these analyses used a rotated stepwise multiple discriminant analysis. It yielded three significant functions. The first was defined primarily by two of the motivations to withhold information: a fear that the negative impressions of the self, partner, or relationship might result and a fear that confidentiality might be violated. Subjects who rated highly on these concerns were more likely to adopt the role of Strategist or Cautious Discloser, while those who were less concerned with negative impressions or confidentiality violations were more likely to be Gatekeepers or Expressives.

The second discriminant function was nearly as strong as the first and showed most clearly the collision of forces that our dialectical perspective envisioned. It was defined by motivations both to with-

hold and to disclose. Thus, the belief that the problem should be solved alone because disclosure would be ineffective or inappropriate was paired with a relational obligation to disclose and with a desire to disclose in order to get the supporter to intervene in some way. A global measure of feeling oneself in a dilemma also loaded highly on this function. Together these measures formed a function that set the Strategists quite clearly apart from Gatekeepers and, to a lesser extent, from Cautious Disclosers and Expressives. That is, the more a subject felt caught in these conflicting motivations, the more likely he or she was to adopt the role of Strategist, and the less likely he or she was to be an Expressive, a Cautious Discloser, or Gatekeeper.

The final discriminant function was defined primarily by the belief that disclosing would improve the relationship with the supporter and by how often the problem had been discussed in the past with this particular supporter. It discriminated the Cautious Disclosers and, to a lesser degree, the Expressives from Strategists and Gatekeepers. To illustrate, the results suggested that people who hoped that disclosing would improve their relationship with the supporter and who had not discussed the problem frequently with the supporter in the past were more likely to adopt the role of Cautious Discloser. Conversely, those who were less concerned with improving their relationship with the supporter and/or who had already discussed the problem with the supporter were more likely to adopt the role of Gatekeeper.

Results of univariate F-tests and cellwise contrasts reinforced the main features of the discriminant analysis, but also pointed to other differences between Strategists, Expressives, Cautious Disclosers, and Gatekeepers. Those who carried concerns about negative outcomes into the support encounter were more likely to adopt a strategic perspective. Thus, our univariate results indicated that, compared to the other groups, Strategists were significantly more concerned about violations of confidentiality, with whether disclosure would be appropriate or effective, with whether disclosure might create negative impressions, and with whether disclosure might place undue burdens on the supporter or their relationship with the supporter. Cautious Disclosers displayed attenuated versions of most of these same differences – having more concerns about confidentiality, appropriateness, effectiveness, and impression management than did Expressives and Gatekeepers. Interestingly, Cautious Disclosers were less concerned with improving their relationship with the supporter than were Gatekeepers. Although those in the Expressive group tended to be more concerned than Gatekeepers that disclosure would be inappropriate,

ineffective, or burdensome, the differences between Expressives and Gatekeepers were generally smaller than the differences between these two groups and the remaining groups.

We believe these results show that the approach taken by support seekers is highly sensitive to their initial concerns and conditions surrounding the encounter. Moreover, it appears to us that approaches to obtaining support are most clearly differentiated by concerns with negative outcomes and by the tension between the risks and benefits of disclosure. When people worry that disclosure might not be appropriate or effective, that it might not remain confidential, but simultaneously feel both a strong desire for support and a relational obligation to disclose, they tend to adopt a strategic perspective. Strategists were also more worried with the risk of negative impressions and that their disclosure might be a burden to the supporter or to their relationship with the supporter. To some extent, these worries might reflect the fact that Strategists had discussed the problem with the supporter fewer times than had members of the other groups.

People tended to adopt an approach of cautious disclosure when they had a strong desire for support counterbalanced by moderate perceived risk. Both Cautious Disclosers and Strategists worried over leaving negative impressions or creating a burden. However, Cautious Disclosers did not worry as much about confidentiality, perhaps because, compared to Strategists, they already had more experience talking about the problem with the supporter.

People who felt little conflict between the risks and benefits of seeking support tended to operate either as Expressives or as Gatekeepers. Expressives and Gatekeepers did not feel such tensions because they had little concern with issues like confidentiality, relational obligation, appropriateness, effectiveness, and relational burden. They did have a high desire for support, though no higher than the members of the other groups, but that desire did not extend to a wish to have the supporter intervene. For the most part, differences in initial conditions did not account for the differences between Expressives and Gatekeepers. There were, however, trends toward Gatekeepers having talked previously with the supporter about the problem more often, being more concerned with impression management, and being more interested in using disclosure of a problem with a romantic partner as a tool to improve the relationship with the supporter.

Strategies and Outcomes
So little previous research has directly addressed the impacts of variations in strategy use that our initial approach was to simply

identify classes of potentially affected outcomes. We developed seven measures based on a literature review, exploratory factor analyses, and our own efforts at conceptual clarification. The first was a satisfaction variable – but a rather specific one representing the satisfaction associated with enhanced certainty and control (see Albrecht and Adelman, 1987b; Parks, 1985). Other outcome measures tapped the degree to which the other person reacted negatively during the encounter itself, the extent to which the subject thought that discussing the problem had actually made it worse, and the extent to which negative impressions had been left regarding the romantic partner or the romantic relationship. The remaining outcome measures focussed on how the encounter may have affected the various relationships between the support provider, the recipient, and the recipient's romantic partner.

The outcomes one obtained along these various dimensions turned out to be relatively independent of how many strategies were used. Our respondents generally believed, however, that using a greater number of strategies only ended up making the problem itself worse. There were also less consistently significant indications that using more strategies was associated with more negative reactions during the encounter, and with negative impressions being left afterward, with negative impacts on the relationship between the subject and support, and on the relationship between the subject and his or her romantic partner.

Strategists, Cautious Disclosers, Expressives, and Gatekeepers were also compared in terms of the seven outcome variables. Our procedures were similar to those used in the previous section – MANOVA and multiple discriminant analysis aided by univariate F-tests to examine cell contrasts. Generally speaking, Strategists, Cautious Disclosers, Expressives, and Gatekeepers were more similar in their perceptions of outcomes than they were in their perceptions of initial conditions. All four groups reported fairly high mean levels of certainty and satisfaction, and felt that the interaction had resulted in improved relationships between the subject and supporter, the subject and his or her romantic partner, and the supporter and the romantic partner.

Nonetheless, the multivariate effect in the MANOVA bordered on statistical significance ($p < 0.06$) and the stepwise discriminant analysis uncovered two significant functions. The first function was defined primarily by greater certainty/satisfaction and lower negative reactions. Expressives and, to a lesser extent, Cautious Disclosers scored higher on this dimension, while the Strategists scored quite low. That is, Strategists reported lower certainty/satisfaction and greater negative reactions during the interaction. The second

function was defined predominantly by the perception that talking about the problem had made it worse. This function sorted between the Cautious Disclosers and Strategists, on the one hand, and Expressives and Gatekeepers on the other hand. Cautious Disclosers and, to a lesser extent, Strategists felt that talking about the problem had made it worse, while the Expressives and especially the Gatekeepers felt that talking about the problem had made it better.

The main themes of the discriminant analysis were echoed in the results of univariate F-tests. Across all these analyses, the largest differences were ones that set the Expressives apart from the Cautious Disclosers and especially from the Strategists. Expressives did not encounter negative reactions or believe that the problem had been made worse by the interaction. Strategists did perceive more negative reactions to their attempts to gain support and perhaps that is why they ended up using more strategies. Both Strategists and Cautious Disclosers perceived some worsening of the problem.

Putting the Pieces Together: Dialectics, Strategies, and Outcomes

When our respondents experienced problems in their romantic relationships, they often turned to friends, family, or other members of their social network for support. Even though they often felt very close to the supporter and genuinely desired support, they also recognized that there were risks in seeking support. Benefits such as receiving emotional validation, advice, direct help, and an improved relationship with the support provider were often balanced by risks. These risks included creating negative impressions, violations of confidentiality, reductions in perceptions of competence, perceptions of inappropriate or ineffective disclosure, and burdens placed on the supporter or the subject's relationship with the supporter. To varying degrees, then, support seekers found themselves in a dilemma defined by conflicting desires to obtain support while minimizing risk.

The communicative options that people exercise in facing this dilemma are more extensive than a simple choice between seeking or not seeking support. Getting at these options involved adapting and extending previous work on the dialectics of personal relationships and the management of conflicting communicative goals (for example, Bavelas, 1985; Baxter, 1988; O'Keefe and Delia, 1982). The result of these efforts was to identify a series of eight strategies and tactics that were actually used in varying degrees by our subjects. Some made a comparatively simple choice between complete

candor and silence, but most of our respondents employed a more complex mix of communicative strategies. These included alternating periods of openness and closedness with a given supporter ('temporal separation'), spreading support requests around one's network ('network separation'), sending mixed messages that conveyed the need for support verbally and downplayed it nonverbally (or vice versa, two ways of enacting 'behavioral separation'), being ambiguous about the problem of one's needs for support ('disqualification'), compromising by being somewhat open and somewhat closed in requests for support ('moderation'), and finding ways to be open without suffering negative consequences ('reframing').

Our open-ended data made it clear that most of our respondents had also been practicing what we might call 'supporter selection' – intentionally selecting a supporter with whom the risks were lower and the benefits greater than they might have been with another. Almost all our respondents had chosen to discuss the problem with someone to whom they felt quite close, usually a close friend of the same sex and age. Perhaps this preference reflects cultural definitions of close relationships that simply obligate intimates to provide support (for example, Roloff et al., 1988; Shapiro, 1980). The characteristics our respondents ascribed to support providers, however, suggested that their choices were based on a great deal more than simple perceptions of obligation. For instance, they generally perceived the person they chose to be 'receptive,' indicating that the support request was not a burden to them. Subjects may have thought that 'sympathetic' supporters would be less likely to develop a negative impression of them, while 'trustworthy' supporters would be less likely to violate confidentiality. The benefit of the supporter's 'expertise' often appeared to flow from either his or her general similarity to the subject or from his or her specific experience with the subject or the subject's problem.

This strategic selection of supporters probably allowed some subjects to adopt the role of 'expressive' in which the problem was disclosed with almost complete candor. Even with careful selection of supporters, however, most of our subjects still experienced risk. A few dealt with it by becoming 'gatekeepers' of their problem – alternating periods of openness and closedness with the supporter. The vast majority adopted even more complex styles of dealing with risk that earned them the labels of 'cautious discloser' or 'strategist.' Quite clearly, then, selecting the 'right' person with whom to share the problem is important, but it does not obviate the need for more specific risk-management strategies.

The communicative behaviors we have called 'strategies' really are strategies: they represent choices about communication made

in response to an individual's experienced dilemma. In our data the best single predictor of the number of communicative strategies a person used was his or her fear that the discussion would leave negative impressions of the self, of the romantic partner, or of the overall relationship. Those who feared leaving such impressions used more strategies. Qualitatively, those with greater fears about negative impressions and those who were more concerned with burdening the supporter were more likely to play the restrained and controlling roles of Cautious Discloser or strategist. Further analysis revealed that the Strategists, the group that used the greatest number and variety of approaches to gaining support, were also the people who most deeply felt conflict between the desires to withhold and disclose. These were people who appeared to realize fully the dialectic tensions we had predicted. At the same time as they wanted to disclose the problem in order to get help and to satisfy relational expectations, they also wanted to keep the problem to themselves because they worried that sharing it might be inappropriate, ineffective, or create negative consequences.

The strategic character of the support process was also underscored by the finding that people used a greater number of strategies when they felt that their problem was more important and when they had a closer relationship to the supporter. These two variables were not, however, associated with qualitative differences in strategy choice. That is, the particular strategies support seekers chose did not depend on problem importance or the relationship to the supporter. We think that people are especially responsive to the support provider when their problem is important and they feel close to the support provider. If so, then particular strategy choices might depend more on the way the conversation unfolded sequentially than on these more general factors themselves. Thus, knowing that the problem was important and that the relationship with the supporter was close would allow one to predict that a greater number of strategies would be used, but not which ones.

To explore such possibilities we need samples of actual conversation between seekers and supporters who have an ongoing relationship. After all, whatever 'support' a seeker receives is ultimately the result of the communication that transpires between the interactants and is no doubt affected not only by the actions of the support seeker, but also by the responses of the supporter, and the ways their behaviors intermesh. Thus, future research should examine the strategies providers use to respond to support requests (See Burleson, Chapter 4, this volume). While these responses were not our primary focus, our open-ended data did reveal a wide range of responses. Many supporters asked questions, gave advice,

disclosed their own relationship problems, and swapped experiences with the support seeker. Some agreed with support seekers, while others expressed disagreement or surprise. Finally, some supporters broached the support seeker's desire for support in indirect ways that allowed the seeker to deny or ignore his or her need for support.

Variations in supporter responses should cycle back to create differences in the number and kinds of strategies used by support seekers. In our data, for example, subjects who perceived that the other person was responding negatively reacted by adopting a strategic perspective and by using a greater number of communicative strategies to manage the situation. The vast majority of our respondents evaluated their support encounter in positive terms regardless of the number and types of strategies they used. While those who used a greater number of strategies reported that the problem had become somewhat worse as a result of the encounter, they did not report being any less satisfied or certain. Nor were they any more concerned than those who used fewer strategies that negative impressions had been left. Nor did they feel that the relationships among the parties involved had been affected any more negatively or positively than did respondents who met fewer negative reactions and used fewer strategies.

We think this pattern of findings is further evidence of our respondents' skill at adapting to their circumstances. Some found themselves in a situation in which there was little cause for concern and little need for strategy, perhaps because they carefully selected their supporters, or the problem was not so important, or because the supporters responded in positive ways. Others found themselves in a situation where risks were serious and a more strategic approach was needed. Those using more strategies may have encountered negative reactions as the interaction unfolded and their greater and more varied use of strategies may be the result of their recognition that they needed to take additional steps to salvage a successful interaction. From this admittedly speculative point of view, the types and numbers of strategies chosen should not be strongly correlated with outcomes. No one strategy or set of strategies should be necessarily more effective or sophisticated as long as it was responsive to the circumstances; and thus, quite different mixes of strategies could yield quite similar outcomes.

Individual-difference variables no doubt play a role, too. How the perceived closeness of the relationship with the supporter and how the importance of the problem translate into perceptions of risk and benefit may be heavily influenced by personality differences (see Pierce et al., Chapter 10, this volume). Differences in

the participants' construct systems may be particularly relevant (for example, Burleson, 1987). People with more differentiated social-construct systems, for example, have been shown to be more effective at creating messages that reconcile conflicting communicative goals (for example, O'Keefe and Shepherd, 1987). People who employ more constructs and who have higher levels of abstraction in their construct systems also appear to be more sensitive and effective in comforting distressed individuals (for example, Burleson, Chapter 4, this volume; Samter and Burleson, 1984). Thus, the level of differentiation and abstraction in the system of constructs used to interpret communicative situations may be one individual difference that begins to account for strategies and outcomes. And because construct-system abstraction and differentiation change according to a developmental sequence, we suspect that there also would be cognitive developmental differences in strategies used to balance risks and benefits of social support.

Beyond the realm of individual developmental differences is the larger developmental cycle of interpersonal relationships. One way to put the results of this study in the context of relational development is to argue that people experience and cope with the risks of seeking support differently as their relationship with a supporter evolves. This is consistent with Baxter's (1989) research on the use of selection, separation, and integration strategies to cope with relationship dialectics. Her subjects were most likely to report using moderation early in a relationship, followed by an increased likelihood of temporal separation and disqualification during the middle stages. Reframing and selection were most likely to be used later in a relationship's history. Our own findings show only that the number of strategies increases with the closeness of the subject–supporter relationship; however, the range of relationship types and perceived closeness in our study was quite limited. The need to examine a broader range of relationships and of levels of relational development is underscored by the finding that for at least some simple support requests (for example, borrowing class notes) increasing intimacy might be associated with simpler, less strategic persuasive appeals (Roloff et al., 1988).

Finally, this study provided further evidence for the utility of linking the development of personal relationships with the dynamics of the participants' surrounding social networks (for example, Milardo and Lewis, 1985; Parks and Eggert, in press). Some theoretical perspectives on relationship development ignore social-network factors completely (for example, Altman and Taylor, 1973; Kelley, 1979), while others emphasize that it is withdrawal from, rather than contact with, network members that promotes intimacy

and commitment (for example, Milardo et al., 1983). The results of this study, however, illustrated the positive role that network members can play in the development of romantic relationships. Regardless of its perceived importance, most of our respondents had found ways to share their romantic problem with an outside supporter in such a way that the romantic relationship was improved rather than damaged. Over half (57 percent) reported that sharing their relational problems had left them feeling closer to, more satisfied with, and more committed to their romantic relationship.

Throughout this project our goal has been to interrelate four root terms: relationship dialectics, social networks, social support, and relationship development. We were able to use each to cross-fertilize our understanding of the other because they all shared something even more basic. All four terms ultimately recognize that our personal relationships and the process of social support are created in and experienced through communication. They exist in it and can be understood in terms of it.

7

The Negative Effects of Informal Support Systems

John J. La Gaipa

Research on personal relationships and on social support has generally focussed on its positive effects and, in my earlier work, so did I. For instance, I identified friendship expectations or stereotypes of friendship as an idealized relationship (La Gaipa, 1977a). Later studies, however, indicated that 'true friendships' are not too common, that they are often brief, and that many people avoid intimacy and closeness, expecting negative rather than positive outcomes (see La Gaipa, 1987 for a review of this research program). Accordingly I have also looked at negative effects in relationships and social support, focussing on the informal systems provided by family and friends. There are clearly negative consequences of lack of support, but less clear and equally important negative consequences of giving and receiving support. In outline, these negative effects can be long- or short-term, but impact both on the individuals and the relationship. The short-term effects include feeling smothered and controlled, feeling obligated to conform, and a sense of inadequacy, whereas the long-term effects include low self-esteem and identity problems, resentment, and depression.

Why study negative outcomes? In addition to the importance of balancing out the present Pollyanna style of thinking about relationships, such research may sensitize us to the nature of constraints on positive outcomes, and facilitate the implementation of strategies to enhance mental health and well-being.

In focussing on the negative effects of social support, this chapter will develop a number of arguments and perspectives. First of all, a systems approach is used which highlights the interdependency or connectedness of personal relationships and social support (see La Gaipa, 1981b). Second, the giving and receiving of support is viewed in terms of a dialectical conflict of independence and dependence. Third, the dialectical tensions associated with the giving and receiving of rewards and benefits are viewed here as major sources of negative effects.

The notion of dialectics is found in various psychological and social theories, from Freud's to Marx's theory of social classes and revolution. The notion of dialectics of human experience is a key feature of the systemic thinking adopted in this chapter. It calls attention to the contradictions, for instance, in the interplay between the individual and society. An approach to informal support systems in terms of dialectic thinking implies that giving and receiving have a 'built-in' and ever-present source of negative effects. In so far as dialectical tension involves both positive and negative poles, it follows that the resolution of such conflict is likely to have negative effects.

Le Fevre (1981), in discussing such dialectics, contends that we experience our world as ambiguous; that ambiguity means insecurity; and that insecurity means anxiety. The question of trust in each other is seen as resulting from the fundamental insecurity of all our lives. For Le Fevre (1981: 11), life ' . . . is both positive and negative. It is joy and sorrow, bondage and freedom, guilt and forgiveness, love and hate, justice and injustice, loneliness and belonging, gain and loss, unity and disunity.' From such dialectics spring one major tension in relationships, that of *Autonomy vs. Dependence.*

Autonomy is a multidimensional concept. It involves the freedom to make your own decisions, to shape long-range goals, and to determine life priorities and commitments. The individuals' need for independence and/or his or her culturally derived belief in the value of independence may be in conflict with needs for resources available through personal relationships. When autonomy is suppressed in the providing of care, the benefits come at a high cost of loss of individuality and freedom.

Dependency is also a multifaceted concept. A common element of dependency is practical or physical helplessness. Tobin (1969) focusses on dependency as a personal, psychological trait as 'characterological dependency.' Dant (1988) suggests that dependency makes a statement about power in a relationship. It is manifested in social relationships in the way people manipulate others or allow themselves to be manipulated (Goldfarb, 1969).

The dialectic of Autonomy–Dependency is likely to be of major significance in the matter of care giving (and is thus given lengthy discussion here), but there are other dialectical tensions in informal support groups that go beyond this. One instance, that is particularly relevant in discussion of coping and support at times of private personal distress, is the need to maintain a balance between privacy and intimacy (cf. Burgoon et al., 1989). Such a dialectical tension even affects relationships in college students, who often have limited personal space available in the residential dormitories. There

may be lack of support for the roommate's need for physical privacy. A dramatic instance is provided in universities where the students are permitted overnight guests of the opposite sex. This sometimes results in one roommate being exposed to the surveillance of love making. La Gaipa (1989) found that both the participants and nonparticipants complained of violations of privacy, though each defined it somewhat differently. The coping strategies used sometimes led to negative effects for the persons and the relationship. A common complaint by the nonparticipants was that the lovers used a detachment strategy. 'They acted as if I wasn't there. They treated me as an object.' The bystanders felt dehumanized. The poor resolution of this dialectical conflict over privacy and intimacy resulted in negative self-concepts, and the deterioration of the relationship. We can easily extrapolate the principle from such a case to those where, for example, seriously ill persons in need of support experience the same delicate dialectic conflict over personal privacy (for example, if they have become incontinent or have lost voluntary control over bodily functions).

In sum, then, I will deal with both the negative effects of lack of support, and the negative effects of the giving and receiving of support. I will do this by highlighting the whole system, the social context, human experience of dialectical tensions, and the process of dependency, which is constantly mentioned by researchers in seeking to explain negative effects. The first part of the chapter will deal with these issues in general, whereas the second part will emphasize the support problems of the elderly. Since the issues of lack of support are covered by the chapter by Berg and Piner (Chapter 8), I will focus here on the negative aspects of giving and receiving of support but illustrate all three in the later sections of the chapter.

Negative Consequences of Giving Support

(In)appropriateness of Support
Support is sometimes discussed as a perfectly matched provision of resources to needs, but the matching of support to the real needs of a person is often not done effectively in real life. When, for example, members of one's social network have no personal experience with a particular crisis, such as cancer, their efforts to be helpful are likely to be strained and clumsy (Chesler and Barbarin, 1984). While a behavior offered by others and intended to be supportive may be seen as helpful by the recipient if provided at the right time, it is nonetheless unhelpful if provided at the wrong time. Duck (1984) has detailed the fact that interventions have

different goals at different points in the process of relational dissolution and shows how support out-of-phase is ineffective.

The most appreciated kind of help in the early stages of illness (that is, at diagnosis or soon thereafter) is emotional support, which often consists simply of providing an opportunity for the patient to express feelings. Dunkel-Schetter and Wortman (1981) found that cancer patients in early stages did not appreciate being given specific directional advice or being told that 'they would be OK,' nor did they view as helpful being provided with material assistance as caretaking.

Little systematic research has been done to determine the kinds of advice that are most appropriate for different kinds of people with different kinds of problems. Rogerian therapists recommend that advice giving is seldom justified. In an experimental study of advice using vignettes, La Gaipa and Klein (1984) found that the most effective advice was where the person emphasized that the friend was not responsible for the problem – the innocent-victim approach was most preferred. It also appears to make very little difference whether the adviser focussed on the gains or the losses arising out of the interpersonal conflict instigating the need for advice.

Advice generally has little harmful effects even when it is ineffective as a support strategy, since it is usually rejected! In some instances the recipients are not really interested in solving the problem; in other cases, the advice may be objectively bad, premature, and inadequate. Certainly, the above studies suggest that advice is often given without an adequate assessment of the problem, and may be strikingly inappropriate and unappreciated.

Cost of Providing Support   Against this background we can begin to understand some of the costs and benefits of relationships and support in a broader sense, as a result of noting the dialectical forces and uncertainties in developing relationships.

Offers of support may be misinterpreted or ineffectual. Wiseman (1986) describes friendship as a unique and fragile relationship containing seeds of its own destruction. Friendship is subject to cross-pressures inevitably impinging on and threatening a sense of autonomy. For instance, actions taken to develop a friendship may be perceived as strategies for the mobilization of a support system, and may be interpreted as exploitative, leading to the disruption of the relationship. Recent research has also clarified instances of ineffectual support. It suggests that negative ties have a greater negative impact than positive ties have a positive effect (cf. Rook, 1984). Pagel et al. (1987) found that the helpful aspect of one's

social network bore little or no relation to depression and overall network satisfaction. By contrast, being upset with one's network was consistently related to depression.

There may also be high costs associated with caring. Females who are highly sensitive to the needs of others experience higher levels of burden and depressive symptoms. Women are more responsive than men in meeting the life crises of network members, and the emotional costs of caring for those in one's network account for a substantial part of the pervasive mental-health disadvantage of women (Kessler and McLeod, 1985). Women with more intimate friends are liable to greater emotional strain than women with fewer. To be genuinely concerned about the misfortunes of others, and open in the expression of empathy, exposes women to more stress. Hobfoll and London (1986), in particular, found that Israeli women whose loved ones were mobilized into the Israeli Defense Forces experienced more stress if they had such high resources.

Furthermore, active participation can be associated with higher levels of some types of distress. The costs of friendship accelerate when the number of friends goes beyond an optimal level. Antonnuci and Akiyami (1988) found that happiness was negatively related to the number of people in women's inner circle, but unrelated for men. A study of adolescent friendship networks noted that students with many social ties in the network had higher systolic blood pressure than isolates (Hansell, 1985). The physiological stress of high reachability was interpreted in terms of the social obligations that friendship implies. To maintain an extensive personal network requires engagement, time, and attention – in short, it brings costs as well as rewards.

If this were not enough, social obligations may override the positive effect of companionship and social support. Such constraints may have a negative effect on mental well-being that may not make up for the beneficial aspects of personal relationships (Gove et al., 1983). Persons who live alone vs. others (never married, separated/divorced, and widowed) tend to be in no worse – and on many indicators are in better – mental health than persons in these same categories who live with others.

There are possible negative effects associated with having a confidant – one who displays unconditional positive regard and accepts the other regardless of the weaknesses revealed. Understanding and encouragement are provided, but such unqualified acceptance has a price in terms of accuracy. Confidants are not likely to provide an accurate reflection of what a person is worth. Rather, one must turn to less intimate friends for more accurate feedback (Simons, 1984).

There are individual differences, of course, in the perception of social exchange, and what kinds of rewards and benefits are sought. High self-esteem widows perceive more emotionally helpful experiences, while low self-esteem widows report more instrumentally helpful experiences (Malkinson, 1987). In a similar study individuals high in self-esteem were found to seek more emotional support than those low in self-esteem (Hobfoll et al., 1986).

Caring others can also undermine a person's value system and deprive one of support in time of crisis. For instance, Ratcliff and Bogdan (1988) looked at unemployed women when social support was not supportive. Nearly half of the women said their friends and kin were not concerned that they had lost their jobs. These people, who should have been 'caring others,' were essentially denying the legitimacy of an activity the unemployed regarded as important.

Negative Consequences of Receiving Support

The possible lack of support at some *future* time may generate feelings of uncertainties in a relationship, a source of anxiety. Berger (1988), Duck (1988), and others have commented on the strong feeling of uncertainty in relationships. To combat such uncertainties various uncertainty-reduction mechanisms are employed, such as the 'relationship audit.' This information gathering, however understandably, makes the other uncomfortable – like a credit search or a tax audit. It makes the other person defensive, and strains the relationship.

A feeling of uncertainty about the reliability of the support system is likely to evoke search behavior. Baxter and Wilmot (1984) write about 'secret tests' as a strategy for evaluating the state of a relationship. Baxter (1988) has focussed attention on dialectical aspects in communication strategies used in relationship development. One strategy used to 'test' a relationship is to exaggerate the need and see what happens. A study of spouses found that 40 percent of them felt that the spouse was acting more dependent than necessary (Barusch, 1988). The responses to such exaggeration are likely to be negative. Mills and Clark (1986) contend that the caregiver may view such exaggeration as exploitative, but the motive may be simply reality testing. These system-maintenance strategies often are self-defeating and may accelerate the disruption of a relationship.

Information Management
Uncertainty about the reliability of resources may lead to information management (see Berger, 1988; Metts, 1989). McCall and Simmons (1978) posit that the social order rests upon errors, lies, and deception as well as upon accurate information. Duck and Sants (1983) have noted that the parties in a dyad do more than send and receive messages, but are engaged in deletion, addition, and rearranging or 'editorializing' of what transpires. Fitzpatrick et al. (1982) argue that what is required in an ongoing relationship is a constant balance between 'hiding' and 'revelation.' Individuals seek an equilibrium between the need to be open and the need to protect themselves from the effects of such openness, and to maintain the stability of the dyad.

The potential positive benefits of social exchange on emerging relationships may be thwarted by cognitive distortion, leading instead to negative effects. Distortions in the perception of the exchange process were reported by La Gaipa (1977b) in a roommate study in which each roommate was asked to describe the rewards received and given by the other roommate. Little relationship was found between what one roommate reported giving and what the other reported receiving. The greater the difference, the less likely the survival of the relationship. This constant error in the perception of exchange, that we give more than we receive, may act as a barrier to the growth of the relationship.

The Family and Support
The extended family is mobilized for support at times of personal crisis such as the breakup of a marriage or when economic resources are limited. To be able to turn to one's family in time of need is a normative expectation. It is what a family is supposed to do, but it does not always do so effectively, with one effect being that of negative attitudes toward the family. In a recent article, Morgan (1989a) reported the results of a study of recent widows using focus groups. Morgan found that 40 percent of the descriptions were negative, and that the 'family' received more negative comments than non-family. One possible reason is that the family unit may constrain the autonomy of its members.

The dilemma for the family is that it wishes that each member is self-supporting, but the person in need is often helpless to achieve this objective. The dependence on the economic security of the extended family limits efforts to be independent. Economic inadequacy may jeopardize a relationship. For instance, when kin feel their own security is threatened by the needs of others, they tend to be ambivalent, if not hostile, about the exchange of goods and

resources. Trust may be less common under conditions of limited resources. Such dependency on the family, then, may be stifling to its members. Martin and Martin (1978) identified some of the determinants of strain in extended families of blacks. These included feeling burdened by obligation, disagreeing over the need, resenting the beneficiary, and feeling cheated by those who want more than they need or deserve.

Receiving Advice from Others

Costs may be incurred in accepting advice – for example, advice may constrain a person's options. Adolescents sometimes reject advice in order to equalize social power in relationship with parents (Tripathi et al., 1986). Reliance on the advice of a more powerful person or one with higher status may also reduce a person's autonomy and personal decision making. Dressler (1985) found that newly divorced, black woman often became depressed when they turned to their family for support. They found themselves to be under close scrutiny from the older support-system members, and were expected to follow the advice of their elders very closely.

Confiding

The benefits of confiding in others depend in part on the type of relationship. Confiding to a good friend may be beneficial, but not to a spouse or relative. Women are often inhibited about confiding in mothers about family quarrels (O'Connor and Brown, 1984). Such confidences are viewed as causing more problems than they solve. Mothers are likely to feel hostile toward the confiding wife's husband, or the confidence may make the mother feel guilty or inadequate for not bringing up the confider to be able to handle such conflicts.

Whether giving and receiving have a positive effect depends, in part, on the degree of reciprocity according to equity theory (see La Gaipa, 1977b). In a recent study, however, Ingersoll-Dayton and Antonucci (1988) found minimal support for this hypothesis. Neither reciprocal nor non-reciprocal confiding relationships predicted life satisfaction or negative affect, regardless of the type of relationship. Nonetheless, the perception of the network as too demanding was characteristic of respondents who said they did not confide in their spouses but that their spouses confided in them. Surprisingly, not confiding to a friend who confided to oneself was associated with the perception of the network as *less* demanding! Negative effects of inequity appear to depend on the type of relationship and the nature of the support.

Personality factors may mediate the impact of the family. A study

of pregnant women found that higher levels of emotional support were associated with lower feelings of well-being and satisfaction for women with low self-esteem (Hobfoll et al., 1986). Gender differences have also been found. Men who socialize with kin or rely on kin feel worse than men less dependent on kin. Dependent men experience higher rates of depression than dependent women. For women, reliance on kin makes them feel better (Gerstel, 1988).

In some cultures, the family emphasizes loyalty and commitment to it by stressing its all powerful significance to the individual. Ierodiakonou (1988) found that the Greek family may foster a sense of inadequacy in its members who seek to be autonomous in the larger community. The individual is indoctrinated with the notion that he or she will fail without family support. Such family strategies are used to foster extreme dependence of the individual on the family.

The North American Indian culture values autonomy, but independence is handicapped by limited economic resources. Indian youth struggle to maintain self-control while surrounded by conditions that undermine their efforts (cf. La Fromboise and Bigfoot, 1988). The high rate of alcoholism, violence, and suicide in adolescent North American Indians may be symptomatic of cultural-value clashes.

Relocation of ethnic groups may constrain positive effects of the family. Adolescents of Southeast Asian refugee parents were found to have identity problems because their parents were preoccupied with their own survival in this new country. These parents were burdened by depression and other emotional difficulties, and were physically and emotionally unavailable to their children (Lee, 1988). These parents were often perceived as objects of pity and shame. Many of their children experienced nightmares, compulsive work, and drug abuse. Others felt an obligation to compensate for their parents' helplessness and sorrow.

Systems Theory and the Alcoholic

Family systems theory may be useful in linking up personal relationships and support systems. Efforts by the family to maintain equilibrium may have unintended, negative effects. This may be illustrated with regard to the problem of alcoholism. Because the family is a system, the alcoholism of one member affects all the others, who develop defensive systems parallel to those of the alcoholic. In seeking to maintain homeostasis in the family, two extremes are possible here. In the first instance, the alcoholic may provide a common problem that serves to make the family more cohesive. The removal of the problem, then, may be disruptive to family

unity, and in this sense family cohesiveness may have a negative effect on the individual in constraining his or her recovery because such a recovery could be disruptive to the family as a unit. In the second instance, the family may sustain denial of alcoholism in an effort to maintain homeostasis. The family is so busy taking care of the alcoholic that they do not have time to examine their own dysfunction. Members tend to isolate themselves emotionally and physically from each other, and are unable to share feelings of resentment, embarrassment, and ambivalence.

The Elderly

The above review has dealt in general with negative consequences of relationships and support. I will now extend these points – and others on lack of support – to the specific population of the elderly. From this following review we shall determine the particular sharpness of the two-edged sword that relationships and support-needs represent for the elderly.

Negative Consequences of Lack of Support

Seniors have recently been the subject of more attention as governments react to the increasing demand of the ageing population on the formal health-care system and try to convince us of the value of independence, autonomy, and human dignity. This has led to funding of studies on independence in the elderly. Given the preceding review on dialectics and systems, we could expect, and we do indeed find, that the negative effects of support groups in the elderly are nonetheless a rich and fertile field.

Most seniors can draw on kin for support. There are, however, pockets of isolated elderly who neither wish for nor are eligible for institutionalization, and rely heavily on social security for subsistence. What can happen to elderly persons with minimal support from family and who live in cheap rooming houses and hotels in urban centers?

A study of the elderly living in a large, metropolitan hotel in a large city was conducted by Stephens (1976). This hotel was located in a high crime area. Many of the seniors living in the hotel were also of questionable character. These seniors were quite vulnerable to crime from 'outsiders' and were fearful of exploitation by 'insiders.' Their priorities were to control deviance in order to survive, goals achieved by the avoidance of close relationships.

The dominant value of these hotel residents was that of privacy and autonomy. Mutual suspicion prevailed. Others were perceived as untrustworthy characters, a threat to their limited resources.

The coping strategies used to survive are quite revealing. They maintained emotional and social distance from each other, an exaggerated inapproachability. The men relinquished their need for intimacy in order to take care of basic needs, whose satisfaction precludes all forms of intimacy and dependence. The women were fearful of both financial and sexual exploitation. Both friendship and courtship were perceived as enhancing vulnerability to exploitation. Within this social context of limited resources, informal relationships were perceived as providing more negative than positive benefits. In brief, the available social network was not actually a support system.

Negative Consequences of Giving of Support

Caregiving   When the giving of support becomes all pervasive in a personal relationship, one person is labeled as a caregiver, and other features of the relationship become almost secondary. The negative effects of such a role are well documented. Feelings of love and respect for the elderly parent easily can turn into guilt, hatred, and disappointment as children attempt to function in their new roles of caregiver.

The analysis of caregiver tasks and problems in accomplishing them is one way to appreciate the burden of caregiving. Clark and Rakowski (1983) identified three major tasks. Direct assistance involving instrumental help generated the least strain. The personal tasks, creating more strain, included compensating for emotional drain, resolving guilt over negative feelings, and compensating for or recovering personal time. The familial and societal tasks included balancing the giving of assistance with responsibilities to other family members, managing feelings toward other family members who are not helping, and interacting with medical, health, and social-service professionals.

The quality of care may depend on the management skills of the caregiver in coping with the multiple demands. One strategy involves delegating responsibility to other members of the family. There are, however, a host of problems associated with it, such as the limits and dilemmas of family responsibility, fears of loss of control, who is competent for a given task, and who should and would take over when one is no longer able to be the primary caregiver.

An important factor in family management is the size of the social network. Some networks may be too large and dense to be useful to particular clients. La Gaipa and Friesen (1984) found that the larger the number of relatives of cancer patients, the greater

the perceived caregiver level of burden. Similarly, a study on the frail aged found that they may have too many relatives, friends, professionals, and others in their network who compete with and undermine one another (Specht, 1986).

Perceived Competence of Caregiver The perceived competency of the caregiver is important because the nature of provided support is influenced by beliefs as to what one is capable of doing. La Gaipa and Malott (1989) identified four dimensions of perceived competence: role management, handling dialectic conflicts, support awareness, and feeling of comfort with ageing. Many of the Alzheimer caregivers expressed considerable competence in overall care, but feelings of incompetence in specific areas of care. It should be apparent that the elderly face increased vulnerability if the caregiver has mistaken notions about his or her competency.

In a study on family and friends of cancer patients (La Gaipa and Friesen, 1984), we sought to identify some of the barriers to support. For the family, problems center around negative emotional reactions to the situation, uncertainty as to how to give support and the personal costs of involvement with the patients. Friends of the patients, in particular, felt the major problem that they faced was task ambiguity – not knowing what to do.

Caregiver Burden Brody (1985) has identified the effects of caregiver burden, in particular the effects of emotional strains. A long litany of mental-health symptoms was identified, including depression, anxiety, frustration, helplessness, sleeplessness, lowered morale, emotional exhaustion, restrictions on time and freedom, isolation, conflict from competing demands, and interference in life style.

Cicirelli (1983) found that caregivers complain most frequently of feeling physically worn out, being emotionally exhausted, and perceiving that the parent 'was not satisfied no matter what one did.' Feelings of frustration, impatience, and irritation were correlated with parental dependency. Similarly, a study of Japanese caregivers found that perceived burden was associated with such negative emotions as depression, anxiety, irritation, and anger (Yatomi et al., 1989). Needless to say, the elderly should not be viewed largely as 'innocent victims.' Their own psychological symptoms add to the family burden. Seward and Gatz (1989) found that most of the variance of family burden was explained by the low interpersonal sensitivity of the elderly rather than physical or cognitive dysfunctioning.

A concern of health-care professionals is that the caregiver may

abuse the elderly person, either emotionally or physically (Hooyman and Lustbader, 1986). Pillemer (1985) found, instead, that the abusers of the elderly are heavily dependent individuals, sometimes children who have been unable to separate from their parents. Rather than having power in the relationship, the abusers are often relatively powerless.

Various adaptive mechanisms by the caregiver have been found (Johnson and Catalano, 1983). The first technique is distancing. About a third of the respondents reported establishing greater physical distance or establishing psychological distance while maintaining physical proximity. A second method is enmeshing: the caregiver increasingly withdraws from prior social involvements, and becomes isolated from others. A related method is role entrenchment in which the caregiver role takes precedence over other social roles, and is accepted as a permanent, full-time role.

Changes in the primary caregiver due to illness or death can create problems within an extended family (La Gaipa, 1986a). The substitution principle posits a serial order regarding the family member who is 'next-in-line.' Though the hierarchical structure does provide guidance, it can be dysfunctional. The person 'next-in-line' is not necessarily the most competent – a source of anxiety for other family members. The position, however, may be used for the self-justification of competence. Moreover, persons not 'next-in-line' may complain about unfair treatment in being asked to 'do more.' Changes in task allocation, then, may introduce considerable strain in the family, and can have an impact on the quality of care given, and the distancing of relatives from the chronic patient.

Impact of Chronic Illness on Relationships   Changes in need play a role in what one looks for in friendship. Health problems induce a strain on a relationship as more and more instrumental support is needed as compared to other types of support. Friends gradually change from tasks involving actualization to tasks involving maintenance. La Gaipa (1986b) found that the instrumental rewards received from friends may lead to reduced feelings of personal competence. La Gaipa (1981a) also found changes in friendship expectations after the elderly reached 75 years of age. Genuineness and authenticity become increasingly important whereas self-disclosure becomes less important. These changes mirror changes in physical health and increased dependency.

There are changes also over time in the support provided by family. Johnson and Catalano (1983) report that initially, hospitalization activates family support as children and relatives increase their contacts. Improved health, however, may lead to a reduction

of such contacts and a decline in morale. This decline in social contact with family members is not compensated by an increase in sociability with friends. So the patient becomes more isolated and depressed.

Friends are rarely helpful in time of severe illness. Weisman (1979) notes that friends tend to withdraw from the sickbed, because their relationships to the patient are fairly circumscribed in time, depth, intimacy, and commitment. Newly diagnosed patients do not rank friends very highly with respect to problems they are experiencing. Weisman suggests this indicates that limited expectations are held regarding friends.

Long-term chronic conditions accentuate the differences between friends and kin in the support provided (La Gaipa, 1984). More specifically, emotional expression and listening showed a significant decrease from 'normal' to 'crisis' situations. Under crisis situations, families and relatives provide much more help than friends, in particular identity confirmation, and somewhat more empathic understanding than friends. In non-crisis, day-by-day interactions, few differences were found between friends and kin with regard to helping, identity, or empathy.

Some attempts have been made to identify the factors leading to assistance by family caregivers. Certainly, assistance is instigated by the needs of the elderly for support, but it is not as simple as this. Horl and Rosenmeyer (1989) found that the need for help (physical and psychological handicaps) has less weight in determining actual assistance by kin than emotional relations between the generations involved.

The giving of support is influenced by the history of social exchange, including what one has received from the other, building up a sort of bank of credits. Research on social exchange has found that feelings of obligation are a major motive for persons aiding the elderly. Typically, studies find that less than a third of the adult children mention love or affection as their motive. Those who function as supporters are not necessarily those toward whom the greatest positive affect is felt.

Emotional investment is influenced by temporal factors. In a study of family visiting patterns, Fisher and Tessler (1986) compared the responses to the younger, mentally ill patients, and the older, Alzheimer patients. Little emotional attachment was evident with regard to the chronically mentally ill. There is little hope for the future with regard to the mentally ill, and families despair and divest themselves of emotional investment. With Alzheimer patients, emotional involvement persists. The greater attachment to the patient is not based on hope but dependence. It is more

difficult to let go of a valued family member who benefited them so greatly in the past.

Negative Consequences of Receiving Support

Ageing and Dependency   The most common definition of dependency used by health professionals is in terms of requiring assistance in one or more activities of daily living (ADL). Nearly 40 percent of the elderly require some assistance in one or more instrumental ADL. Mental or physical infirmity may result in lowered competence in such ADL activities as bathing, dressing, and feeding. Neither the caregiver nor the elderly person is prepared for the change in role that often accompanies the increased dependence of the elderly person (Brody, 1985).

The caregiver, feeling more responsible and/or manipulative, may exert more personal control over the caregiving situation and become restrictive in interactions, and, perhaps, may insist on making all decisions without consulting the elderly person. It is not uncommon for a caregiver to extend control from areas where the elderly person is incompetent to areas where competency has not been reduced. One justification is that managing the care is easier if most of the decision making is handled by one person, the primary caregiver. Communication barriers also add to the problem. Dependency may have different meaning to the participants. While the elderly person often defines dependency in terms of physical circumstances, the caregiver is equally or more concerned with emotional dependency, often more stressful than the physical demands (Steinmetz, 1983).

A basic conflict in supporting the frail elderly, then, is between paternalism and dependence. Paternalism is usually defined in terms of the intention of protecting them from harm. But such paternalism may deny the elderly the right to manage their own affairs, and may question an elderly person's status as a free, rational, moral, and autonomous being (Kleinefelter, 1984).

Adult children or spouses may create or induce dependency in order to increase control by creating feelings of incompetence in other. A child may, deliberately or unknowingly, exaggerate failings of a parent and impose unwanted controls over the actions of ageing parents. Carried to extreme this is defined as one major type of elder abuse, such as in gaining financial control over parent's money and house. On the other hand, the need to maintain a dependent relationship may influence perception of the needs of others. Verwoerdt (1981) found that some adult children deny the needs of ageing parents. A parent may neither want nor be capable

of self-care, but may be burdened by a child's need to see him or her as unrealistically self-reliant.

The elderly are motivated by a desire for independence and autonomy, but they may not be in the position to refuse assistance from kin – the elderly may not want support, but have little choice. Rodehoever and Datan (1986) suggest, however, that the desire to avoid becoming a burden does not constitute a personal ethic of independence. In their study of Appalachian elders they found that the elders wished to avoid becoming a burden on others, but simultaneously exhibited a dependence on others for tangible services. Rodehoever and Datan suggest that the need for independence among the elders is a personal myth, and recommend that attention be given instead to the interdependence of their lives with the lives of others.

As the elderly person becomes increasingly dependent and more and more instrumental aid is provided, the elder may present reactance to this loss of control. For the elderly person the visible reactions to loss of personal control can include withdrawal, imposing guilt, manipulation, crying, and refusing medication or food (Steinmetz, 1983). Elders who perceive themselves as dependent and the causes of stress may retaliate by engaging in abusive behavior themselves (Stein, 1989).

The elderly may be met with reactions from others that only magnify their feelings of anxiety, confusion, and isolation. One unfortunate aspect of social encounters between the elderly and others is that the topics most beneficial for an elderly person to discuss may be the very topics most likely to threaten and upset others. For example, the elderly may be especially interested in focussing on past conflicts or present distresses in order to view them from a meaningful perspective and resolve them. However, listening to accounts of these problems may heighten others' feelings of vulnerability and helplessness.

The loss of autonomy has been shown to be related to a depressive symptomatology among the elderly (Gimbert et al., 1989; Richman and Flaherty, 1985). Instrumental support has been shown to be related to lower scores on mental-health measures. A study of stroke victims found that instrumental support had a significant negative effect in that the stroke patient continued to rely on the caregiver beyond the point where it was necessary (McLeroy et al., 1984).

Finally, too much support may be problematic for people in dependent roles. Optimal results are obtained from environments that afford opportunities for autonomy to the maximum extent tolerable for the individual's level of competence and simul-

taneously provide support in areas where the individual cannot exercise autonomy. The environment for older people must maintain the right mix of support and challenge for each person: an environment that provides too much support and too little challenge for a well functioning older person may foster dependency and deterioration, although the same environment may provide too little support and too much challenge for someone who is frail (Shinn et al., 1984).

Conclusions

In this chapter I have called attention to the conflict between the dependence on necessary resources provided by the support system and the needs of the individual for autonomy. What seems characteristic is the trade-off that occurs between this need to rely on others, and the need to 'do your own thing.' Maintaining a reliable resource system often comes at a high price of jeopardy to personal integrity.

In this chapter dependency has been treated as a negative condition. But efforts to avoid dependency may have negative consequences and attempts to reduce it do not necessarily lead to the achievement of autonomy. Autonomy is not the absence of dependency. Moreover, autonomy is not necessarily a positive state of being. A study of elderly widows who were relatively self-sufficient found that high levels of autonomy were not related to psychological well-being or life satisfaction. Living alone and being independent were not fulfilling roles for them (O'Bryant, 1989).

Some of the negative effects of informal support systems may be better understood if looked at in terms of such dialectical conflict resolution. I have touched on resolution of such conflicts in terms of movement in one direction or the other. But, there are various other kinds of resolution, including synthesis and creative change, that need to be addressed.

Negative effects have generally been viewed as unexpected findings, subject to much speculation and interpretation. Such negative findings appear to be predicted from information on the social context and dynamics of the caregiver–carereceiver relationship. Little research has been done on the negative effects of informal support systems from a social-psychological perspective. More direct, and well designed studies on negative effects are warranted. Of particular importance is the need to examine the coping mechanisms that underlie the negative effects and the social context in which dependency occurs.

Research on the negative effects of support systems suffers from

some methodological problems. One problem is that such terms as 'autonomy' are used in different ways by researchers. Autonomy can refer to a person's self-perception of autonomy, the opinion of others, what a person can do, what a person could do under certain conditions, and what a person actually does (Vetel and Papin, 1984). Another problem in dealing with such constructs as autonomy and dependency is that neither is well integrated into any well established theory. It would be useful, for instance, if dependency were treated in terms of a helping model such as that of Brickman et al., in which dependency is the outcome of a medical model that locates responsibility in neither the source or solution to a problem (Brickman et al., 1982).

Efforts to deal with the dialectics of autonomy and dependence apart from the social context are likely to be unproductive. The problem of dependency goes beyond the psychological. Personal autonomy is achieved through a delicate balance of physical, economic, psychological, and social factors. This balance is easily disrupted in old age, often leading to dependency. More effective intervention strategies are needed. But structural dependency requires changes in social policy and reform in the distribution of wealth and power, and improvement in housing options.

In a literature review of the limitations of formal support systems, Schilling (1987) calls attention to the complexity of social support, and that in some circumstances the costs of social support may outweigh the benefits. Policy makers and practitioners are advised that in developing support strategies, care must be taken to consider the possible associated risks of social-support interventions.

The intervention strategies likely to minimize the negative effects of informal support systems are not self-evident. Certainly, one implication is the importance of assessing negative effects of adult children's services to their elderly parents and finding practical ways of minimizing them. But this is not easily done. There is a serious lack of research on intervention strategies used by informal support systems. For instance, little is known about what kind of advice should be given by people who spend most of their time giving advice.

8

Social Relationships and the Lack of Social Relationships

John H. Berg and Kelly E. Piner

In a volume that attempts to integrate concepts drawn from the personal-relationships literature with ideas drawn from social support, some of the most basic questions involve the effects the very existence of relationships may have on the social support a person can receive. This chapter attempts to relate relationship characteristics to different types of social support and subsequent differences in psychological well-being. In describing characteristics of relationships, a distinction is made between 'quantitative' factors (for example, number of acquaintances or number of close friends) and social-behavioral characteristics (for example, intimacy of interaction). The aspect of adjustment that we will be most concerned with will be feelings of loneliness, and after attempting to theoretically integrate concepts drawn from the social-support and relationship literature, we will review recent work linking these constructs with loneliness. Finally, we will indicate what appear to us to be promising directions for future investigations.

Types of Social Supports

Social supports are the resources that are provided to one by other people. Various taxonomies have been proposed of the different types and functions of social support. Without going into the specifics of these various categorization systems, we note that all seem to include some mention of tangible or instrumental aid, emotional support, and informational support. According to Rook (1985), the approaches differ in terms of whether or not they include such things as shared behaviors or expressions of liking as a type of social support. Rook (1985, 1987) has argued that such actions are best described under the heading of companionship and that they be distinguished from other types of social support. For Rook, the important difference is that other types of social support occur *in response* to learning of another's problem whereas behaviors classi-

fied as companionship would be a part of normal interaction that would occur regardless of whether or not one person knew of another's specific problem. It is argued that different types of social support will be related to different aspects of health and well-being (for example, Cutrona and Russell, 1987).

A second major approach to studying social support is through investigation of a persons' social network. The types of social support noted above are generally measured through assessing subjects' perceptions that they have received certain supports and/or their satisfaction with them. In a social-network approach, the emphasis has been on obtaining valid and reliable quantitative measures of the structure of relations within a group. The assumption is made that these structural attributes reflect the extent to which a person receives social support from members of that group. Specifically, network analysis is concerned with assessing the connections or ties between a group of individuals and how these ties influence an individual's well-being.

Three aspects of the social network are generally distinguished. Network *range* or *size* reflects the number of different people in a persons' social network. As network size increases social support should increase. However, it has also been noted in several places that such an assumption is questionable because not all the ties between one individual and others in the network will be sources of support or pleasure (for example, Cohen and Syme, 1985; Rook, 1985). Recognizing this, Berg and McQuinn (1989) argued that attention be restricted to examining a person's *support* network or the number of people an individual felt would or had rendered aid.

The second aspect of social networks that is generally distinguished is termed 'multiplexity.' This refers to network members serving multiple roles or functions. If attention is restricted to the support network, multiplexity would involve others being frequent sources of support.

The third network factor generally distinguished is network *density*. Density refers to the extent to which members of a network are connected to each other. Increased density within a network should contribute to feelings of solidarity and cohesiveness among network members (Albo and Moore, 1978; Domhoff, 1970). Just as companionship, emotional, informational, and tangible support may each be related to different types of stress, so too different network variables may impact differently on well-being depending on the particular samples or particular stresses being studied.

Types and Characteristics of Relationships

The factor that is used most often to distinguish different types of relationships is their closeness. Berg and Clark (1986) noted a number of factors that distinguish close relationships from those that are not close. In addition to increased interdependence and amounts of exchange, relationships also differ in the quality of the resources that participants exchange. In a similar vein, the quality of communication (intimacy) will increase in close relationships and those with a close relationship are more likely to think of themselves as a unit, to find the relationship intrinsically satisfying, expect it to continue, and experience stronger affect.

A second approach to looking at friendship is found in Weiss (1969, 1974) who distinguishes six needs/provisions that are important in social relationships. These six needs are:

1 the opportunity for *being* nurturant (feeling needed by others);
2 attachment (emotional closeness);
3 social integration (a sense of belonging to a group who share similar interests, concerns, and activities);
4 reassurance of worth (recognition of competence, skill, and value by others);
5 guidance (advice or information); and
6 reliable alliance (persons who can be counted on for tangible assistance).

Social Support, Social Networks, Social Needs, and Interaction

Table 8.1 presents a hypothesized summary of the relations between various types of social support, network characteristics, relational needs, and characteristics of interaction. (For slightly different proposals relating some of these variables see Cutrona and Russell [1987] and Rook, 1985.) Although no empirical data exist to offer a direct test of these hypothesized relationships, consider the conceptual linkages. First, as regards emotional support, the network variable of density should be more relevant than other network factors (at least as regards the total social network) because density will be related to feelings of solidarity and cohesiveness among network members. If one restricts one's focus of attention to a respondent's network of *close* friends, or *supportive* others, feelings of cohesiveness and solidarity should already be present between members of this reduced network, so the factors of network size and multiplexity in the smaller network should be related to emotional support. In other words, in a very cohesive network

(one of close friends), I am more likely to receive emotional support. In my total social network, the amount of emotional support I receive will be less related to network size and more related to network density (solidarity and cohesiveness within the *total* network). The social needs that appear most relevant to emotional support are attachment and reassurance of worth. These needs can be met best through relationships and interactions with close friends and family. Interactions with these people involve giving and receiving intimate self-disclosures, particularly of feelings.

In the case of informational support, all three of the network factors appear relevant, depending on the intimacy and amount of information needed. Close friends, casual ones, or even strangers can provide simple directions, hence the relation to network size. However, if I require guidance about a more personal matter, only close friends, family members, or those who share a feeling of solidarity with me are likely either to be asked or to provide it. The role that relationship closeness can play is suggested by findings demonstrating that disclosure breadth and intimacy increase over time and as relationships become closer (Berg, 1984; Berg and McQuinn, 1986; Hays, 1984, 1985). Also, persons who are familiar with me in multiple contexts will be in a better position to provide reliable and useful information because they know me best. Consequently, relationships' multiplexity and disclosure breadth seem especially relevant.

Table 8.1 *Hypothesized relationships of support, network characteristics, relational needs, and interaction characteristics*

Type of support	Network characteristic	Social need satisfied	Available through:
Emotional support	Density	Attachment	Intimate interaction and disclosure
Informational	All	Guidance	Breadth of disclosure
Instrumental	Multiplexity	Reliable alliance	Increased exchange of needed resources
Companionship	All	Social integration, Reassurance of worth	Increased interaction

In terms of tangible aid, the network variable of multiplexity

seems most relevant since by definition this refers to being able to call upon others frequently and/or in multiple contexts. Similar arguments apply regarding the need for reliable alliance. In terms of interaction characteristics this would be reflected by both the increased amount of exchange between close friends and the increased concern of close friends with each others' needs (Berg, 1984; Clark et al., 1986).

Network size, multiplexity, and density would all appear related to companionship. Knowing more people, knowing them in multiple contexts, and sharing a feeling of solidarity all make it more likely that the joint activities important for companionship will occur. Such companionship would satisfy a need for social integration and being chosen as a companion by another should also help meet the need for attachment. In terms of behavior, this would be reflected through an increased amount of interaction. In line with this link between companionship and attachment, Hays (1984) reports that companionship was more consistently related to the intensity of friendship than either affection, consideration, or communication.

Although no study has attempted to look simultaneously at social supports, networks, needs, and interaction in relation to well-being, indirect support for the relationships that we hypothesize might be found across studies. Concentrating on a single indicator of well-being, we can compare studies that have examined the influence of different types of support to studies that have looked at different network variables or different needs or interaction characteristics. If studies looking at social support find that companionship is important, indirect support is provided when studies looking at social needs find integration and attachment to be important factors. It is this type of inductive approach that we will take in the remainder of this chapter. The aspect of well-being on which we focus is loneliness. A large amount of past research on loneliness exists, not all of which is consistent. Nevertheless, by focussing on those studies that have examined particular support, network, needs, or interaction variables, we hope to 'triangulate' loneliness and find indirect support for some of the relations depicted in Table 8.1.

Relation to Loneliness

Loneliness is defined as a discrepancy between the quantity and/or quality of social relationships one has and the quantity and/or the quality that one desires (Perlman and Peplau, 1981). Previous attempts to relate loneliness to differences in individuals' social

milieux have produced equivocal and inconsistent results. For example, while some investigations have found that lonely individuals have fewer social contacts than nonlonely people (Brennan and Auslander, 1979; Peplau et al., 1978), other studies suggest that it will be the number of *close* friends, rather than the total amount of social contact, that will be important (Russell et al., 1978). Still other studies (for example, Jones, 1981; Williams and Solano, 1983) fail to find a relationsip between loneliness and either of these factors.

An alternative approach has been to attempt to relate loneliness to characteristics of the interactions that a person has with others in his or her social network. Again, results have been equivocal. While Williams and Solano (1983) found that loneliness was related to the perceived intimacy of interactions, Jones (1981) could not find this relationship. Similarly, although some studies link loneliness to deficiencies in self-disclosure or the absence of a confidant (for example, Cutrona, 1982; Solano et al., 1982), other work finds no relationship between disclosure and loneliness (Jones et al., 1981) or find it only for women (Berg and Peplau, 1982; Franzoi and Davis, 1985).

The fact that previous findings regarding antecedents of loneliness have been inconsistent highlights the need for more sophisticated theoretical development. An approach taken in recent years that appears promising is to relate loneliness more directly to aspects of social support and social networks. This has an immediate intuitive appeal because, by definition, loneliness involves a perceived deficiency in a person's social relations.

Such an approach, although appealing, is not problem free. While *perceived* social support has been linked with loneliness (Corty and Young, 1980; Sarason et al., 1985), this, in itself, does not tell us what types of support, what network features, or what interaction characteristics will be important for preventing or treating loneliness.

An analagous problem exists throughout the social-support literature. Heller and Lakey (1985: 291) state that 'previous research has treated the social support construct in too global and unifactorial a manner.' A more promising approach may be to relate specific aspects of support and loneliness.

Social Support and Loneliness
Investigators of social support often view it as being a buffer that protects a person against life stressors. Thus, an individual threatened by illness can gather informational and emotional support from others who have been confronted with a similar threat

and friends are able to render tangible support in such forms as trips to the doctor and help with meals and housework. In the case of loneliness, however, it is the support system itself that is threatened. Relational stress refers to events that disrupt personal relationships (Jones et al., 1985). Jones et al. found five general causes of relational stress: (a) emotional threats to relationships (for example, arguing with a friend); (b) social isolation (for example, not having any friends); (c) extraneous constraints (for example, when I'm too busy to be with others); (d) social marginality (for example, when I'm with others with whom I have little in common); and (e) romantic conflicts (for example, when I broke up with my boy or girlfriend). All these are events that disrupt or threaten important personal relationships. In relating this concept to types of social support, we would hypothesize that those experiencing relational stress are especially lacking in companionship and emotional support. If the relationships depicted in Table 8.1 are correct, this would mean that needs for integration, and attachment are felt most. Partial support for this is given by Jones et al.'s finding that relational stress was negatively related to feelings of integration and alliance and that loneliness was significantly related to relational stress.

Although this study begins to tie the social support and loneliness literature together, it does not directly examine the effect of different types of support. If Jones et al.'s findings linking relational stress to loneliness, integration, and alliance needs are correct, Table 8.1 suggests that companionship and instrumental aid should be the types of support most related to loneliness. Rook (1987) holds that it is primarily companionship that protects people from loneliness. She supported this in a series of studies that consistently found stronger correlations between loneliness and the frequency of companionship than the frequency of either emotional or instrumental support. Companionship also showed a stronger relation to subjects' satisfaction with their friendships than did either emotional or instrumental support.

Rubenstein and Shaver (1980) report results from a survey of newspaper readers that fit well with Rook's ideas on companionship. In this survey, loneliness was significantly related to the hours per week that respondents spent socializing, the number of organizations they participated in, and the frequency of seeing close friends. All of these correlates represent companionship activities.

Taken together, these findings provide rather strong evidence linking companionship to loneliness. Note, however, that this is different from previous work that has attempted to link loneliness with a person's total amount of social contact. Activities that have

some extrinsic end as their main goal (for example, work-related activities) while representing opportunities for social contact would not be considered instances of companionship. Activities included under companionship are those interpersonal activities that are (a) mutually chosen and (b) persons find rewarding in and of themselves (for example, shared leisure, conversation). Some activities that seem to be excluded from Rook's view of companionship would, however, be included in what we believe the term should encompass. For example, while Rook (1987: 1133) explicitly excludes actions that convey a sense of belonging or embeddedness, we maintain that they should be included with other companionship activities because the general social rewards (being told that one is liked or having another disclose *to* you) are an intrinsic and integral part of the activity itself. Activities such as these would seem much closer to the events that Rook describes as companionship than to those she describes as support, in which the emphasis is on the person *receiving* something to help cope with a stressful event. Note that your response to the other (for example, expressing sympathy or giving advice or tangible aid when he/she discloses to you) may constitute support for him or her (cf. Chapter 4 by Burleson, this volume). The benefits you receive, however, are intrinsic to the interaction and would seem more like companionship. In Weiss' (1974) terms, the interaction itself has reaffirmed your attachment to the other.

Aspects of Social Networks and Loneliness

In terms of network characteristics, Derlega and Margulis (1982) hypothesize that loneliness should be negatively related to network size, network multiplexity, and network density. Derlega and Margulis appear to have been referring to the total social network when they made these hypotheses. However, not all the ties an individual has with network members and not all members will invariably be sources of support or pleasant companionship. Consequently one should not be too surprised that attempts to relate loneliness to the total number of social contacts a person has (size) or the total number of close friends (multiplexity) have found inconsistent results. Similarly, intimate interactions or disclosure will not always be welcome and so one cannot expect studies to invariably find that these factors are negatively related to loneliness. The inconsistencies in the loneliness literature, noted above, bear witness to this.

Derlega and Margulis' (1982) predictions are consistent with the relations depicted in Table 8.1, but seem more appropriate if attention is restricted to an individual's network of *friends* or *supporting* others. In a similar vein, Stokes (1987) suggests that it is self-

disclosure to a particular person (for example, romantic partner or best friend) that will be important in loneliness rather than disclosure per se. If the other is a close friend, disclosure should reaffirm the friendship and attachment that you have to him or her and provide an instance of the more personal interactions that we wish to include under the heading of companionship.

The importance of various types of social support and various network characteristics may not, however, be the same for all people. In an intriguing article on sex roles and loneliness, Shaver and Buhrmester (1983) drew on Weiss' (1973) distinction between social and emotional isolation. They suggest that loneliness will be more related to social isolation for men than for women while emotional isolation will be more important in determining women's loneliness. In terms of the varieties of social support distinguished here, this implies that activities included under the heading of companionship, although they may influence feelings of loneliness for both sexes, will show a stronger relation to men's loneliness. Similarly, activities important for emotional support may be more important in affecting women's loneliness.

In line with this view, it has been proposed that loneliness will be related to both masculinity and femininity, but for different reasons (Berg and Peplau, 1982; Wittenberg and Reis, 1986). Wittenberg and Reis identified two different clusters of skills that mediated feelings of loneliness. The first of these (relationship-initiating skills) should influence the amount of social contact a person has and was found to be related to the instrumental aspects of masculinity. The second group (relationship-maintaining skills) should influence the development of intimacy and was related to femininity. Wittenberg and Reis found that both masculinity and femininity were significantly related to loneliness, but the correlation between masculinity and loneliness disappeared when relationship-initiating skills were partialed out and the correlation between femininity and loneliness disappeared when relationship-maintaining skills were controlled for. These latter findings support the contention that for individuals high in masculinity, the amount of social contact will be more central to loneliness, while for individuals high in femininity, the intimacy of contacts will be central. In a similar manner, Berg and Peplau (1982) reported that loneliness showed a significant relationship with the ability to elicit disclosure and the extent to which subjects had disclosed only for women. This again implies that for more feminine subjects, interaction intimacy, disclosure, and emotional support will be determinants of loneliness.

Other studies provide additional support for the link between

social isolation and deficits in masculine characteristics. For example, Borys and Perlman (1985) had subjects evaluate lonely and nonlonely male and female characters. The descriptions of the lonely characters highlight social isolation. Borys and Perlman's finding that subjects were more rejecting of the lonely male than of the lonely female is consistent with the hypothesis that the *number* of close friends one has (network size) will be more important in men's loneliness than in women's. Finally, Schultz and Moore (1986) found a significant correlation between loneliness and risk taking (a variable that should be related to both masculinity and the number of relationships one attempts to form) only for male subjects.

Taken together, these findings suggest that the relationship between loneliness and network size should be stronger for men than for women. Given our earlier comments on the activities that would and would not constitute companionship and the difference between the total social network and the friendship or support network, we expect this primarily when it is characteristics of the friendship or support network that are being considered. In the case of interaction intimacy or self-disclosure, we expect to find a stronger relationship to loneliness for women.

Several recent studies have investigated the relationship of loneliness to network characteristics. When studying the *total* social network, Stokes (1985) found that density was the only factor to show a significant relationship to loneliness. Also, Stokes (1985) did not examine potential sex differences in the influence of these factors on loneliness. Our above reasoning suggests that focussing on the total network may have masked relationships that would be found if one looked specifically at support or friendship networks. It also suggests that structural factors such as size and density may be more important in men's loneliness than in women's.

Berg and McQuinn (1989) looked specifically at the relationships between loneliness and the size, multiplexity, and density of support networks. They also included a social-behavioral factor related to interaction intimacy (the amount of reciprocal disclosure with the most central member of the network) and analyzed results separately for men and women. For men, all four variables were significantly correlated with loneliness, while for women, only disclosure and cohesiveness were significantly correlated with loneliness. In addition, multiple-regression analyses indicated that all variables explained significant independent amounts of the variance in men's loneliness, while only self-disclosure made a significant independent contribution to predicting women's loneliness. This latter fact is understandable if women's loneliness results mainly

from emotional isolation as Shaver and Buhrmester (1983) suggest or is more influenced by receiving emotional support. Table 8.1 suggests that disclosure should be primarily related to emotional support. The fact that the structural features of support networks influenced men's loneliness is consistent with our earlier reasoning and Shaver and Buhrmester's hypothesis that social isolation is more important in determining men's loneliness.

Several factors may have contributed to finding that disclosure affected loneliness for both sexes. First, Berg and McQuinn (1989) measured reciprocal disclosure with a specific other (the most central person in the support network). This is reminiscent of Cutrona's (1982) finding indicating the importance of having a confidant in overcoming loneliness. Also, because the other was central in subjects' support network, disclosure may be instrumental for receiving support. That disclosure can have this purpose is suggested by Berg's (1984) finding that subjects who disclosed more to their roommate received more of the resources they needed most.

By concentrating on the support network, and considering factors separately for men and women, considerably more of the variance in loneliness was explained (32 percent for men and 19 percent for women) than when Stokes (1985) examined the total social network and analyzed data collapsed over subject sex (14 percent). Stokes and Lewin (1986) reanalyzed the earlier Stokes (1985) data separately for men and women. In this reanalysis, the variables of network size, network density, and the number of people in whom subjects could confide were significantly correlated with loneliness for men, but not for women. When Stokes and Lewin performed the regression analyses of loneliness on the network variables and perceived social support, they were able to explain 19.6 percent of the variance in loneliness for men and 10.6 percent for women. The fact that both these percentages are lower than those found by Berg and McQuinn (1989) for a comparable sample of undergraduates is most likely due to the fact the studies focussed on different networks (total vs. social support).

A final study relevant to the relation of network factors to loneliness was conducted by Berg and Piner (1989). Both lonely and non lonely undergraduates kept records of their interactions for two seven-day periods. After each interaction, they completed a brief record on which they indicated: who they had interacted with, their relationship to these people, how intimate, important, and satisfying the interaction had been, and what they had talked about. While we will discuss the interaction variables below, what concerns us here are the number of people in different categories of relate-

ness to subjects that subjects interacted with three or more times in a week.

Romantic partners, best friends, and close friends are people to whom college students turn most often for different kinds of social support and particularly for companionship. The closer the relationship, the more important the other should be to receiving such supports. Thus, we would expect that lonely subjects will have fewer people in these categories in their interaction network. However, they are not expected to have fewer friends, casual acquaintances, or kin in their networks. Moreover, results reported above suggest that lonely men will be particularly deficient in the number of close (supportive) others in their interaction networks. In line with this, Jones (1981) reported that lonely individuals had more social contacts with casual acquaintances and strangers than non-lonely people while having fewer with friends. Berg and Piner's (1989) study expands on this by (a) allowing finer discrimination in the types of relationships considered, (b) focussing on those others who are frequently encountered and who would thus have frequent opportunities to provide social supports, and (c) exploring potential sex differences.

Main effects of loneliness were found for the number of best friends, close friends, and casual acquaintances. Lonely subjects had fewer best friends and fewer close friends but more casual acquaintances with whom they frequently interacted. The fact that lonely subjects had more casual acquaintances and an equal number of central others in other classes again suggests that it is not interaction with just anyone that is important, but rather, interaction with certain kinds of people. Best friends and close friends are particularly likely to be sources of companionship, support, and a sense of social integration – thus supporting one of the hypotheses suggested in Table 8.1. Borderline interactions between loneliness and sex were found for the number of romantic partners and close friends that subjects frequently interacted with. Although both lonely men and lonely women had fewer romantic partners and close friends, as expected, the difference was somewhat greater for men.

Given Rook's (1987) findings indicating the importance of companionship in preventing loneliness, Table 8.1 suggests that all of the network variables should be relevant. The work we have just reviewed suggests some qualification of this. Specifically, it suggests that one will need to specify the network under study (total or support), the nature of loneliness (social or emotional), and the sex of respondents. These qualifications make theoretical sense

and, if they are made, support is found for the relations we hypothesize.

Social Needs and Loneliness

Although the results reported above on types of social support and social networks imply that the need to be integrated into a network of close, supportive others will be maximally important in preventing loneliness, they do not test this directly. Studies that provide more direct evidence regarding social integration were performed by Cutrona (1982) and Russell et al. (1984).

Cutrona (1982) administered measures assessing subjects' feelings that current relationships satisfied each of the six needs distinguished by Weiss (1974). Loneliness scores were then regressed on these six measures. In Cutrona's study three variables made significant contributions when they entered. Social integration entered first, followed by reassurance of worth, and then guidance. The implication that social integration is the most important of these needs as regards loneliness, together with findings regarding companionship and social networks (discussed above), is consistent with the relationships hypothesized in Table 8.1.

Russell et al. (1984) obtained separate assessments of social and emotional isolation. When they regressed each of these types of loneliness on the extent to which each of the needs distinguished by Weiss (1974) was met, it was found that each type of loneliness was maximally related to different needs. Attachment and the opportunity to be nurturant were significant predictors of emotional isolation, while for social loneliness, reassurance of worth and social integration were the best predictors. Although separate analyses for men and women are not available, given results we reported above, it is tempting to speculate that the former pattern will be more characteristic of women while the latter is stronger for men. Both, however, seem consistent with the relationships between types of social support and social needs hypothesized in Table 8.1.

In addition, Russell et al. also measured subjects' reports of the amount of interaction with (a) friends, (b) a romantic partner, and (c) family members, during the previous two weeks as well as their satisfaction with each of these types of relationship. When social loneliness was regressed on these six measures, the extent of interacting with friends and satisfaction with friendships were significant predictors. Rook's (1987) findings indicating the importance of companionship in preventing loneliness are quite consistent with this. For emotional loneliness, closeness and frequency of interaction with a romantic partner were the best predictors, although satisfaction with friendships also had a significant effect. If attach-

ment needs are best met through having a romantic relationship, as Weiss (1974) suggests, it is quite reasonable that the closeness of the relationship and the frequency of contact with the romantic partner would be most important in preventing emotional loneliness. The fact that satisfaction with friendships (but not frequency of interaction with friends) remained a significant predictor may have resulted from the fact that some of these friendships were close and so might also be able to help meet needs for attachment and provide more intimate forms of companionship. If so, satisfaction with friendships would increase, as would the ability of these friendships to prevent emotional isolation.

Aspects of Interaction and Loneliness

The work reviewed above indicates that lonely and nonlonely people will receive different amounts of *some* types of support, differ in *some* aspects of their social networks, and show differences in the extent that *some* social needs are met. They do not, however, indicate *what* it is about the actual interactions of lonely and nonlonely people that lead to these differences. To what extent are they due to quantitative factors such as the number and/or length of interactions? To what degree are social-behavioral factors such as intimacy of interaction or the amount disclosed responsible? Is it that lonely and nonlonely people differ in how they evaluate their interactions (for example, their importance and satisfaction with interactions)? The extent to which different aspects of interaction are related to loneliness has important implications both for understanding loneliness theoretically and for its treatment.

To some extent, inconsistencies in the loneliness literature between studies searching for interactional correlates of loneliness (see above) arise from the fact that social interaction is a multidimensional process. As implied above, the intimacy of interactions, the identity of participant, the relationship existing among participants, the amount of disclosure that occurs, and subjective appraisals of interaction importance and satisfaction may all affect the relevance of the interaction to support. In contrast, most studies of loneliness and interaction have studied only one or two of the numerous parameters. Just as social-support researchers have recognized that the relationship between support and well-being will vary with the types of support, and stresses studied, so too, the relationship between loneliness and aspects of interaction may vary depending on just who is interacting and just which aspects of interaction are being considered. Recognizing this complexity, Jones et al. (1985) called for more systematic and thorough attempts to assess the connections between external events and

loneliness. In this section, we will review some recent studies that attempt more through assessments.

Wheeler et al. (1983) took a multidimensional approach investigating interactional correlates of loneliness. In this study, subjects kept diary-type records of each interaction they had in which they reported not only its length, but also several qualitative aspects and the sex of the person they were interacting with. Wheeler et al. hypothesized that the relation of loneliness to quantitative aspects of interaction (for example, frequency and length) and qualitative aspects (for example, initimacy, disclosure, satisfaction) would vary depending on the gender of participants. In this regard, Wheeler et al. hypothesized that loneliness should be related to quantitative aspects of interaction primarily when the interaction *partner* is a female. Such a prediction is based on findings demonstrating that women are generally more socially responsive, empathic, and intimate (for example, Deaux, 1976; Miller et al., 1983). Women should consequently be better at providing various types of support to those they interact with. Thus, increased amounts of interaction with females increases the likelihood that one will receive the resources necessary to prevent loneliness. This prediction was confirmed by finding that loneliness had significant negative correlations with the number of interactions with female partners but not with the number of interactions with males. Consistent with this is Jones and Moore's (1987) finding that the social networks of subjects reporting greater loneliness contained proportionally fewer women. Wheeler et al. (1983) also found that for male, but not female, subjects, a significant negative correlation existed between loneliness and the average length of interactions with female partners. Thus we again find evidence suggesting that loneliness will be influenced by the existence of some kinds of interactions but not by others and that these interactions may have greater relevance for men. While direct measurements of the constructs are not available, it is tempting to speculate on whether the observed differences are due to interactions with women providing more support, greater amounts of the more intimate aspects of companionship, or both.

Wheeler et al. (1983) found that regardless of partner's gender, disclosure, interaction intimacy, pleasantness, and satisfaction had significant negative correlations with loneliness. Additionally, they found that these qualitative aspects of interaction were lower if both participants were males than when either or both were women. To the extent that these qualitative aspects of interaction are important in guarding against loneliness, these results suggest that men interacting primarily with other men may be at greater risk.

Berg and Piner (1989) found that overall, lonely subjects had fewer interactions per day than nonlonely subjects and interactions involved less disclosure breadth, and were less satisfying. Overall, men saw their interactions as more important perhaps because the provided companionship is more important for men. Women reported their interactions as more intimate and satisfying, and as having greater disclosure breadth. This latter finding is consistent with the results of Wheeler et al. (1983) as well as results indicating that females disclose more than males (for example, Berg, 1984) and are more socially responsive (Miller et al., 1983).

Interactions between loneliness and sex were found for the average length of interactions, interaction importance, and disclosure breadth. For importance, the interaction is due to nonlonely men rating their interactions as more important than nonlonely women. Recall (from the results presented when discussing networks) that nonlonely men had more close friends and romantic partners in their networks. Interactions with these people are likely to be more important than interactions with others who are less close. For disclosure breadth, the interaction was due to nonlonely women having interactions of greater breadth. This is consistent with the view, expressed above, that the disclosure–loneliness relation will be stronger for women. Regarding interaction length, lonely women had shorter interactions than other subjects. We noted above that women are often responsible for injecting interactions with meaningfulness. One aspect of this may be maintaining interactions. If lonely women are deficient in some of the social skills necessary to maintain interaction, this finding becomes understandable. While a number of previous studies (for example, Jones et al., 1981) have shown that lonely people are generally deficient in social skills that help maintain interaction, an additional measure collected in this study suggests that lonely women may be particularly affected. Before they began keeping records of their interactions, subjects completed the Openers Scale (Miller et al., 1983). This scale appears to measure a respondent's general responsiveness and goals as well as his or her ability to elicit disclosure from others. In addition to the expected main effects for loneliness and sex, analysis of this measure also revealed a loneliness by sex interaction. This interaction was due to the fact that while lonely and nonlonely men did not suffer, lonely women had lower Opener scores than nonlonely ones. To the degree that the responsiveness of women is important in maintaining interactions and increasing interaction quality, these women should be at a deficit. In the present case, they not only had shorter interactions than their

nonlonely counterparts, but ones that were less satisfying, and lower in disclosure breadth.

A final set of analyses performed by Berg and Piner (1989) looks at these various interaction characteristics in people with closer and more casual relationships with the subject. For these analyses, only dyadic interactions are considered and relationships are grouped into four categories: close (romantic partners and best friends), friends (close friends and friends), casual (casual acquaintances and strangers), and family members or relatives. While we are unable to go into all the effects involving relationship closeness here, a few are quite relevant to the present discussion.

First, the closer the relationship, the more frequent, longer, intimate, important, and satisfying were the interactions and the greater was disclosure breadth. Thus, interactions with closer friends should be better able to meet various social needs and provide various types of social support. This leads to the expectation that lonely individuals (who may lack these social supports) would have fewer interactions with those with whom they have close relationships. Because interactions with more casual acquaintances do not provide supports or meet social needs as well, decreased interaction with casual acquaintances should not lead to loneliness.

In support of these expectations, a loneliness by relationship closeness interaction was found for the frequency of interaction. Lonely subjects had fewer interactions than nonlonely subjects with those others in the two closest relationship categories. However, they had more interactions with casual acquaintances (persons less likely to satisfy social needs or provide social supports). So while results presented when discussing networks indicated that lonely subjects had fewer others in their network whom they considered close, these findings indicate that they did not compensate by interacting more with those who were close. In fact, fewer interactions with such potentially supportive others occurred.

The Berg and Piner (1989) study provides additional evidence that lonely people suffer deficits in some types of relationships, but not in others. As did Wheeler et al. (1983), their study also begins to investigate just what it is about interactions with some people that makes them important in preventing loneliness. Future explorations that directly relate various types of support and social needs to these interaction differences are now needed. Such multivariate investigations fit well with the idea expressed by Jones et al. (1985) that studies of the external correlates of loneliness should begin to deal with more complex issues.

Conclusions

In the preceding pages, we have reviewed a group of studies that all suggest that the presence of social relationships is an essential component of well-being. Taking loneliness–nonloneliness as our measure of well-being, research from a number of specific theoretical orientations appears to have a common thread. This is that the important causal factor appears to be the type of relationships that exist and the nature of the interactions that these relationships occasion.

While the ability of relationships to provide social support is important, evidence is found indicating that the most important aspect of such support as regards loneliness is companionship. Sharing activities with others may be the most effective indicant that one is not alone, but is a part of an integrated group of people. Evidence also suggests that such feelings of companionship and integration will be more effectively provided by some people (for example, women or close friends) than by others. Thus, the number of certain types of people in one's social network and the number of interactions one has with such people become important. Moreover, some evidence exists to suggest that this may be particularly true for males.

We move then to a truly social-psychological answer to the question of whether social support and social relationships affect loneliness. This answer is that it depends. Just as Jones (1985) advised, we suggest that answers to this question (and the question itself) be phrased in a more complex and sophisticated fashion. The more appropriate question would be: 'What types of social support and social relationships affect loneliness and how do they accomplish this?'

Early in this chapter, we hypothesized a number of relationships between types of social support, aspects of social networks, social needs, and aspects of interaction. While a number of the studies we have reviewed provide evidence consistent with these hypotheses, they have not been directly tested as yet. We believe that such direct tests would go far in advancing our understanding of the relationships among support, relationships, and well-being.

To the extent that personal relationships are essential for social support, a second promising direction is suggested by a recent study of Sarason et al. (1986). These researchers suggest that social support can also be viewed as an individual-difference variable. In other words, people exhibit stable differences in the amount of social support they receive. Are the same individual differences that are important in forming relationships (for example, self-disclosure,

responsiveness, proximity, attractiveness) important in receiving social support? Do people lacking in social support show social-skill deficits similar to those observed in lonely individuals? Taking such a view of social support opens up a whole new direction for attempts to link support and relationships.

Although extensive literatures already exist dealing with social support on the one hand, and personal relationships on the other, as noted in other places in this volume, they have developed rather independently of each other. We believe future attempts to tie these areas more closely with each other are both promising and exciting. Here we have tried to note some similarities in the two lines as regards loneliness and to suggest some others.

The Contribution of Social Networks, Work-shift Schedules, and the Family Life Cycle to Women's Well-being

Stephen Brand and Barton J. Hirsch

It is eminently reasonable to assert that the study of ongoing personal relationships could add considerably to our understanding of the mechanisms underlying social support. Yet few such investigations have been undertaken: hence was born this volume. It is also quite reasonable to assert that relationships are embedded within larger social contexts which, in turn, can affect the nature and supportive value of interactions with network members. Few would argue with this position. But again, only a handful of relevant studies have been conducted. It is this gap in the literature which is addressed by this chapter.

We will focus our attention on one such critical social context: the work environment. One way in which we shall do this is by considering the supportive value of relationships at work, especially with one's immediate supervisor and closest co-worker. There has not been a great deal of attention paid to such relationships among those who study either personal relationships or social support. Rather, the predominant concern has been with intimate relationships, especially with family members. The relative inattention to work is difficult to justify given the importance of work, for better and for worse, to most adults. Relationships at work are a source of stress and support for work concerns. Ecologically, they can also be drawn on for coping with non-work stress and, in turn, ups and downs from the workplace often spill over to affect relationships with family members and friends.

In addition to studying relationships at work, we will also consider in some detail the effects of work-shift schedules. By work-shift schedules, we mean the time of the day or night during which a person works: whether an employee works on the day, evening, or night shift, or on different shifts (for example, shifts that change from week to week). At first glance, work-shift schedules may seem quite irrelevant to the purposes of this volume, yet a moment's

reflection will suggest that shiftwork could have profound and pervasive effects on personal relationships and social support.

Consider, first, how the time of day structures social interaction. There are certain times, typically breakfast (in the early morning) and dinner (late afternoon or early evening), when family members are expected to eat together. In the evening, spouses can have some time together. Nor are friendships immune from time constraints. Restaurants and movie houses, for example, are open at some hours and not others. Indeed, among a wide variety of non-work settings, there is a pervasive orientation to the leisure time of day-shift workers: weekday evenings and weekends. Finally, let us not forget that most people are asleep at night, providing a limited range of interactional possibilities! All of this structure is convenient and enabling for those of us who work something like a 9 to 5 schedule. But what about those who work evening or night shifts? When and where do they get together with their social network? Work-shift schedules do more than mark the starting and ending hours of work: they can have drastic effects on the nature of personal relationships and, potentially, on the support that is available from them.

The disruptive potential of work-shift schedules on relationships may be most severe for women with children at home. Job requirements can be equally as demanding for women as for men, yet women and men are not equally responsible for home and child care (for example, Belle, 1982b; Haw, 1982; Vanfossen, 1981). Conflict between work and family roles is therefore of special concern for married women, particularly at stages of the family life cycle that entail care for young children. This inter-role conflict clearly has considerable potential in its own right to affect relationships and support in both work and other settings. For women with young children, shiftwork might further complicate efforts to combine family and work roles, for example by interfering with routines in the household, as well as family outings and access to community services.

Accordingly, by studying women shiftworkers across the family life cycle, we can examine a concrete, real-world example of the impact of larger social contexts on support provided in work and other relationships. We will report findings from research we recently conducted on one group of women shiftworkers, married women employed as nurses in hospitals. In-patient health-care facilities require staffing during evening and night hours. Approximately 42 percent of all married registered nurses are employed on non-day or changing work-shift schedules (Presser, 1984). Over the past two decades, much of the increase in labor-force participation

among married women has taken place in service-sector occupations, such as nursing, that utilize non-day shifts quite extensively (Presser, 1986). Before turning to our study, we will briefly review findings from previous research with married women employed in paid jobs.

Married Women with Paid Jobs: Social Support and Psychological Well-being

We begin by considering how supports provided in work and other relationships are related to the psychological well-being of married women with paid jobs outside of the home. We will then examine the possible effects of work-shift schedules and stages of the family life cycle on supports and on the relationship between support and well-being.

Most previous studies have focussed on the spouse as a potential source of support. Paid employment has shown a stronger link with married women's psychological well-being when arrangements for sharing household work and child care are more satisfactory (Kessler and McRae, 1982; Ross et al., 1983). Conversely, the relationship with the spouse can also constrain efforts to balance work and family roles (Holohan and Gilbert, 1979a; Lewin and Damrell, 1978). Negative spouse attitudes toward employment have been linked with higher job dissatisfaction (Andrisani and Shapiro, 1978), lower marital satisfaction (Hirsch and Rapkin, 1986a), and higher levels of psychological symptoms (Berkowitz and Perkins, 1984). Thus, support and negativity from the spouse seem to have strong effects on the psychological well-being of married women who are employed outside of the home.

Though the marital relationship has been the predominant focus of most studies, relationships outside of the family also affect the well-being of married women with paid jobs. Close friends are a major source of support, and higher levels of support from the closest friend has been linked with lower levels of psychological symptoms (Hirsch and Rapkin, 1986b). In the workplace, greater support from work associates, particularly the immediate supervisor, have been related to better well-being (House, 1981). Indeed, interactions with the supervisor appear to have a greater impact on work outcomes (for example, job satisfaction) than do interactions with the spouse (Hirsch and Rapkin, 1986b).

Are work-shift schedules likely to affect the social support available to married women? We will focus on three non-standard shift schedules that are markedly discrepant from normal working hours in most communities: fixed night, rotating, and variable schedules.

Fixed night shifts involve regular hours that span the period from the late evening to the following morning (that is, starting at 10–12 p.m. and ending at 6–8 a.m.). Women on *rotating schedules* change shifts on a regular sequence and pattern (for example, five day, five evening, then two night shifts), while *variable schedules* involve shift changes in a less structured sequence (Adler and Roll, 1980; Staines and Pleck, 1983).

We are especially interested in the hypothesis that married women working non-standard shifts will report less social support than those working on day shifts. One of the undesirable aspects of working on non-standard shift schedules is the disruption of family ties. Initial studies have examined global ratings of work--family conflict. Women on non-standard shift schedules reported greater conflict between work and family roles (Pleck and Staines, 1985). In addition, specific aspects of work–family conflict have been linked to shift schedules. Women on rotating and variable schedules were less satisfied with the amount of time they spend with their spouse (Tasto et al., 1978) and, more generally, with the amount of time they have for family activities (Staines and Pleck, 1984). Women on evening and night shifts had more difficulty scheduling their non-work time with other family members (Staines and Pleck, 1984).

Shiftwork might also constrain activities with close friends. The leisure activities of women on rotating and variable shifts have been compared with those of women on fixed (predominantly day) schedules. Women on rotating and variable shifts report that they spend more time in solitary activities (Jamal and Jamal, 1982), and are less involved in voluntary organizations, such as social and civic groups (Jamal, 1981). These findings are generally consistent with a large-scale survey of nurses in the United States (Tasto et al., 1978) that found less satisfaction with the amount of time that shift schedules allowed for organizations, sports, and personal interests among women on evening and rotating schedules.

Some attention has been given to the nature of interactions with work associates among women who work on rotating and variable schedules. Tasto et al. (1978) found that long-term day, evening, and night shift workers discuss work-related concerns with co-workers more frequently than workers who have recently changed shift. Lower job satisfaction has been found repeatedly among workers who spend less time on the same shift (Frost and Jamal, 1979; Jamal, 1981; Tasto et al., 1978).

These findings are certainly consistent with the hypothesis that married women working non-standard shifts receive less social support than those who work day shifts. Non-standard work shifts

might have adverse effects on relationships with friends and work associates, as well as the spouse.

There are good reasons to expect that the negative effects of non-standard shifts are especially severe for married women who have young children at home. Major changes in family roles take place as the worker moves through successive stages of the family life cycle (Lewis and Cooper, 1987; Pleck et al., 1978). Stages of the life cycle are differentiated by the presence and age of the youngest child. In the first stage, the worker is married with no children. In the second stage, there is at least one pre-school aged child at home. In the third stage, after the youngest child attains the age of six, the household contains children in school. In the final stage, all of the children have entered adulthood.

Stages of the family life cycle have been linked with differential levels of conflict between work and family roles. This inter-role conflict is of greatest concern for employed women with children at home (Holohan and Gilbert, 1979b; Pleck, 1977; Pleck and Staines, 1985), particularly when the youngest child is less than 6 years old (Staines and Pleck, 1983). Working on non-standard shifts may be especially difficult for parents. For example, the shiftworker might be awoken repeatedly from daytime or evening sleep by children's activities and the preparation of meals (Gadbois, 1980). Indeed, women night shiftworkers, who sleep during daytime hours when they work, often revert to nocturnal sleep and daytime waking on their days off to have more time to spend with family members, resulting in a substantial reduction in the quantity and restfulness of sleep (Weitzman, 1976). Thus, the problems in managing work and family roles that accompany shiftwork might be even more pronounced for women with young children at home.

In spite of these disadvantages, many married women with children at home work on non-standard shift schedules (Presser, 1986). Shiftwork might provide two significant benefits. First, shiftwork can be used by dual-earner parents for child care (see Morgan, 1981; Nock and Kingston, 1984; Presser and Cain, 1983). When parents work on different shifts, one parent can provide child care while the other is at work. In occupations that have a large number of women shiftworkers (for example, nursing), the husband is a major provider of child care (Presser, 1982). Second, shift workers typically receive additional pay to compensate them for working during inconvenient hours (Presser, 1986). This extra income can help women shiftworkers to provide for their children financially.

In turning to consider relationships at work, findings from previous studies suggest that the effects of non-standard shifts on work ties might again be more negative for mothers of young children.

Even on the day shift, work associates may have negative attitudes toward the mothers who work, particularly mothers of pre-school aged children (Gilbert et al., 1981; Lewis and Cooper, 1987). For women on non-standard shifts with young children at home, these attitudes might be even more pronounced. In many countries, for example, shiftwork is subject to more restrictive labor regulations for mothers than for other women, because it is assumed to have harmful effects on the mother and family members (Carpentier and Cazamian, 1977). Negative attitudes toward maternal employment may persist even though an increasing proportion of married women with children have entered the labor force. In the United States, over half of the mothers of pre-school children, and over two-thirds of the mothers of school-aged children, are employed or are seeking work (Waldman, 1983). Though precise data on changes in maternal shiftwork are not yet available, much of the increase in maternal employment has taken place in service-sector occupations that utilize non-day shift schedules quite extensively (Presser, 1986).

These cumulative findings are consistent with the hypothesis that married women working non-standard shifts receive less social support than do those who work day shifts, and that the negative effects of non-standard shifts are likely to be especially severe for women with young children. Although this is plausible, there are two major problems with this line of reasoning.

First, these studies do not directly address the provision or perception of social support itself. Most investigators focussed on the frequency, variety, or duration of social contact, rather than qualitative differences in social support. These are not equivalent dimensions of personal relationships. Nor is it clear that greater work—family role conflict necessarily results in less support from the spouse. No significant differences have been found between women on different shifts in levels of marital and family satisfaction (Staines and Pleck, 1984). Thus, the findings reviewed earlier are merely suggestive of a negative relationship.

An alternative perspective might draw attention to the possibility that women and their network members adapt to the non-standard work schedule over time. They may come to focus more on the quality of the time that they spend with each other, rather than the amount or variety of their social activities. Thus, non-standard shifts might not result in a diminished quality of perceived support.

The second major problem with the negative effects hypothesis as formulated is the exclusive attention to possible differences between shifts in mean scores on measures of support. No attention is given to the possibility that the salience or value of interactions

might differ across work shifts. Here, we would be concerned with differences in the correlation between support and psychological well-being among women on different shifts. These differences in correlation might be in addition to or instead of differences in mean levels of support.

Might support matter more for women on non-standard shifts? Tasto et al. (1978: 12) suggest that 'because of the unique pressure on shift worker's families, feelings of cohesion and support may be more important to them than to other families.' More generally, we have seen that non-standard shifts constrain the nature and amount of interpersonal contact. There simply are fewer opportunities to interact. Women in these circumstances are likely to be much more dependent on the quality of any given interaction. In addition, their closest personal relationships might assume greater importance given the diminished contact with a more extensive set of social-network members. Thus, supportive interactions with key network members may have a greater impact on psychological well-being.

Furthermore, in addition to having less time available for relationships, women on non-standard shifts face greater stress. In particular, there is likely to be more conflict between work and family roles for women with young children in their household. The stress-buffering hypothesis would lead us to expect a greater relationship between support and adjustment for women in these circumstances than would be the case for women on day shifts.

In summary, for women working on non-standard shifts, there may be a decrease in the supportive quality of their personal relationships as well as an increase in the impact of these relationships on their psychological well-being. These effects may be particularly strong for women with young children. However, there is a paucity of empirical data which bear on these concerns.

Relationships in Context: Empirical Findings

In this section, we report findings from a study we recently conducted with married women nurses (Brand and Hirsch, 1989). The study addresses whether those who worked on non-standard shifts report less social support, especially if they have pre-school children at home. We also consider whether the correlation between support and psychological well-being is greater for nurses on non-standard shifts.

Data for this study were drawn from a larger investigation of social networks, multiple roles, and women's well-being (Hirsch and Rapkin, 1986a, b). The following analyses focus on 148 nurses

who worked in in-patient hospital units, were married and currently living with their spouse, and provided data on all of the relevant measures.

Nurses were classified as working on one of three schedules: day shift, evening shift, and non-standard shifts (that is, fixed night shift, shift rotation, two or more different shifts in the same week). The family life cycle was coded into four stages: (a) No children; (b) At least one pre-school aged child in the house; (c) at least one school-aged child, but no pre-school aged children, in the household; (d) parents of adult children. Stages in the family life cycle have been found to be correlated with the age of the mother (Staines and Pleck, 1983), and age was partialed out from all analyses of the family life cycle.

The measure of social support, developed especially for nurses, assessed perceived positive (support) and negative (rejection) qualities of key relationships that bore on both work and nonwork concerns (for a more extensive discussion of this measure, see Hirsch and Rapkin, 1986b). Interactions with five key network members were assessed: spouse, the adult family member to whom they felt closest (other than the spouse), closest friend outside of work, supervisor, and the co-worker to whom they felt closest. These five network members were selected to represent the most salient relationships in family, friendship, and work spheres.

Shift Differences in Network Interactions
The following analyses examined potential differences between shift schedules in mean levels of support from specific network relationships. The first stage of analysis focussed on differences between shifts. For each of five network relationships, a one-way ANOVA was conducted to test shift differences in mean scores on support. None of these analyses found significant shift differences.

The second stage examined the combined effects of shift schedules and family-life-cycle stages. Here, we hypothesized that non-standard shift schedules would have more negative effects on network interaction among married women with pre-school aged children in the household. In five ANOVAS we examined the two-way shift by family-life-cycle interaction on support. Two-way shift by cycle interactions were not related to support from the closest adult family member, friend, co-worker, or supervisor. However, the two-way shift by family-life-cycle interaction accounted for a significant proportion of the variance in spouse support. Day-shift schedules were linked with more spouse support among women who did not have children at home (that is, had no children, or only adult children). Among women with children at home, spouse

support did not differ between shifts. Staines and Pleck (1983) report similar findings for the two-way shift by family-life-cycle interaction on work–family conflict.

These findings do not support the hypothesis that women on non-standard work-shift schedules experience lower levels of support, nor do they support the hypothesis that non-standard shifts have more deleterious effects on network interaction among mothers of pre-school aged children.

Shift Schedules and Correlates of Support and Negativity
The preceding analyses focussed on differences in network inter-actions between shifts, as well as stages of the family life cycle. The following analyses examine differences between shifts in psychological symptom levels and the linkage between network interactions and symptoms.

Five one-way ANOVAs tested differences between shifts in symptom levels. No significant differences were found between the day, evening, and non-standard schedules. These negative findings were contrary to past studies, which suggest that women employed on rotating shift schedules exhibit somewhat higher levels of psychological symptoms (Frost and Jamal, 1979; Jamal, 1981; Jamal and Jamal, 1982), negative mood states (Tasto et al., 1978), and rates of in-patient hospital admissions (Koller et al., 1980). However, shift schedules might not have negative effects on psychological well-being among shiftworkers who have positive interactions with network members (Dunham, 1977; Tasto et al., 1978; Wedderburn, 1967).

To examine shift differences in the correlates of support, five multiple regression analyses tested two-way interactions between work-shift schedules and support from each specific network member on symptoms. Specifically, moderated regression analyses (Cohen and Cohen, 1975) were conducted to test the significance of two-way interactions.

The two-way interactions of shift by co-worker support, and shift by adult-family-member support, were not significant. However, two-way interactions of shift by supervisor support, shift by closest friend support, and shift by spouse support, were significantly related to symptoms. Consistent with our hypothesis, in all three analyses the relationship between support and lower symptom levels was stronger among nurses on non-standard shifts than it was among nurses on fixed day or evening shifts.

Analysis of the three-way shift by family life cycle by network interaction on symptoms might uncover further effects of work and family contexts on the correlation between support and symptoms.

However, in the present study, the sample size did not permit a meaningful test of these effects.

Relationships in Context: Discussion

The findings of this research (Brand and Hirsch, 1989) provide mixed support for the hypothesized effects of non-standard shifts on married women nurses. To our surprise, there were no significant shift differences in mean levels of support among any of the five work and nonwork relationships. In particular, nurses on non-standard shifts did not report less support. We expected to find lower support because prior studies of women who worked on non-standard schedules revealed marked constraints on the amount of time and the settings available to them for interaction, as well as increased conflict between family and work roles. In the present study, women on these schedules seemed to adapt successfully, in terms of social support, to their specific set of opportunities and constraints. They appear to have carved out a niche for themselves, perhaps with considerable effort, in which they were supported by key members of their social network. How they managed to do so would be a useful topic to explore in further research as it would address a central issue in the study of support and well-being: the creation of supportive networks under difficult circumstances.

When we turn to the correlational data, findings are clearly consistent with the hypothesized effects of working on non-standard shifts. The correlational findings suggest that shift schedules have important contextual effects on the relation between social support and psychological well-being. Supportive interactions were linked more strongly with psychological symptomatology among women on night-, rotating-, and variable-shift schedules. The supportive quality of their personal relationships matters more to these women than to women on day shifts. As nurses on non-standard shifts are more restricted in when and where they can interact, and so presumably need to put more effort into creating and maintaining supportive personal relationships, they are likely to be more sensitive to the nature of their interactions. The time spent had better be spent well. We suspect that there are some differences in how this process is reflected in different personal relationships.

Spouse support might be of greater importance for women who work on non-standard schedules because of the constraints that their work schedule place on the integration of work and family roles. Women on non-standard shift schedules experience greater conflict between work and family roles (Staines and Pleck, 1986; Tasto et al., 1978). Women who work on rotating- and variable-

shift schedules report less satisfaction with the total amount of time that their schedules allow for family activities, and women who work on night shifts have difficulty in coordinating their time off with other family members. Support from the spouse could be of critical importance in addressing these concerns.

Personal relationships outside of the family also seem to be of greater importance for women who work on non-standard shift schedules. Specifically, supportive interactions with the closest friend outside of work seems to be more closely linked with the psychological well-being of women on night, rotating, and variable shifts. Because their hours off do not match those of other community residents (Dunham, 1977; Tasto et al., 1978), women on these schedules have fewer opportunities to actively participate in civic and benevolent organizations, sports, social gatherings, and other nonwork interests. Rotating and variable schedules might interfere with consistent attendance in these groups. The night shift imposes a difficult choice between sleeping or participating in social and civic life. In such circumstances, interpersonal time may become focussed around a more limited friendship network, and so supportive interactions with the closest friend can make a greater contribution to psychological well-being.

Relationships at work were also found to have a considerable impact on mental health. Specifically, supervisor support was more important for the psychological well-being of nurses on non-standard schedules. Nurses on the night shift might be more dependent on their supervisor to influence decisions made on other shifts that impact on the night shift. Night-shift workers commonly have little contact with clinical and administrative staff who work during daytime hours. To the extent that the supervisor represents their needs and concerns, night-shift nurses can see themselves as an integral and valued part of in-patient services, rather than marginal workers who merely provide coverage during less desirable working hours. Nurses on rotating and variable shifts might experience the same concerns about communication between shifts, and also depend more on their immediate supervisor for orientation to a new set of co-workers and procedures (Caplan, 1976; Tasto et al., 1978).

We have thus seen that work relationships can have an important influence on women's sense of psychological well-being via mechanisms that appear to be different from those of the spouse or closest friend. In part, this may be due to different characteristics of the social systems in which these relationships are embedded. Some of these findings, and possible directions for future research, might be clarified by our consideration (below) of Bronfenbrenner's (1979)

delineation of different ecological units: the *microsystem, mesosystem, exosystem*, and the *macrosystem*.

Microsystem

The microsystem consists of a set of two or more ongoing relationships between the individual and other occupants of a setting, such as the family or the work group. Positive outcomes follow to the extent that the setting promotes positive relationships and goal consensus (Bronfenbrenner, 1979). The current study calls attention to the importance of the match between the adaptive demands of a setting and interactions with other occupants. For example, among women on non-standard shifts, a supportive relationship with the immediate supervisor of the work group might address needs for greater influence and recognition at work.

Further research in this area could provide a more focussed look at the match between network relationships and the adaptive demands of specific microsystems. For example, a subsequent study (Brand et al., 1989) found that supervisor behaviors directed toward career development and mentoring had a stronger linkage with psychological well-being among workers on non-standard schedules who, as we noted above, might otherwise be seen as marginal employees. Attention could also be given to the match between the adaptive demands of nonwork settings and relationships with the spouse and friends.

Mesosystems

Network interactions can be examined in the context of multiple settings. Bronfenbrenner (1979) suggests that dyadic relationships might be greatly affected by 'mesosystem' variables, or the relationship between two or more settings that an individual occupies, such as the workplace and the family. Positive outcomes are expected to the extent that the roles and regularities of the two microsystems are congruent with one another.

In the present study, the two-way interaction of work shift by spouse support on symptoms can be viewed as a mesosystem process. The linkage between symptom levels and support in one microsystem (the family) varies, depending on attributes of another setting (the workplace). Lack of spouse support might result in greater incongruity between work and family roles, and hence in symptom levels, for women who are working on non-standard shift schedules.

Further research might build on the findings of this study by further delineating the nature of conflict between work and family roles, and examining the contribution of specific relationships to

resolution of incongruity. For example, perceived flexibility in work schedules has been linked to lower levels of work–family conflict (Staines and Pleck, 1983). The supervisor might have greater influence on the flexibility of work schedules (for example, frequency of rotation), while the spouse may be able to address other aspects of work–family conflict, for example by increasing flexibility in the scheduling and sharing of household tasks.

It might also be of interest to examine how the spouse affects the ability of nurses on non-standard shifts to manage their friendship networks. The difficulties involved in friendship relations due to shift schedules can be minimized or exacerbated by spousal behavior. More generally, the nature of the family–friendship mesosystem can have an important impact on social support for multiple roles (see especially, Hirsch et al., in press).

Exosystems

The exosystem consists of the microsystems that the individual does not occupy, but is nonetheless affected by. Positive outcomes can be expected to the extent that the individual has an effective relationship with another person who can mediate between these systems. For example, nurses on non-standard shifts do not have a regular direct relationship with administrative offices and clinical services that are open during the daytime. Thus, the supervisor may play an important role as an advocate and mediator between the work group and other parts of the hospital. Findings from a related study by Brand et al. (1989) provide additional support for this model. Among health-care workers on non-standard shifts, supervisor loyalty to subordinates and advocacy with higher echelons of the organization are associated with lower levels of psychological symptoms. In addition, nonwork relationships might also provide support through ecosystem processes. The spouse or closest friend of a woman working on a variable schedule might be able to participate in a wider variety of nonwork settings. These relationships might provide an indirect link with these settings that keeps her informed, for example about alternative job opportunities, forthcoming social activities, and ongoing civic concerns.

Macrosystem

The fourth and final unit of analysis, the macrosystem, encompasses cultural or subcultural beliefs and ideologies that shape the form of lower level micro-, meso-, and exosystems. For example, social norms concerning sex roles might affect the linkage between maternal employment on shift schedules and levels of support from work associates. In the current study we did not find lower levels

of support among mothers employed on night, rotating, and variable shifts. However, maternal employment on non-standard shifts may be more acceptable in a traditionally female profession such as nursing. There is a clear need for nurses to work in hospitals and to have them staffed around the clock due to the precarious health status of many of the patients. Maternal employment on these shifts might be less acceptable in industries that have employed a predominantly male labor force, or in occupations for which the need for shiftwork is not as compelling.

Conclusion

Little attention has been given to the effect of larger social settings on the supportive qualities of personal relationships. The present study examined the effects of shiftwork and the family life cycle on levels of support, as well as on the correlates of support, in five key work and nonwork relationships. Supportive interactions with the spouse, best friend, and the work supervisor were more strongly linked with lower symptom levels among nurses on night, rotating, and variable shifts.

The results of this study suggest that the correlates of support differ according to: (a) match between support and the adaptational demands of a setting (that is, microsystem effects); (b) the extent to which support addresses potential incongruities between settings and resulting conflict between roles (that is, mesosystem effects); and (c) the role that the other person in the relationship plays as a link to settings with which the individual has no regular contact (that is, exosystem effects). Levels of support for mothers employed on non-standard shifts might also vary according to prevailing sex-role ideologies (that is, macrosystem effects).

Note

Funding for this research was provided by an award from the University of Illinois to the second author, who is currently supported in part by the Center for Urban Affairs and Policy Research (Northwestern University).

10

Integrating Social Support Perspectives: Working Models, Personal Relationships, and Situational Factors

Gregory R. Pierce, Barbara R. Sarason, and Irwin G. Sarason

Research on social support reflects a variety of approaches. Unfortunately, this diversity of focus and of guiding assumptions has led to fragmentation of research efforts and difficulty in interpreting available evidence. This chapter argues for the need to adopt an interactional framework to guide research on social support. This framework emphasizes that social support, however defined, is a product of interacting influences among persons, their personal relationships, and the situations they help to create and to which they respond.

Although many definitions have been proposed for the social support construct, most researchers seem to agree that social support refers to social transactions that are perceived by the recipient or intended by the provider to facilitate coping in everyday life, and especially in response to stressful situations. However conceived, the impacts of these social transactions on responses to stressful situations are mediated by the *personal meanings* that individuals attach to these social experiences (cf. Cutrona et al., Chapter 2; Morgan, Chapter 11; and Leatham and Duck, Chapter 1 – all in this volume). These personal meanings, in turn, are products of the intrapersonal, interpersonal, and situational contexts in which social transactions occur. The *intrapersonal context* includes the individual's stable, unique patterns of perceiving social relationships which are based on working models of self, important others, and the nature of personal relationships. The *interpersonal context* refers to the distinctive quantitative (for example, network size) and qualitative features (for example, interpersonal conflict) of both specific relationships and larger social networks in which supportive behavior and personal coping efforts take place. The *situational context* includes the events (for example, death of a loved one, loss of a job) to which relationship participants respond.

In this chapter we review research on social support that deals with these contexts and we point out strengths and weaknesses of current approaches. We give special attention to the need for theories of social support that incorporate what is known about these interacting intrapersonal, interpersonal, and situational contexts. The chapter concludes with some suggestions for future research that reflect this focus.

Research on Social Support

A wide variety of approaches has been used to investigate social support and this had made it difficult to integrate the diversity of published findings. Researchers (for example, B. Sarason et al., 1987) have acknowledged this state of affairs by attempting to clarify the nature of the social support construct. Such investigations frequently have focussed on deciding which of several current approaches leads to the most valid conceptualization of social support. However, this chapter is concerned not with arguing for the value of one current approach over another, but rather with highlighting the merits of several approaches with an eye toward integrating their important contributions and avoiding their individual pitfalls. We review three prominent conceptualizations of social support that focus on (a) structural characteristics of social networks, (b) social support as categories of helping, or (c) social support as a generalized perception. Rather than discarding one approach in favor of another, we advocate integrating each of these perspectives into an interactional theory of social support. An important conclusion of this review is that a comprehensive theory of social support will need to address aspects of social behavior and cognition emphasized by each of these approaches.

Structural Characteristics of Social Networks

Orientation of the Approach   The network approach focusses attention on the social matrix in which supportive efforts take place. This emphasis on interpersonal context has been operationalized by relating quantitative descriptions of the social environment (for example, network size and density) to personal adjustment (for example, Homel et al., 1987). An example of how this approach has been operationalized is Stokes' (1983) Social Network List. This instrument, which was modeled after Hirsch (1980), asks each subject to list, on both axes of a matrix, up to twenty people important to the subject and with whom contact is made at least once a month. The subject then indicates network members who

are significant in each other's lives and identifies which network members are relatives and which are confidants. The instrument yields measures of several social network variables, including size, density, and number (and percentage) of friends, relatives, and confidants.

The social network approach is based on the assumption that quantitative features of a social network influence the impact that interactions have on network members (Gottlieb, 1981). For example, Vaux and Harrison (1985) have suggested that low-density networks (that is, ones in which few network members know each other) may be effective in facilitating transitions and adjustment to new circumstances (for example, women returning to college), while high-density networks may be helpful when 'retrenchment, recuperation, and validation is the appropriate response' to the stressor (p. 262).

Theoretical Limitations   Accumulating research suggests that qualitative, rather than quantitative, features of personal relationships are related to well-being (for example, Blazer, 1982). Sandler and Barrera (1984) found that measures of social network characteristics (for example, total network size, proportion of unconflicted relationships) were unrelated to personal adjustment. In contrast, involvement in conflicted relationships was related negatively to personal adjustment. Mounting evidence suggests that interpersonal conflict may be particularly important in determining the impact of potentially supportive efforts on well-being (Barrera, 1981; Fiore et al., 1983; Rook, 1984; Sandler and Barrera, 1984; Stephens et al., 1987). These studies indicate that receipt of social support from conflicted or ambivalent relationships plays a negative role in personal adjustment. Requests for support (as well as its receipt) from ambivalent relationships may cause feelings of guilt and indebtedness which increase rather than decrease distress. Support that is initially provided by family members and friends in response to a stressor may be beneficial. Nevertheless, stressful events that lead to long-term needs for social support can also result in overinvolvement on the part of support providers and subsequent decrements in psychological well-being for both the support recipients and the providers (Coyne et al., 1987; Coyne et al., 1988; Silver et al., in press).

Methodological Limitations   As mentioned earlier, several researchers have concluded from available evidence that perceived aspects of personal relationships (in contrast to structural characteristics of social networks) play a more important role in processes

by which personal relationships have impact upon coping and adjustment (B. Sarason et al., 1987; Wethington and Kessler, 1986). This conclusion suggests the need to incorporate the assessment of qualitative, as well as quantitative, aspects of personal networks. It may be that perceived aspects of personal relationships interact with structural features of one's network in determining the enactment and perception of social support (cf. Leatham & Duck, Chapter 1; and La Gaipa, Chapter 7, this volume). For example, the presence of conflictful relationships in dense networks may be particularly problematic because an individual may have little opportunity to interact with other network members without being upset and frustrated by ambivalent relationships.

Conclusions While the network approach has, by itself, not led to consistent or substantial empirical findings, it can help to emphasize the need to consider the interpersonal context in which supportive efforts take place. For example, investigators frequently have conceptualized social support mechanisms (that is, mechanisms by which potentially supportive transactions impact an individual's coping efforts and well-being) in terms of dyadic relationships in which one individual is identified as the support recipient and another person is designated as the support provider. However, this view fails to consider the larger social network in which potentially supportive transactions occur. Consider the dilemma faced by an individual who is making arrangements for his upcoming wedding and must ask one of his friends to be the best man. Although the person whom he eventually asks may be pleased to have been singled out for the honor, other male friends in the future groom's network may feel rejected and even angry. The groom's relationship with each male friend in his social network may be subtly influenced by these friends' perceptions of the groom's relationships with other network members. Thus, while one person (that is, the best man) may provide support to another (that is, the groom), this support does not occur solely in a dyadic context. Instead, this transaction has implications for other members of the support recipient's network. This point highlights the fact that the interpersonal context in which supportive efforts take place involves a network of personal relationships, rather than simply a dyadic relationship (Morgan, 1986 and this volume).

Social Support as Functional Components

Orientation of the approach Initial conceptualizations of the processes by which social transactions facilitate adaptation were

focussed on the specific functions served by personal relationships, especially social functions performed by network members. For example, Cobb (1976) conceived of social support as information within a network leading individuals to believe that they are cared for and loved, esteemed and valued, and active participants in social communication that implies mutual obligation. Weiss (1974) proposed six specific functions of personal relationships: attachment, social integration, opportunity for nurturance, reassurance of worth, a sense of reliable alliance, and guidance. This perspective disaggregates personal relationships in terms of specific social provisions. This approach grows out of the *buffering hypothesis*, which posits that social support has beneficial effects only when available support or support actually received is appropriately matched to a person's specific needs engendered by a particular stressor (Cohen and McKay, 1984; Cohen and Wills, 1985).

The Interpersonal Support Evaluation List (ISEL; Cohen et al., 1985) illustrates an approach to the assessment of social support based on this perspective. The ISEL was developed to assess four aspects of social support: tangible support (for example, material aid), appraisal support (for example, someone to talk with about one's problems), self-esteem support (for example, someone who thinks positively of the individual), and belonging support (for example, someone to do things with). Although the subscales have some face validity as measures of specific facets of social support, thus far, strong evidence of discriminant validity for these scales has not yet been provided (Brookings and Bolton, 1988; Cohen et al., 1985; B. Sarason et al., 1987).

Another illustration of the functional approach to social support is Cutrona and Russell's (1987) Social Provisions Scale (SPS) which is based directly on Weiss' (1974) description of six provisions of social relationships described earlier. Their work suggests that the interaction between the needs engendered by specific stressful experiences and the type of support either available to the individual or actually received from support providers may influence the impact of social support on coping and adjustment. For example, reassurance of worth, but not other types of support, was found to buffer the stresses of work and to prevent burnout among some teachers and nurses (Constable and Russell, 1986; Russell et al., 1987).

The functional approach also is useful because it suggests that the nature of stressors, as well as the needs that they engender, may change over time. Cutrona (1984) conducted a longitudinal study to investigate the relationship between specific components of social support and postpartum depressive symptoms. Of the six

provisions assessed by the SPS, 'guidance' was significantly related to depressive symptoms two weeks following the birth of a child, while 'social integration' significantly predicted depression eight weeks postpartum.

Theoretical limitations   Although researchers have argued for the need to consider the interaction between stressful situations (that is, situational context) and the specific needs that they engender, most researchers have failed to explicate specifically which aspects of social support are likely to be beneficial to individuals who are experiencing particular stressful events. For example, if Robert loses his job, will he need a loan of money, leads on potential jobs, or a companion to distract him from his worries? Even more problematic is that the functional approach fails to recognize that the impact of specific categories of social support on coping and adjustment is a product, not only of the situation, but of the personal relationships from which support stems.

This conceptual shortcoming may explain why researchers have had a difficult time obtaining support for the position that specific social provisions are beneficial to individuals confronting distinct categories of life events (see Cohen and Wills, 1985, for a review of relevant research). For example, several investigators who have examined the relationship between functional components of social support and unemployment have failed to find an association between tangible assistance (for example, monetary support) and personal adjustment (Bolton and Oatley, 1987; Mallinckrodt and Fretz, in press). Although there are likely to be other negative consequences associated with unemployment, it seems reasonable to assume that a need for some form of tangible assistance might arise from losing one's job. The lack of association between tangible support and measures of adaptation may result because researchers have failed to consider the personal meanings that individuals attach to supportive experiences (cf. Leatham and Duck, Chapter 1, this volume). Two individuals might both lose their jobs and subsequently receive assistance from important persons in their lives. One of them may perceive the receipt of aid from others as reflecting a lack of confidence in his or her ability to deal effectively with the situation and this perception may threaten the individual's self-esteem, thereby undermining personal coping efforts (Fisher et al., 1982). Similar provisions of assistance from the other person's network might be perceived as reflecting care, empathy, and commitment. Thus, the personal meanings that an individual attributes to the 'supportive' responses of network members are likely to

influence strongly the contribution made by these relationships to the individual's coping efforts and adaptation.

Implicit in the functional approach are two assumptions: that both the support provider and the recipient should be in agreement regarding the supportive provisions that are most likely to be of help to the recipient; and that this agreement should be reflected in the supportive exchanges that occur between support providers and recipients. Recent evidence indicates that support providers frequently do not provide the kinds of support that are seen by the potential recipient as helpful (Lehman et al., 1986; Wortman and Silver, 1989). Further, while some research indicates that providers and recipients may sometimes agree on the types of social exchanges that are needed to facilitate coping with specific challenges, this research also makes clear that this agreement often does not get translated into actual behavior (Lehman et al., 1986). Supportive behaviors frequently are not forthcoming from support providers because their own needs also influence their efforts to assist potential recipients. Some stressful situations (for example, serious health problems such as cancer and heart problems or the death of a child) may also cause distress on the part of potential support providers. In these situations support providers may orient their behavior toward reducing their own distress rather than the distress of the afflicted individual. Coyne et al. (in press) found that the spouses of men who had recently suffered an uncomplicated myocardial infarction frequently engaged in behaviors that, rather than supporting their spouses, increased the patient's chances of suffering further cardiac problems. Coyne and his colleagues noted that the behavior of the spouses reflected their own needs to reduce anxiety associated with their husband's recent heart attack. Thus, not only did the event have implications for the needs of the patients, but it also engendered needs on the part of potential support providers. For some couples these needs appeared to exert a stronger influence on the supportive efforts of the spouses than did the actual needs of the potential recipients. This finding highlights the need for theories of social support to reflect the complex interactions among an individual's personal resources, the life events which confront him or her, and the implications that these events have for other network members. These factors, and the personal relationships upon which the potential recipient must rely for support, together help to determine the supportive efforts of providers and the impact of their efforts on the recipient's response to challenging situations.

Methodological Limitations   In addition to failing to consider

explicitly the interpersonal context in which various social provisions are enacted, researchers employing the functional approach have had difficulty in demonstrating the empirical distinctness of various categories of social support. For example, the four subscales of Cohen's ISEL are found consistently to be highly intercorrelated (Cohen et al., 1985; B. Sarason et al., 1987). Brookings and Bolton (1988) also recently performed a confirmatory factor analysis of the ISEL which suggested a general factor of social support. Cutrona and Russell (1987) also found evidence for a general factor of social support underlying responses to the SPS described above. These findings suggest the need for further efforts to determine the viability of conceptualizing discrete categories of social support.

Conclusions The functional approach is important because it focusses attention on the situational context in which coping efforts occur. For example, support providers probably gauge their efforts based upon the needs that they believe are engendered by the specific stressor confronting the potential recipient. However, factors associated with the stressful situation do not operate in isolation. Regardless of the type of support that is offered, the impact of potentially supportive behaviors reflects the interpersonal context in which supportive efforts occur.

These observations suggest that the functional components approach to social-support research is a useful one. Nonetheless, further research is needed to identify salient features of situational contexts that influence supportive efforts and perceptions of social support. For example, negative events that are perceived as personally threatening or socially stigmatizing by potential providers may undermine their support attempts (Silver et al., in press; Wortman and Dunkel-Schetter, 1987).

Social Support as the General Perception of Being Supported

Orientation to the Approach In contrast to the functional approach which attempts to divide social support into distinct components, social-support researchers also have assessed global perceptions of available resources and satisfaction with these resources (Henderson et al., 1980; Procidano and Heller, 1983; I. Sarason et al., 1983). From this perspective, social support can be viewed as the generalized perception that there are people available to provide assistance regardless of the nature of the specific situation confronting the potential support recipient. This generalized perception of potential social support is consistent with the prominent global

factor found to underlie a number of social support instruments (Brookings and Bolton, 1988; Cutrona and Russell, 1987; B. Sarason et al., 1987).

For example, the Perceived Social Support from Friends and from Family measure (Procidano and Heller, 1983) is intended to assess the extent to which friends (Friend Support) and family (Family Support) fulfill an individual's need for support, information, and feedback. The PSS asks subjects to answer *yes*, *no*, or *don't know* to a list of 40 statements (20 items per scale) and include items such as the following: 'My friends (or family) give me the moral support I need,' and 'My friends (or family) are sensitive to my personal needs.'

Another example of this approach is the Social Support Questionnaire (SSQ; I. Sarason et al., 1983). This twenty-seven-item instrument is a measure of both perceived available support and satisfaction with perceived available support. Each of the items consists of two parts. The first part asks a subject to report up to nine individuals to whom the subject can turn for support in each of a variety of situations and includes items such as the following: 'Who accepts you totally, including your worst and your best points?' and 'Who helps you feel that you have something positive to contribute to others?'. The number of individuals who are listed for each item on the SSQ is summed across all of the twenty-seven items to assess the amount of support perceived to be available by the subject. The second part of each item measures, on a six-point Likert scale (ranging from very dissatisfied to very satisfied), the person's degree of satisfaction with the perceived available support.

The important feature of these general or global measures of perceived support is that they focus primarily on the sense of being accepted and valued by others (I. Sarason et al., in press). According to this view, relationships that provide this feeling also will provide specific supportive behaviors. This approach reflects the assumption that feeling cared about by others enhances personal coping and lessens performance impairing anxiety.

A recent study concerned with the development of a short form of the SSQ (I. Sarason et al., 1987) further clarified the nature of the general perception of being supported. The results of this study indicate that interpersonal acceptance (the sense of being loved, valued, and accepted by others) may be a critical ingredient in social support. A short-form of the SSQ was developed from the six items loading most strongly on the perceived availability dimension of the SSQ. Inspection of these items makes clear that they do not assess the availability of specific categories of support. Instead, these items appear to measure the extent to which individ-

uals believe that others love and value them, even if they might perform poorly or behave in a less than desirable fashion.

The general perception of being supported may reflect a personality characteristic. Sarason and his colleagues (I. Sarason et al., 1986) advanced this view based on a study in which they found perceptions of social support availability (and satisfaction with that support) to be stable over periods of up to three years, even during transitional events that led to major changes in network composition. Several researchers have argued that stable differences in the general perception of social support might be explained by individuals' working models of self and important others (I. Sarason et al., in press). Research is accumulating to buttress the hypothesis that perceptions of social support may be influenced by working models of self and important others (Mankowski, 1989; B. Sarason et al., 1989). For example, individuals who perceive high levels of available support believe (a) that they possess many positive attributes and few negative characteristics; (b) that others hold similarly positive views of them (B. Sarason et al., 1989).

Working models guide expectations regarding the behaviors of others and influence the interpretation that these behaviors have when they are enacted. People who believe they have something positive to contribute to relationships are confident that others will find them to be desirable relationship partners. These expectations motivate and direct social behavior to achieve these goals. These expectations are also likely to lead to positive attributions regarding the behavior of others. In this manner, working models achieve stability as expectations and perceptions of social interactions confirm one other.

Theoretical Limitations   The concept of the global sense of being socially supported is useful because it recognizes the importance of the *intra*personal context in which social support occurs. However, just as the functional approach focusses too much on the potential supportive needs engendered by specific classes of situations, so the 'general perception of being supported' approach emphasizes the contribution of personality and does not sufficiently consider the *inter*personal context in which supportive efforts occur.

Recent research on social support highlights the need to take account of its interpersonal context (Hobfoll et al., 1986; Pagel et al., 1987; Pierce et al., 1988). The point is illustrated by a series of studies conducted to clarify the independent contributions of interpersonal context and social support to personal adjustment (Pierce et al., 1988, 1989). Results from these studies indicate that multiple categories of personal relationships (for example, mother

and friends) each independently contributed to the prediction of personal adjustment. In addition, several qualitative aspects of these relationships (for example, interpersonal conflict and positiveness) made independent contributions.

These findings are consistent with the idea that the quality of the relationship between support providers and recipients strongly influences the impact of social support on personal adjustment. They also indicate that although measures of perceived social support (for example, ISEL, SPS, SSQ) typically aggregate these perceptions across specific relationships, it may be important to disaggregate the perceptions in terms of the specific relationships from which these resources are perceived. For example, in the Pierce et al. (1989) study cited above, both parents and friends contributed independently to subjects' global perceptions of available support and satisfaction with it. Such studies call attention to the need to conceptualize perceptions of social support as an interpersonal experience which occurs in the context of specific relationships. Also, the impact that these experiences have on an individual is strongly influenced by the quality of the relationships in which they occur.

Taken together, these studies suggest that although the intrapersonal context (for example, working models of relationships) may influence potential recipients' perceptions of social support, other factors are important as well. Perceptions of social support are also a product of interpersonal and situational factors; therefore, fuller understanding of the processes by which social support facilitates coping and adjustment will require the inclusion of all three sets of factors into theories of social support.

Methodological Limitations   Accumulating evidence suggests that the concept of working models represents a promising framework from which to investigate the role of personality characteristics in perceptions of social support. However, although this represents an important conceptual contribution, this body of research relies heavily on the inference that responses to perceived social support instruments reflect differences in working models, a construct which these measures were not developed to assess. What are needed currently are new methods to assess relevant working models directly. For example, Mankowski (1989) developed a set of rating scales to describe members of a family portrayed in a series of photos depicting ambiguous family interactions. He found subjects' perceived social support to be positively related to their appraisals of the feelings, motives, and personality characteristics of the family members depicted as well as the supportiveness of the family

environment. The results of this study suggest that projective techniques represent a psychometrically sound approach to the assessment of working models. Other promising approaches include semi-structured interviews (Main et al., 1985) and self-report questionnaires (Hazan and Shaver, 1987).

Conclusions   The general perception approach to social support is important because it focusses on the role of personality characteristics (for example, working models) that influence perceptions of social behavior and situations to which individuals respond. This perspective emphasizes that the need for social support and the interpretation of supportive efforts of others are not simply a function of situational context. Instead, working models of self and important others also guide interpretations of and responses to stressful situations and the social behavior of others. However, further research is needed to investigate existing approaches to the assessment of working models and to develop new measurement techniques.

Integrating Current Approaches to Social Support

In reviewing several prominent approaches to social support research, a number of contributions deserve special emphasis. The structural network approach has recognized the need to conceptualize supportive efforts as taking place within an interpersonal matrix composed of dyadic relationships. Although social support researchers typically have investigated this topic from the perspective of the potential support recipient (and occasionally from the support provider's perspective), this represents an incomplete picture of the interpersonal context in which supportive efforts occur. Just as Duck and Sants (1983) have conceptualized relationships as process, the same approach is appropriate in understanding social support. For example, there are at least three important perspectives to consider when conceptualizing potentially supportive transactions. These include the interaction as viewed by: (a) the recipient, (b) the support provider, and (c) other potential support providers.

Traditional conceptualizations of supportive transactions incorporate only the first two perspectives mentioned above. For example, when confronted by a challenging situation, individuals (that is, potential support recipients) are believed to engage both in self-monitoring and monitoring of those important others from whom they believe aid might reasonably be expected. Support providers monitor the potential recipient's behavior in the context of the

situation which confronts the individual, and based upon these observations, decide what might be done to aid the individual within the parameters established by the personal resources of the support provider. However, this conceptual framework neglects another important aspect of this interpersonal transaction – the potential support provider's evaluation of what others are doing for the potential recipient. The provider's decision to give social support reflects an assessment of: (a) what the individual might need; (b) what the potential provider is willing and/or able to do for the individual; and (c) what others are likely to do or are actually doing for the potential recipient. From this perspective, supportive efforts take place and have implications not only for specific dyadic relationships, but also for the interpersonal matrix in which the dyadic relationship is embedded.

Just as the structural network approach has provided a needed focus, an important question identified by researchers employing the functional approach concerns the situational contexts in which specific supportive efforts are likely to contribute to an individual's current coping efforts. However, this approach considers only part of the picture and the question remains: 'What type of support will be effective'. An answer will not be found by reference only to the challenging situation that confronts an individual. Instead, to answer this question it is necessary to consider the goals which the behaviors are intended to facilitate. For example, when individuals are faced with a situation that threatens to exceed their capacity to cope, they may evaluate the potentially supportive behaviors of important others in terms of their relevance to the goal of reducing current stress and frustration. On the other hand, potential support providers may orient their supportive efforts toward the goal of assisting the individual to resolve successfully the long-term implications of the situation. These differences in perspective may lead to considerable discrepancies in the evaluation of whether the potentially supportive transactions actually are supportive – it will depend upon the goal that one uses to evaluate the efforts of potential support providers. This observation suggests that it will not be possible to define behaviors as supportive or not supportive with reference only to a specific situational context. Instead, researchers need to recognize that potentially supportive efforts must be evaluated in terms of the goals to which they are directed as well as the quality of the specific relationships in which they occur.

Research focussing on general perceptions of social support has highlighted the role of personality characteristics in social support processes. Although this approach, like the social network and

functional components approach, has not led to a comprehensive theory of social support, it has made an initial contribution by identifying the role of working models in social-support processes. For example, when individuals cope with challenging situations, they evaluate the supportiveness of others' behaviors. These evaluations are in part a product of working models which guide individuals' coping efforts and their expectations about the appropriate behavior of others in response to their present circumstances (Mankowski, 1989; I. Sarason et al., in press). In addition, the working models of potential support-providers will strongly influence their evaluation of the needs of the potential recipient as well as their own ability and willingness to provide aid. From this perspective, potentially supportive transactions reflect a complex series of personal evaluations on the part of potential support-providers and recipients which are a product of the unique ways in which individuals view themselves, important others in their lives, and the meanings that these relationships have for them.

In summary, the social network approach has emphasized the need to consider the interpersonal matrix in which supportive efforts take place. The functional components approach draws attention to the need to examine the role of situational factors in determining the nature and impact of potentially supportive transactions. The general perception approach highlights the important influence personality characteristics (for example, working models) have on perceptions of social support. These contributions represent an accumulation of efforts that have revealed important aspects of social behavior and perceptions. The following section discusses the implications of these insights for future efforts in social support research.

Future Directions for Research and Theory

Researchers are now calling for increased attention to theory development in the area of social support (B. Sarason et al., in press). However, we believe that significant theoretical contributions are unlikely to be made unless researchers adopt a theoretical framework that both recognizes important contributions and acknowledges significant limitations to all the current empirical and theoretical approaches to this topic. We encourage researchers to move beyond current debates that pit one approach against another and to utilize multiple approaches to investigate social support. A broader, integrative approach to social support research suggests that the impact of supportive efforts reflects the contributions of both environmental provisions and personality characteristics. Such

a perspective would make a valuable contribution to current efforts to develop integrative, interactional theories of social support (B. Sarason et al., in press).

The following section will focus on two important issues which have received little attention in the current literature. These include the need for (a) further conceptualization and measurement of constructs related to the link between social support and personal relationships, and (b) laboratory studies that permit direct observation of interacting dyads in situations in which support provision is likely to occur.

Conceptualization and Measurement

As mentioned earlier in this chapter, the literature on social support is characterized by a plethora of definitions and measurement strategies, many of which are idiosyncratic and without a firm theoretical base. Many instruments designed to assess social support lack adequate psychometric properties (Heitzmann and Kaplan, 1988) and, more important, lack a theoretical base. This state of affairs calls strongly for further efforts aimed at clarifying constructs relevant to social support. For example, work is needed to develop empirically distinct measures of functional components of social support that are not strongly confounded by the general factor of social support.

We should recognize the contribution of specific relationships to coping efforts and well-being and direct further efforts (a) to conceptualize important aspects of personal relationships that influence the provision and impact of supportive efforts and (b) to measure these constructs. Efforts to measure social support in the context of relationships should incorporate the observation that supportive efforts can be viewed from several vantage points. Reliance on a single viewpoint on supportive efforts may lead to a biased understanding of the role of social support in coping and well-being. For example, researchers need to assess potentially supportive transactions from the point of view of potential recipients, providers, and other important network members. In addition, the potential supportiveness of these transactions should be evaluated with reference to the specific goals held by each relationship participant – goals that may not be shared by all network members.

Research is also needed to investigate the role of situational factors in giving and getting support. For example, are there classes of situations that are likely to inhibit the supportive efforts of potential providers? Can aspects of these situations be modified to provide an optimal environment in which social support might

occur? Answers to these questions are crucial in order to develop effective interventions.

Further research to investigate the role of personality characteristics in social support is also needed. Although preliminary findings suggest that working models of self and important others may play an important role in social support processes, direct assessment techniques are needed for these constructs. Initial efforts toward the development of research instruments for this purpose suggest that comparison of the results of projective techniques, interviews, and self-report questionnaires used with the same individuals may provide valuable information regarding these constructs.

Studies of Social Support as an Interactive Process
Further research efforts also are needed to explore the role of interactive factors in social support processes. For example, although most research on social support has focussed on situations in which one relationship participant can be identified as the 'support recipient' and the other individual is identified as the 'support provider,' research is needed to establish whether these findings will generalize to situations in which each individual acts both as a support provider and a recipient. When a student must take an important examination, for instance, the student can be seen as the focal individual who must confront the stressful situation. Other network members may offer support (for example, strategies for taking the test, opportunities to distract the student from thinking about the upcoming exam) but they cannot take the test for the student. However, some situations may require that an individual provide support as well as receive it. The same college student who must take an important final examination also probably has a roommate or other friend who is facing a similar situation. The student must then coordinate efforts to prepare for the upcoming exam with efforts to provide support to the other person. An important aspect of this situation is likely to be the individuals' perceptions of support reciprocity, an issue that has received considerable attention in the social support literature (Antonucci, 1985; Heller et al., in press). Individuals who perceive that they are providing more support to specific others than they are receiving from those others may experience ambivalence and resentment. These feelings may undermine personal coping efforts and subsequent perceptions of social support from these important others. An understanding of the role of social support must also take into account the developmental stage of the relationship because the perceptions of the need for equity in support provision may change over time as the duration of the relationship increases. Available

evidence suggests that the need for concurrent reciprocity may decrease over time as relationship participants adopt a longer term view of their relationship (Antonucci and Jackson, in press; Clark and Mills, 1979; Hays, 1989).

As mentioned earlier, it is our view that specific behavioral transactions cannot be evaluated as supportive (or not supportive) without reference to their interpersonal context and the personal goals which motivate the potentially supportive efforts. This does not mean that the assessment of observable features of potentially supportive transactions will not contribute to our understanding of social support processes. Instead, what is needed are studies that incorporate behavioral observation methods with assessments of the perceptions of each relationship participant regarding the observed transactions. This approach has the potential to increase our understanding of the roles of intrapersonal and interpersonal factors that influence supportive efforts and perceptions of behavioral exchanges. Thus, while they are interrelated, perceived and observable aspects of social interactions are distinct and both have implications for our understanding of the role of personal relationships in cognition and human behavior.

In this chapter we have reviewed research that suggests the importance of adopting a broader perspective on social support phenomena. An important aspect of this perspective is the recognition that social support is not simply an objective property of social interactions. Instead, social support reflects interactive influences among the intrapersonal, interpersonal, and situational contexts in which supportive efforts take place. Emphasis on the interactive contexts in which social support occurs not only can enhance the contributions of present approaches to social support but also can help to avoid some of their deficiencies.

Note

The authors wish to thank Roxanne C. Silver and Steve Duck for their helpful comments on an earlier draft of this chapter.

11

Combining the Strengths of Social Networks, Social Support, and Personal Relationships

David L. Morgan

Most of the chapters in this book begin from the assumptions common to either social support or personal relationships. In this chapter I widen the focus to include the field of social network analysis as well. I do so partly because social network analysis overlaps with both social support and personal relationships, but also because an emphasis on networks provides fresh insights into the strengths and weaknesses of the two fields that are at the core of this book. Indeed, I argue that social networks, social support, and personal relationships are each just different perspectives on the broader topic of social relationships.

I have borrowed the umbrella term 'social relationships' from a review of the social support literature by House et al. (1988). Although these authors use social relationships to describe the broader field that includes social support and social networks, they fail to include personal relationships. This omission is conspicuous because the volume in which their article appears also contains a review of the sociological literature on personal relationships by Blumstein and Kollock (1988), who, in turn, ignore the topic of social support. This mutual obliviousness is particularly apparent in the two bibliographies, where there is not a single item in common in a combined total of well over 200 citations. Fortunately for the present argument, both articles do devote attention to social networks, and I use this as license to extend the umbrella of social relationships to cover personal relationships as well as social support and social networks.

This does not, however, mean that there actually is a field of social relationships. Instead, we have three separate perspectives on one, larger topic. By treating social networks, social support, and personal relationships as three perspectives on social relationships, I am explicitly denying that it is subject matter that separates them. Instead, I see differences in subject matter as derivative: using a perspective inevitably means paying more attention to some

topics and less to others. Most work investigating sets of social relationships relies on the social networks perspective. Most work emphasizing the coping benefits of relationships relies on the social-support perspective. Finally, most work focussing on the development of specific relationships relies on the personal relationships perspective.

It is relatively easy to agree with the goal of bringing any two of these areas into closer contact – indeed, this book is devoted to just this purpose. But I maintain that a three-way sharing of perspectives can generate even greater benefits to each field. Broadly speaking, the argument is that each field has unique strengths and notable limitations, but that the limitations of any one field are matched by the strengths of the other two.

Throughout, I argue for recognizing the distinctiveness of the three fields and the benefits of applying more than one perspective to whatever one is studying. In other words, rather than advocating a unified approach to theory, I am pushing for a diversified approach to research. I develop this general argument by concentrating on the connections among social networks, social support, and personal relationships in my own area of interest, lifecourse transitions. Aside from personal familiarity, life events provide a valuable emphasis on the dynamic interconnections among the three perspectives.

After developing this argument, I will present an illustration using my research on caregivers for family members with Alzheimer's Disease. Because caregiving is a life event that both affects and is affected by the other relationships in the caregiver's life, it fits the theme of multiple linkages between life events and social relationships. One goal of this illustration is to produce specifics that add substance to the general argument, but the larger point is that the changes associated with life events need to be approached from multiple perspectives. Focussing on the changes that accompany major life events reveals the conceptual connections among social networks, social support, and personal relationships. Focussing on these connections provides a broader understanding of the changes associated with life events.

Three Perspectives on Social Relationships

In the next three sections, I give a sense of both what is unique to each perspective and how they overlap. Underlying this presentation is a matching of each perspective to a particular approach to social relationships: networks and the structure of relationships,

social support and the benefits of relationships, personal relationships and processes within relationships.

This approach to relationships in terms of structure, content, and process is common enough (cf. Kelley, 1987). But if the literature on intra- and intergroup processes is any guide, many readers will be dissatisfied by matching their chosen perspective to only one approach – at the same time that they are willing to accept my caricatures of the other two perspectives. In truth, each perspective does make some use of all of these approaches to relationships, even if it also emphasizes one approach above the others. By overstating the narrowness of each perspective's approach to social relationships, I hope to give a clearer sense of the strengths and weaknesses of each.

In my view, no one of these perspectives takes precedence over the others. Still, it is necessary to begin somewhere, and I start by examining the perspective that is unique to this chapter, social networks, followed by similar summaries of social support and personal relationships. The goals in each section are, first, to delineate the strengths and weaknesses of each perspective, and then to show how the strengths of the other perspectives can be combined to overcome the limitations of each.

The Social Networks Perspective

The unique approach that social network analysis offers to the study of social relationships comes from its emphasis on the structure of sets of relationships. This perspective refuses to view relationships in isolation; nor is it sufficient to possess a simple inventory of how both partners in a relationship are tied to others in the network. Rather, we must locate the partners to any one relationship within the structure of a larger network. This preoccupation with the structure of social networks is also, however, the chief limitation of this perspective. Although a single-minded emphasis on network structure points to topics that are largely ignored in either social support or personal relationships, it also discourages attention to many of the important issues raised in those two fields.

Strengths   By emphasizing a structural approach, the networks perspective is the most likely to pursue the goal of explaining relationships in terms of interactive features that go beyond the attributes of the partners. This reliance on structural, rather than individual-level, explanations is not surprising, given the large number of sociologists and anthropologists who make up the core of this field. While the goal of operating beyond the individual level of analysis

is acknowledged in most work on social relationships, it is the networks perspective that pursues it most fully.

The concentration on the study of network structure has produced a highly technical field that includes several variant conceptualizations (cf. Burt, 1980; Knoke and Kuklinski, 1982), a wide range of different measures (for example, Albrecht and Adelman, 1987a; Israel, 1982; Sokolovsky and Cohen, 1981), and several complex computer packages (Freeman, 1988). Fortunately, many of the better known aspects of network structure can be appreciated at an intuitive level in terms of connectedness or close-knit and loose-knit networks (Goldenberg, 1987; Hammer, 1983; Morgan, 1986). Among the aspects of network structure subsumed under connectedness are the density of ties among network members, whether networks are broken into separate cliques, and the extent to which networks are composed of strong versus weak ties.

Limitations The emphasis on structure within social network analysis ignores the fact that to study either structure or process in isolation is senseless. Just as the current structure of a network constrains the possible processes that occur within it, processes in networks maintain some aspects of that structure and modify others. Unfortunately, the lopsided emphasis in social network analysis has resulted in increasingly sophisticated methods for detecting network structure, but surprisingly few paradigmatic research questions that demonstrate the application of these methods.

The general inattention to issues of process is a major reason why social network analysis has yet to produce a research program that fits within the standard lexicon of independent and dependent variables. Seen in this light, processes in social networks are the independent variables that produce network structure, while network structure is the independent variable that influences the likelihood that a given process will occur. Interestingly, those studies that do pay attention to processes that are either inhibited or facilitated by network structure are some of the most cited work in the field, with Granovetter's (1973, 1982) work on weak ties being the exemplar.

Contributions from Social Support One way to introduce an emphasis on process to the social networks perspective can be found in work on how social support operates within social networks. The key point here is the recognition that the supportive content of relationships operates across the full set of relationships that make up a social network. The social support perspective thus shares the

interest in sets of relationships that is a key characteristic of the social networks perspective. By narrowing its interest to only one content area, however, the support perspective is able to devote attention to both structure and process in networks.

An important question for investigating how support operates in social networks is which relationships in the network are supportive. For example, an emerging body of evidence (Schuster et al., 1986; Wellman et al., 1987) finds that if one first elicits the membership in a social network and then asks which members provide various forms of support, only about half of these relationships are actively supportive. But the question of where supportive and non-supportive relationships are located within the overall structure of the network remains open. Under what circumstances is it better to have support spread throughout the network and when should it be concentrated in one segment – or are small but separate clusters of supporters generally optimal?

Similar issues also occur with regard to activating or mobilizing social support. Here, the question is how people modify the membership and structure of their networks in response to life events. For example, losses such as divorce and widowhood may lead people to reshape their networks toward the smaller, denser set of contacts associated with emotional support, while events such as unemployment or relocation may create a shift toward the loosely connected networks associated with effective information searches. As several authors have pointed out (for example, Dunkel-Schetter et al., 1987; Gottlieb, 1985, 1987; Hobfoll and Stokes, 1988), research on the mobilization of support, both within relationships and across networks, would go a long way toward unifying elements of these three perspectives.

Contributions from Personal Relationships   Work on the development of personal relationships provides another alternative for supplementing the structural emphasis of the social networks perspective. In comparison with social support's focus on how one content domain operates across a range of relationships, work on the development of relationships typically looks at how a wide range of processes influences the course of a single relationship.

The development of intimacy in relationships has always been central to the personal relationships perspective, but recent work has begun to look at the development of closeness across social networks (for example, Adams, 1987). Studies deal with changes in networks after moves to college (Berg and McQuinn, 1986; Hays and Oxley, 1986; Shaver et al., 1985), to a retirement complex (Shea et al., 1988), and to a new town (Starker et al., 1989).

Another set of studies looks at how existing relationships respond to life events such as divorce (Rands, 1988), parenthood (Gottlieb and Pancer, 1988; McCannell, 1988), and widowhood (Morgan, 1989a).

In these recent studies, questions about how life events affect relationships are generalized to questions about the membership and structure of the wider network. I must note, however, that the question of how changes in relationships create changes in networks typically remains implicit in most research on how life events influence personal relationships. One important step toward generating the kinds of mutual benefits that I am advocating would be to make this connection more explicit in future work.

Prospects for Connecting Perspectives How likely is it that developments in either social support or personal relationships will stir social-network analysis from its single-minded pursuit of network structure? Sadly, the answer is that this is not very likely, as evidenced by the relatively small role that network analysis plays in this volume. All too often, the division of labor pursued by networkers is one whereby they provide conceptual and methodological tools that others are free to adopt, thus placing the onus on the other two perspectives. Without a more even-handed recognition of the strengths that exist elsewhere, social network analysis may well remain bound by its own limitations.

The Social-Support Perspective

The social-support approach to social relationships is unique because of its detailed examination of one specific content domain, the benefits that relationships supply when coping with stressful life events. Concentrating on this content domain allows this perspective to pursue a wide range of questions concerning the positive (and negative) outcomes that people receive from social relationships. By casting its net widely, the support perspective is not bound to one level of analysis, with some proponents emphasizing psychological factors (for example, B. Sarason et al., 1987) and others behavioral factors (for example, House at al., 1988). This focus on a single aspect of relationship content is also, however, the major limitation of this perspective. At the same time that concentrating on the benefits of support provides a systematic set of hypotheses with regard to social networks and personal relationships, it also provides a view of these fields that can be irritatingly incomplete.

Strengths If one were to limit one's consideration of social

relationships to a single content area, it would be hard to argue with the choice of the benefits that relationships provide. From a social networks point of view, positive affect or exchange is almost always included among the forms of relationships studied. From a personal relationships point of view, the discovery of positive outcomes from associating with a partner is one basis for relationship formation, while increases and decreases in the benefits received from an ongoing relationship influence its development or dissolution.

Any attempt to understand the perspective that the social support field uses to investigate social relationships must consider its emphasis on explaining the health outcomes of stressful life events. By focussing on the mental- and physical-health benefits of relationships, the social-support perspective has been able to generate concrete summaries of the functions of relationships, and the range of beneficial functions included in typologies of support (for example, Gottlieb, 1978; House, 1981) is admirably large. As a result, we know a great deal about how this one particular content domain performs across a wide variety of social relationships.

Limitations   The single most limiting feature of the social support perspective derives from its origin in studies of stress, rather than in studies of relationships. Because most studies of social support investigate whether relationships counteract stress, there has been a tendency to ignore the negative effects of relationships, even though this topic appears in some of the earliest work on support (for example, Maddison and Walker, 1967). Fortunately, researchers have now recognized that the negative aspects of relationships can be just as important as their positive ones (see reviews in Rook, 1989; Rook and Pietromonaco, 1987; Wortman and Dunkel-Schetter, 1987). A different problem caused by seeing support as the result of stress has been the neglect of how relationships can prevent stress, although this topic is beginning to receive some attention under such headings as the regulation of behavior (House et al., 1988) and social control (Rook and Pietromonaco, 1987).

A further limitation on the content of the support perspective comes from the fact that relationships are so often studied for their health-related aspects. This limitation has had relatively little effect on studies of the psychologically supportive aspects of relationships, which are typically examined through a broad-based interest in subjective well-being. The limitation is more severe for the social dimensions of relationships, which are too often reduced to a series of instrumental exchanges. Thus, the emphasis on the health-

related benefits of relationships provides a useful organizing principle, but it also has the unfortunate side-effect of producing even narrower limits on how the social-support perspective approaches social relationships.

Contributions from Social Networks From a social networks perspective, the key issue in studying positive outcomes in relationships is how the structure and composition of the larger social network affect the availability of support. A major stumbling block has been the issue of distinguishing between the perceived or psychological aspects of support (cf. B. Sarason et al., 1987) and the enacted or behavioral aspects of social support (cf. Gottlieb, 1985). In reality, this is not an either–or question, as social networks affect both perceived and enacted support.

For perceived support, one broad hypothesis is that different structures in networks promote different perceptions about support. For example, the interlocking ties in close-knit networks should lead to greater perceived availability of support than in loose-knit networks. Another broad hypothesis is that the same amount of enacted support will be perceived differently in different networks. For example, if close-knit networks facilitate comparisons across the behaviors of their members, receiving a moderate amount of support will also draw attention to those who are not supportive.

With regard to enacted support, an important set of questions centers on the changes in social networks following a major life event. The most basic prediction would be a decrease in contact with those who are not supportive and an increase in contact with those who do provide benefits. Such a strategy would, however, be easier to pursue in a loose-knit network than in a tight-knit one (Hirsch, 1981). Such flexibility is also more likely in friendship networks than in family networks (Johnson and Leslie, 1982; Morgan, 1989a). Overall, the structure and composition of the network affect both the perception of support and the strategy that is used for activating whatever support is available (just as we saw, in the previous section, how the perception and enactment of support could affect the structure of the network).

What is surprising about the potential connections between the network and support perspectives is the rarity of research that brings these two fields together (for example, Cutrona, 1986a). Even when the two sides agree about the source of their differences, as with perceived versus enacted support, there are too few attempts to use empirical research to resolve these differences. The

failure to convert competing claims into empirical tests does not bode well for the possibility of combining these two perspectives.

Contributions from Personal Relationships   The major contribution that the personal relationships perspective can make to social support would be to broaden its range of topics, most notably in terms of the negative effects of relationships. As already noted, the social support perspective has begun to deal with negative aspects of relationships, and borrowing from the experience of the personal relationships field can further this integration. In the recent past, the personal-relationships field has moved from an emphasis on positive processes such as attraction and the development of intimacy to a more balanced view that includes conflict (cf. Kelley, 1987) and the dissolution of relationships (Duck, 1982).

One outcome of the broadened view of relationships has been an emphasis on the path that relationships follow through time (cf. Neimeyer and Neimeyer, 1985). Seen in this light, both the current state and the future direction of a relationship depend on the mix of positive and negative elements in that relationship. Applying a similar view to social support would emphasize the timing of support across the course of major life events. What we need are not just studies of support over time, but studies that follow how the positive and negative aspects of relationships affect the trajectory of the event, leading to successful coping in some cases and failure in others. Some work on the timing of support already exists (for example, Jacobson, 1986; O'Brien, 1984), but borrowing from the models available in the personal relationships perspective could speed the advance of this area.

Another important expansion of the content considered within the social support perspective would come from increasing the range of life events studied. Although health outcomes are best studied in terms of negative life events, any major life event, either positive or negative, is likely to cause changes in how one relates to significant others. This insight leads to a view of social support that not only pays equal attention to obtaining positive outcomes and avoiding negative outcomes in relationships, but also shows equal awareness of the changes following both positive and negative life events. The study of how positive and negative elements of relationships respond to both positive and negative life events is a good example of the mutual benefits from combining perspectives.

Prospects for Connecting Perspectives   A combined perspective on social support would place equal emphasis on maximizing the positive aspects of relationships and networks and minimizing their

negative aspects. In addition, the field would move beyond treating networks and relationships as static pools of resources; instead, it would investigate the features of both that affect the experience of benefits and losses throughout the course of major life events (for example, Gottlieb, 1990). I have more faith in the connection between social support and personal relationships as a means to this end. In contrast to the troubled ties between social support and social networks, the link between social support and personal relationships is still developing in a positive direction. Volumes such as this one foster hopes for a mutually beneficial future.

The Personal Relationships Perspective

The personal relationships approach is unique because of its focus on the processes occurring in specific social relationships. The personal relationships perspective has expanded to a conceptualization of personal relationships as sequences of events and perceptions (Duck and Sants, 1983). This has led to the study of a broad range of processes that occur within relationships (Clark and Reis, 1988) and has been extended to conflict (Kelley, 1987) and to intimacy (Reis and Shaver, 1988). Concentrating on what occurs within relationships has also, however, limited the personal relationships perspective to operating only on a self-contained, dyadic level of analysis. Despite calls to consider the wider social context that surrounds any given relationship (for example, Dunn, 1988; Ginsburg, 1986; McCall, 1982, 1988), the field has been slow to deal with either the networks in which relationships are embedded or the external influences such as life events that shape the content of relationships.

Strengths The process-oriented approach has been most apparent in personal relationships through work on the natural history of relationships, most notably by Duck and his colleagues (Duck, 1982, 1984, 1988; Duck and Perlman, 1985; Duck and Sants, 1983). As already noted, this increasing emphasis on the variety of paths (Neimeyer and Neimeyer, 1985) that relationships can follow has been an important step in moving this field beyond a narrow concern with the development of intimacy in romantic relationships (for example, Huston and Levinger, 1978). That earlier view of relationship development is now understood as being about the beginning stages of one type of relationship. The situation is somewhat analogous to the emergence of life-span developmental psychology (for example, Baltes and Schaie, 1973) as a field that encompasses childhood development, adult development, and aging by drawing attention to the continuity of basic processes across the lifecourse.

To say that the personal relationships perspective relies solely on a process approach would, however, be misleading. In fact, there is a fair degree of reciprocation between an emphasis on processes in relationships and an emphasis on their content. Thus, this perspective has studied both how the past development of relationships affects their current content and how their current content affects their future development. In general, however, it is the dominant interest in processes within relationships that has led to a further interest in their content.

Limitations   Despite its admirable ability to combine process-oriented and content-oriented approaches, the personal relationships perspective is limited to studying these factors in one relationship at a time. Although one can find theoretical discussions of the structure of relationships (for example, Ginsburg, 1986), such discussions are largely metaphorical. In point of fact, actual studies of personal relationships are typically concerned with their attributes (for example, intimacy, duration, and so on), rather than their structure (for example, Perlman and Duck, 1987). Although the pattern of co-occurrence of the key attributes of relationships can generate a structure in the sense of a typology, this still leaves the issue of structure within relationships at a metaphorical level.

Aside from ignoring the broad theoretical challenges posed by a structural approach, the tendency to study one relationship at a time creates problems in dealing with the social context in which any one relationship is embedded. There are many calls for more attention to the larger social structure that surrounds individual relationships (Gottlieb, 1985; La Gaipa, 1982; McCall, 1982; Morgan, 1986). While it is unfair to say that this issue has been ignored, it is one of those perennial candidates for future research that always remains on the far horizon of the personal relationships perspective. Stimulating more research on the social context of personal relationships would bring this topic closer to the core of the field, and both the social networks and social support perspectives provide a means to achieve this goal.

Contributions from Social Networks   Social networks are an obvious source for an infusion of structure into the personal relationships perspective. Because a network is defined as a set of relationships, it inherently links the partners in any one relationship to other actors and thus places the relationship in a structure based on relationships. One way to generate a concrete agenda that links personal relationships to network structure is through the distinc-

tion between social networks as independent and dependent variables.

With regard to social networks as dependent variables, several studies have documented how the development of a romantic relationship influences the partners' networks (for example, Johnson and Leslie, 1982; Milardo, 1982). This is a useful foundation to build upon, but we need to move beyond the development of romantic relationships to studies of how relationship disruption and dissolution affect social networks. We have a modest amount of this work with regard to divorce (see review in Rands, 1988), but in large part this is a neglected area. As the field of personal relationships has expanded to processes and content domains other than intimacy, it appears that the study of how events in relationships affect wider networks has not kept pace.

With regard to social networks as independent variables, there has been a consistent emphasis on how the connectedness of social networks influences relationships. My own work (Morgan, 1986) points to differences in social-learning processes: loose-knit networks provide a wider range of information, but tight-knit networks provide a better base for converting this information into usable knowledge. Gottlieb (1985) emphasizes that although we know that activities within loose-knit networks are different from those within denser networks, we have not uncovered why this should be so. He bases his challenge on Hirsch's (1981) often-cited, but still little-understood, finding that a disconnection between the friend and family components of the network led to better adaptation for young widows and for women returning to school. Both here and in the work on networks as dependent variables, the problem is not a complete absence of work that links networks and relationships; rather, it is a scattering of intriguing findings that have never coalesced into a coherent program of research.

Contributions from Social Support   The social support perspective goes beyond processes within single relationships by examining how support operates across different types of relationships. By asking about an individual's involvement in different types of relationships, we are essentially asking about that person's social roles. Treating these roles as bases for shared activities allows us to investigate how different types of relationships emphasize one type of content over another. The goal for such research would be to compare types of relationships according to both the likelihood that support is provided and any differences in the processes that produce support.

The comparison of how family and friends affect the adaptation

to major life events is one research area where differences in types of relationships have been matched to differences in social support. In my analysis of adaptation to widowhood (Morgan, 1989a), I have argued that we can account for these differences through the greater commitment to family relationships and the greater flexibility of friendships. For family, the commitment to continuing the relationship means tolerance for not only a lack of supportiveness but even for outright interference (Coyne et al., 1988; Lehman et al., 1986). In addition, even those who are themselves quite distressed will attempt to meet their support obligations to other family members (Hobfoll and Stokes, 1988). For friends, the first line of flexibility is an attempt to assure the supportiveness of the relationship, maximizing positive aspects and minimizing negative ones. Further flexibility, in terms of increasing or decreasing involvement, follows from the friend's actual supportiveness.

An emphasis on general principles such as commitment and flexibility allows us to move beyond the essentially typological distinction between friends and family. One goal would be to develop measures of commitment and flexibility as general properties of relationships, based on what we know about the differences between family-based and friendship-based relationships. Determination of the actual utility of these two particular dimensions will require moving beyond the negative, family-centered event (widowhood) in which they were developed. The larger point, however, is that investigating the supportiveness of different types of relationships can provide us with insights into the underlying characteristics of these relationships.

Prospects for Connecting Perspectives   There are excellent opportunities for advancing work in personal relationships by incorporating insights from the other two fields. In each case, there is a reasonably solid base of preexisting work that utilizes elements of the personal-relationships perspective. What remains is to raise the visibility of work that links personal relationships to changes in both social networks and social support.

Combining Perspectives
The combined perspective on social relationships that I have been advocating requires attention to, at a minimum, the structure of relationships across social networks, the crucial content associated with social support, and the developmental processes that occur within personal relationships. In fairness, however, the job of simultaneously studying issues of structure, content, and process in relationships is dauntingly large.

Realistically, it is not surprising that each of the three perspectives considered here has taken only a partial approach to covering this range. The network perspective has done the most to develop the tools necessary for studying a single aspect of social relationships through its concentration on structure. But by being so single minded, it has left it up to the proponents of other perspectives to find uses for these tools. The support perspective has done the most to combine approaches involving structure, content, and process. But it has done this at the price of studying a severely restricted set of topics. The personal relationships perspective has managed to work back and forth between issues of process and content. But this connection has been established only at a dyadic level of analysis with too little regard for the broader social context in which relationships occur.

The safest conclusion one can draw is that it is hard to do everything at once, so it is not surprising that each field has concentrated on doing a few things well. The result is that each perspective provides a rich set of resources that is available to researchers who seek to combine perspectives.

Throughout this section, I have highlighted a number of research opportunities that would combine perspectives. The common element in many of these suggestions has been a connection between social relationships and life events. In the next section, I will follow up on some of these suggestions in discussing my own research on caregiving as a life event. While I believe that caregiving is particularly useful for this illustration, the range of life events that could be considered is extraordinarily broad. No matter what life event is selected, however, the message is the same: more can be gained by combining these perspectives than by pursuing any one of them in isolation.

An Illustrative View from Multiple Perspectives: Caregivers for Family Members with Alzheimer's Disease

This section explores how perspectives from social networks, social support, and personal relationships can be used to understand the dynamics of a major life event: becoming a caregiver for a person with Alzheimer's Disease (for reviews of the literature on caregiving, see Gallagher, 1985; Horowitz, 1985; Ory et al., 1985). My goal in presenting these results as an illustration is modest. I promise neither a definitive analysis of caregiving nor a paradigmatic model for combining perspectives on social relationships. Instead, I seek a convincing demonstration of the value of combining

perspectives when studying the interplay between life events and relationships.

To avoid confusion, it should be clear at the outset that this research devotes relatively little attention to the actual relationship between the caregiver and the care receiver. This is indeed an important topic, but the care receiver's essential inability to interact with the caregiver in ways that we associate with meaningful social relationships poses a critical difficulty that would take us well beyond the realm of issues considered here.

Even though the emphasis here is not on the relationship between the caregiver and the care receiver, the events in that relationship are central. In essence, it is the transformation of that relationship into a caregiving relationship that leads to the reorganization of the caregiver's life. Mace and Rabins (1981) aptly describe the lives of Alzheimer's caregivers as a '36-hour day.' When a spouse or parent develops the disease, therefore, becoming a caregiver means making an intense commitment to this one relationship in a way that reshapes other relationships around the demands of caregiving.

This reshaping of relationships around caregiving responsibilities operates in two directions. As a life event, becoming a caregiver has a profound impact on social networks, social support, and personal relationships. In turn, social networks, social support, and personal relationships all have major effects on how a caregiver experiences this life event (Fiore et al., 1983). Caregiving is thus an excellent demonstration of the mutual interpenetration of life events and social relationships.

Data Collection and Measures

I have labeled this section of the paper 'illustrative' because these data were not collected for the purpose of making connections across the three perspectives considered here. From a network point of view, there should be more data on the structure of each caregiver's network of relationships. From a support point of view, there should be more detail about the supportive content of the relationships considered here. From a personal relationships point of view, there should be more information on the development of these relationships.

Fortunately, these weaknesses are partially compensated for by the strengths of the data: parallel quantitative and qualitative measures of relationships. For networks, this means that an unusually wide range of relationships can be investigated. For support, this means that data are available on both the positive and negative aspects of relationships. For personal relationships, this means that different types of relationships can be compared.

Both the quantitative and qualitative data come from sessions where groups of caregivers spent forty-five minutes completing questionnaires, then another forty-five minutes in tape-recorded focus groups. The thirty focus groups varied in size from four to eight and were conducted with little direct leadership from moderators (cf. Morgan, 1988). The participants were first asked to discuss things that made their caregiving either easier or harder. After about twenty minutes of discussion of this topic, they were asked to talk about how caregiving at home differs from caregiving in formal care settings such as a nursing home. (For more information on data collection, see Morgan, 1989b.)

Quantitative data were generated from questions where participants listed up to ten people who were important in their lives, along with their relationship to each person. A separate question obtained a seven-point rating of each person's supportiveness, ranging from making things much easier to much harder for the caregiver. Those receiving the two highest scores were counted as positive relationships and those receiving the two lowest were considered negative; to further comparisons to the qualitative data, those receiving neutral scores were omitted from the present analysis.

Qualitative data come from a computer-assisted content analysis (Siedel, 1988) of the transcripts from the focus groups. Each mention of another person was coded, along with their relationship to the caregiver. Supportiveness was also coded for each such mention of a relationship, according to whether the person was mentioned positively or negatively; mentions where the caregiver gave no clear positive or negative evaluation were omitted.

In comparing the quantitative and qualitative data, it is important to realize that two very different units of analysis are being counted. In the quantitative data, the numbers refer to specific individuals and each individual is counted only once. In the qualitative data, the numbers refer to how often others are mentioned, and any particular person may have been mentioned more than once. Thus, the quantitative data begin with questions about the social network and then assess the supportiveness of each member, while the qualitative data begin with questions about caregiving and then count which network members are mentioned in this regard. The advantage of the quantitative data is that caregivers provide an equivalent picture of each person in their social networks. The advantage of the qualitative data is that caregivers focus their discussion on those who did the most to make things either easier or harder. Comparing the two forms of data allows us to distinguish between the relationships that caregivers report as important in

their lives and the relationships they mention when discussing their caregiving.

The Range of Caregivers' Social Relationships: A Social-Networks Perspective

Table 11.1 presents data on the composition of the social network according to type of relationship. For both the quantitative and qualitative data, all forms of kin are listed as family, other forms of personal relationships are listed as non-family, and role-based relationships are listed as formal. For non-family relationships, friends make up the clear majority, with co-workers, neighbors, friends of the care receiver, and support-group members also appearing. For the formal relationships, formal-care staff make up the clear majority, with doctors, ministers, and daycare providers also appearing.

Table 11.1   *Average number of relationships reported by caregivers*

Relationship	Quantitative data	Qualitative data
Family	2.49	1.69
Non-family	0.68	0.50
Formal	0.18	1.49
Total	3.35	3.68
	(N=173)	(N=179)

In Table 11.1, the quantitative data show that these caregivers, on average, name a total of 3.35 people who make things either easier or harder, and nearly three-quarters of those they name (2.49) are family members. In the qualitative data, they average 3.68 positive or negative mentions of other people, but less than half of these mentions (1.69) are of family members. The networks derived from questionnaires contain many family members, a few friends, and hardly any formal ties, while formal relationships are much more likely to be mentioned in the focus groups. In other words, these two data collection strategies give different pictures of the range of relationships in caregivers' social networks. If we use the specific experience of caregiving as a standard, the general measures of social networks and social support from the survey data produce too many family relationships and too few formal relationships.

Based on these results, we would do well to avoid the assumption that networks composed of personal relationships are the predominant feature in every life event that we investigate. Instead, we need to investigate the relative importance of personal relationships

across different life events. This conclusion is reinforced by a comparison of these qualitative data to similar data produced by groups of widows (Morgan, 1989a), where mentions of formal relationships were very rare. Further, the rate at which the widows mentioned personal relationships was almost five times as high as in the present data. In other words, the discussions among widows involved proportionately more mentions of personal relationships, while discussions among caregivers generated more mentions of formal relationships.

The prevalence of formal relationships in these data is, of course, greatly influenced by the emphasis on the transition from home-based to formal-care-based caregiving. As the comparison to widowhood demonstrates, however, the key issue is the variability across life events. Depending on the demands associated with a specific life event, networks may be reshaped to place more emphasis on family, non-family, or formal relationships.

It is also worth noting that the importance of caregivers' formal relationships was not apparent in the survey data and would not have been detected without the focus groups. This issue is not merely methodological. Each of these data-collection strategies has its place in assessing the composition of social networks, but these results demonstrate the difference between general questions about networks and discussions of specific life events. A determination of how social networks respond to a life event may well mean beginning with questions about that event, rather than relying only on general questions about the composition of the network.

Overall, these results emphasize the importance of studying networks that are composed of many different types of relationships, including both personal and formal relationships. More than this, we need to recognize that the type of relationship that is most relevant depends on life events. But uncovering differences in network composition requires an explicit investigation of the life event under consideration. To study how life events reshape relationships, we need to direct both our research participants' attention and our own attention to the specific circumstances that we wish to understand.

The Positive and Negative Aspects of Caregivers' Social Relationships: A Social Support Perspective

Table 11.2 builds upon what has already been established by expanding Table 11.1 to show a percentage breakdown between people who made things easier and those who made things harder. Once again, there are notable differences between the two types of data. For the total data, the survey shows more than six times

as many people named as making things easier rather than harder, whereas the focus groups discussions are almost evenly divided between positive and negative mentions.

Table 11.2   *Caregivers' reports of positive and negative relationships*

Relationship	Quantitative data	(%)	Qualitative data	(%)
Family	2.49		1.69	
Positive		84		41
Negative		16		59
Non-family	0.68		0.50	
Positive		98		71
Negative		2		29
Formal	0.18		1.49	
Positive		88		58
Negative		12		42
Total	3.35	87	3.68	52
		13		48
	(N=173)		(N=179)	

But are the two sets of results genuinely incompatible? Examining the actual content of the qualitative data shows that much of their greater attention to negative relationships came from repeated mentions of the same people. In other words, caregivers devoted more time in their open discussions to problem people rather than supportive people. It is thus quite likely that there were more people who made things easier than people who made things harder, as indicated in the survey data, but that the problem people made more difference in the caregivers' lives, as indicated in the qualitative data.

This conclusion is reinforced by a comparison of how family members were mentioned in the two data sets (such comparisons are more difficult for the other two categories due to the small numbers). The greater prevalence of negative mentions in the qualitative data than in the survey data is most apparent in family relationships, as negative mentions are a majority of all discussions of family members in the focus groups. A more detailed examination of the two sets of data strongly suggests that the same family members are being mentioned negatively in both, but that they receive much more attention in the qualitative data. It also shows that many of those whom caregivers list as making things easier in the quantitative data are ignored or receive only minimal attention in the open-ended discussions.

These results indicate that people who make things harder for the caregiver may be relatively rare, but they have strong effects.

This finding that negative relationships have a larger effect than positive ones fits well with what is known in the support literature (for example, Rook and Pietromonaco, 1987). I believe, however, that the present results suggest a need to look at this conclusion more deeply.

The basis for the conclusion that negative relationships have a stronger effect is typically a regression analysis where the coefficient linking the number of negative relationships to subjective well-being is larger than the parallel coefficient for the number of positive relationships. What is overlooked, however, is that the total contribution to well-being depends on both the size of the co-efficients and the number of relationships. Each negative relationship does, on average, make a large contribution, but they are rare (in the survey data, 0.4 per participant). Each positive relationship does, on average, make a smaller contribution, but they are much more numerous (here, 2.9 per participant). Regression analyses on these data show coefficients that fit the pattern just described (Morgan, 1989b), but Table 11.2 provides a more intuitive demonstration. Even if negative relationships are relatively rare, they affect participants so intensely that they dominate the discussion in the focus groups. Thus, the total impact of positive relationships arises from many relationships that each have a relatively small effect, while the total impact of negative relationships comes from fewer relationships that each have a strong effect (for a related discussion, see Rook, 1989).

Overall, these results demonstrate the importance of studying social support in terms of both the positive and negative aspects of relationships. This is also true for making connections between social support and the other two perspectives. At the social network level, there are substantial differences between the composition of the positive and negative components of the support network. At the personal relationship level, the inescapable conclusion is that very different processes are operating in positive and negative relationships. Further progress in understanding the supportiveness of both social networks and personal relationships requires investigating the different dynamics of their positive and negative aspects. Examining these dynamics within specific life events, such as caregiving, is a step in that direction.

Differences in Caregivers and Different Types of Social Relationships: A Personal Relationships Perspective

So far, this analysis has treated all of the caregivers as if they were alike. This is particularly problematic when investigating personal relationships, because the type of relationship varies according to

who is receiving the care. This set of data is divided almost evenly between those who provide care to a spouse and adult children who provide care to a parent. The question in this section is whether there are differences in how caregiving affects the social relationships of spouses and children.

Table 11.3 continues the process of building upon what has already been established by expanding Table 11.2 to distinguish between children and spouses as caregivers. This distinction makes little difference in the quantitative data, but in the qualitative data children as caregivers are both more likely to mention family members and more likely to mention them negatively.

Table 11.3   *Children's and spouses' reports of positive and negative relationships*

	Quantitative data				Qualitative data			
Relationship	Child		Spouse		Child		Spouse	
Family	2.68		2.22		2.17		1.03	
Positive		81%		88%		38%		51%
Negative		19%		12%		62%		49%
Non-family	0.74		0.60		0.48		0.53	
Positive		97%		100%		72%		70%
Negative		3%		0%		28%		30%
Formal	0.12		0.22		1.64		1.28	
Positive		88%		88%		57%		59%
Negative		12%		12%		43%		41%
Total	3.54		3.04		4.29		2.84	
		85%		90%		49%		58%
		15%		10%		51%		42%
	(N=100)		(N=73)		(N=103)		(N=76)	

Examining the relevant sections of the transcripts shows that these differences between children and spouses are partially due to their relationship with the care receiver and partially due to where these two categories of caregivers are located in the lifecourse. For spouses, the transcripts show that their discussions are largely about the specific tasks they face in their relationship with the care receiver, and not about other people. For children, the transcripts show problems in other relationships that are due in part to being at a stage in life where they have other family and work roles.

With regard to the caregiving relationship, transcripts of spouses' discussions emphasize the extent to which they become absorbed

by this role. In large part, this is due to a steadily increasing involvement in caregiving, which matches the often gradual onset and progression of Alzheimer's Disease. In many cases, a spouse's high level of commitment to caregiving is the final development in a relationship that has evolved steadily over three or more decades. This absorption with the caregiver role means that spouses devote their discussions to the specifics of their caregiving and spend relatively little time talking about other people, including family. While these data are not sufficient to claim that spouses withdraw from their other relationships, it is clear that their thoughts about what makes caregiving easier or harder are not thoughts about other people.

Compared to a spouse, a child's assumption of the caregiver role is more likely to require an abrupt redefinition of not only that relationship but also of other family relationships. In these data, this is most apparent in relationships with siblings, who provide the single largest block of negative mentions. The most frequent complaints about siblings are their refusal to assist in home-based caregiving and their interference in decisions to seek nursing-home care. When one child becomes the primary caregiver for a disabled parent, the nominal equality between siblings can be severely tested.

Not all of the differences between spouses and children can be attributed to the difference in the relationship with the care receiver, however. For spouses, their stage in the lifecourse is what makes their absorption into the caregiver role possible. The time they devote to caregiving is largely time that is lost to personal activities, rather than to demands from other roles. In essence, the role losses that older spouses are likely to have experienced (Rosow, 1974) allow a freedom to reallocate effort to the caregiving relationship without penalty from competing commitments.

Compared to spouses, children as caregivers are at a point in the lifecourse where they must contend with many demands from other roles. Brody (1985) refers to middle-aged daughters as women in the middle, due to the demands of both their parents and their children, compounded with their own needs in terms of marriage, career, and so on. Performing the caregiving role at middle age, when it must compete with many other responsibilities, is very different from doing it in old age, when it may be the sole center of one's life. Accordingly, these transcripts show that children are more likely to mention family because they need to make adjustments in relationships with their own spouses and children. While children do not mention these relationships nearly so negatively as relationships with their siblings, their increased attention to these

relationships is an important reason why they are more likely to mention family members as part of their caregiving.

Overall, these results illustrate the importance of differences in relationships for understanding life-changing events such as becoming a caregiver for a family member with Alzheimer's Disease. For a relationship-centered life event such as caregiving, the nature of the relationship affects the way that the life event itself proceeds, either as an extension of the existing basis for the relationship or as a major revision of that relationship. In terms of social networks, differences in relationships may lead to either a disconnection from others or a conflictual redefinition of the composition of the network. In terms of social support, different types of relationships can generate conflict in some circumstances and support in others. By paying attention to the intersection of differences in relationships with differences in life events, we learn more about both the response to life events and the development of personal relationships.

Caregivers' Social Relationships: A Combined Perspective

In taking stock of this illustrative discussion of caregiving as a life event, I will downplay what each separate perspective has accomplished and concentrate on the ways in which combining multiple perspectives leads beyond what is available from any one perspective. In moving beyond the usual limitations of the social networks perspective, we have seen how support processes and changes in relationships affect the content of caregivers' networks. In moving beyond social support, we have seen how caregiving affects the wider network that constitutes the potential sources of support and problems. In moving beyond personal relationships, we have seen how changes in the wider network affect not only the caregiving relationship but caregivers' other relationships as well.

Taken in combination, these perspectives lead us to uncover the mutual influences between social relationships and a life event such as caregiving. Approached from any one perspective, there is a natural tendency to run our causal arrows in only one direction: from life events to changes in relationships or from relationships to the outcomes of life events. Each of these is a large and important question, and the point is not to belittle either of these separate connections between life events and social relationships. Instead, the goal is to emphasize how much more can be learned through a combined outlook.

Finally, it is appropriate to recall that these data were not collected with any prior goal of combining perspectives. Still, as the

progression from Table 11.1 to Table 11.3 demonstrates, such combinations are often possible within existing data sets. In assessing this illustration, I hope that the reader shares my sense that, if it is possible to accomplish this much in a study that was not explicitly intended to incorporate multiple perspectives, then there is so much more that could be done in a study designed for this purpose.

Conclusions

In this final section, I will make the rash assumption that I have proven my case, both for making connections among perspectives and for generating research that combines perspectives. If so, then the next question is how best to accomplish these goals. The answer to this question is somewhat different, depending on whether we look at intellectual goals or research goals.

Beginning with the intellectual goals, even if it is immediately possible to pursue connections across these three fields, it is still unwise to try and do everything at once. Instead, we need to locate the areas where immediate progress is most accessible. In the concluding paragraph of my treatment of each specific perspective, I gave my sense of how realistic it was to expect connections between this perspective and the other two. The clear conclusion that emerges from these comparisons is that the personal-relationships perspective offers the most opportunities for building bridges to each of the other two perspectives.

Does this mean that the personal relationships perspective is a first among equals? If the question is whether personal relationships are the preeminent means for studying the broader field of social relationships, then the answer is no. In this regard, I stick to my original assertion that these are three partial and co-equal perspectives. But the answer is yes, if we mean that the work now being done in the field of personal relationships offers the best starting point for creating connections among the three different perspectives.

If we go further and ask which other perspective personal relationships is most likely to pair-up with, this volume itself suggests that the obvious next step lies in connections between personal relationships and social support. I would like, however, to call attention to a danger that exists in combining only personal relationships and social support. Because the most obvious overlap between these two perspectives is in the development of positive aspects of relationships, we risk losing the hard-won insights that have arisen from consideration of either the negative aspects of relationships or the multiple trajectories that occur when relation-

ships can develop both closeness and conflict. Fortunately, the essays in this volume are remarkably free of this narrow view.

Bringing in the social networks perspective is one way to avoid this narrowness. Adding the social networks perspective to the personal relationships perspective forces us to realize that no relationship is an island. Instead, we need to consider how relationships are connected to each other. Adding social networks to the combination of personal relationships and social support also draws attention to a wider variety of relationships, both positive and negative, both formal and informal. Reaching for the additional contributions from a social networks perspective will keep us from congratulating ourselves prematurely about combining personal relationships and social support while missing the broader intellectual integration that we could achieve.

Such progress with regard to intellectual goals is necessary for progress on research goals; it is not, however, sufficient. Pragmatically, the fact that it is both possible and desirable to combine perspectives is not enough to generate research. What that requires is a coherent collection of questions that are of interest to those who are already active in the field. In other words, we need a research agenda, and life events are the most likely basis for such an agenda.

The simplest reason for selecting life events as the basis for a research agenda is that all three perspectives already share some interest in how life events fit into their approach to social relationships. More than any other potential topic, the study of life events provides a common core of substantive interests across the three perspectives. In practical terms, this also creates a way to recruit researchers who are primarily interested in substantive life events, by giving them a better means to study their specific topics.

A central focus on the intersection of life events and social relationships also avoids the trap of having any one perspective claim that it alone provides the necessary theoretical and methodological tools. Instead, the goal of understanding both how life events influence relationships and how relationships influence life events requires insights from all three perspectives. This means that researchers whose primary commitment is to one of the perspectives, rather than to a substantive topic, must combine perspectives in order to prove that their approach can make a unique contribution, above and beyond what other perspectives can accomplish.

Whether our research on life events is motivated by theoretical or substantive interests, demonstrating that an approach which combines different perspectives on social relationships produces more powerful results will create a demand for further research.

The illustrative account of caregiving provided here is a step in that direction, as are many of the other chapters in this volume. The next step is to prove that we can do even more with research which is consciously conceived to take advantage of combined perspectives.

The message of strength through unity, despite diversity, is a familiar one, and the motto, 'United we stand, divided we fall,' goes back at least to Æsop. Still, as academics, we come from a tradition that is far better known for splitting hairs than for uniting around common interests, so the kinds of combined perspectives that I have advocated here are not going to appear without a considerable amount of work. I can only hope that I have convinced you that the rewards are worth the effort.

Notes

I would like to acknowledge the helpful comments of Roxy Silver, Steve Duck, and my colleague, Kerth O'Brien. Portions of this work were sponsored through a grant from the AARP Andrus Foundation.

References

Acitelli, L.K. (1987) 'When spouses talk to each other about their relationship,' *Journal of Social and Personal Relationships* 5: 185–99.

Acock, A.C. and Hurlbert, J.S. (1990) 'Social network analysis: a structural perspective for family studies,' *Journal of Social and Personal Relationships* 7: 245–64.

Adams, R.G. (1987) 'Patterns of network change: a longitudinal study of friendships of elderly women,' *The Gerontologist* 27: 222–7.

Adelman, M.B., Parks, M.R., and Albrecht, T.L. (1987) 'Supporting friends in need,' in T.L. Albrecht and M.B. Adelman (eds) *Communicating social support.* Newbury Park, CA: Sage. pp. 105–25.

Adler, A. and Roll, Y. (1980) 'Proposal for a standard shift notation,' in A. Reinberg, N. Vieux, and P. Andlauer (eds) *Night and shift work: biological and social aspects.* New York: Pergamon Press. pp. 19–23.

Albee, G.W. (1980) 'A competency model to replace the defect model,' in M.S. Gibbs, J.R. Lachenmeyer, and J. Sigal (eds) *Community psychology: theoretical and empirical approaches.* New York: Gardner Press. pp. 213–38.

Albo, B.D. and Moore, G. (1978) *Sociological Methods and Research* 7: 167–88.

Albrecht, T.L., Adelman, M.B. (and Associates) (1987a) *Communicating social support.* Newbury Park, CA: Sage.

Albrecht, T.L. and Adelman, M.B. (1987b) 'Communicating social support: a theoretical perspective,' in T.L. Albrecht and M.B. Adelman (and Associates) *Communicating social support.* Newbury Park, CA: Sage. pp. 18–39.

Albrecht, T.L. and Adelman, M.B. (1987c) 'Dilemmas of supportive communication,' in T.L. Albrecht and M.B. Adelman (and Associates) *Communicating social support.* Newbury Park, CA: Sage. pp. 240–54.

Alloy, L.B., Abramson, L.J., and Viscusi, D. (1981) 'Induced mood and the illusion of control,' *Journal of Personality and Social Psychology* 41: 1129–40.

Altman, I. and Taylor, D. (1973) *Social penetration: the development of interpersonal relationships.* New York: Holt, Rinehart, & Winston.

Altman, I., Vinsel, A., and Brown, B.B. (1981) 'Dialectic conceptions in social psychology: an application to social penetration and privacy regulation,' in L. Berkowitz (ed.) *Advances in experimental social psychology.* New York: Academic Press. pp. 107–60.

Andrisani, P. and Shapiro, M. (1978) 'Women's attitudes towards their jobs: some longitudinal data on a national sample,' *Personnel Psychology* 31: 15–34.

Antaki, C. (1987) 'Performed and unperformable: a guide to accounts of relationships,' in R. Burnett, P. McGee, and D. Clarke (eds) *Accounting for relationships.* Methuen: London.

Antonucci, T.C. (1985) 'Personal characteristics, social networks and social

behavior,' in R.H. Binstock and Shanas (eds) *Handbook of aging and the social sciences* (2nd edn). New York: Van Nostrand Reinhold. pp. 94–128.

Antonucci, T.C. and Akiyami, H. (1988) 'The negative effects of intimate social networks among older women as compared with men,' paper read at meeting of the Gerontological Society of America, San Francisco, November.

Antonucci, T.C. and Israel, B. (1986) 'Verdicality of social support: a comparison of principal and network members responses,' *Journal of Consulting and Clinical Psychology* 54: 1–25.

Antonucci, T.C. and Jackson, J.S. (in press) 'The role of reciprocity in social support,' in B.R. Sarason, I.G. Sarason, and G.R. Pierce (eds) *Social support: an interactional view*. New York: Wiley.

Applegate, J.L. (1980) 'Adaptive communication in educational contexts,' *Communication Education* 29: 158–70.

Applegate, J.L., Burke, J.A., Burleson, B.R., Delia, J.G. and Kline, S.L. (1985) 'Reflection-enhancing parental communication,' in I.E. Sigel (ed.) *Parental belief systems: the psychological consequences for children*. Hillsdale, NJ: Erlbaum. pp. 107–42.

Asher, C.C. (1984) 'The impact of social support networks on adult health,' *Medical Care* 22: 349–59.

Baltes, P.B. and Schaie, K.W. (eds) (1973) *Life-span developmental psychology: personality and socialization*. New York: Academic Press.

Barbee, A.P. (1989a) 'The effects of mood and attributions on the interactive coping process in female friendships,' manuscript in preparation. University of Louisville.

Barbee, A.P. (1989b) 'The effects of positive and negative mood on cheering-up processes in female friendships,' paper presented at the 2nd Iowa Conference on Personal Relationships, Iowa City, Iowa, May.

Barbee, A.P. and Cunningham, M.R. (1988) 'The effects of mood on the cheering-up process in romantic couples,' paper presented at the annual convention of the American Psychological Association, Atlanta, GA, August.

Barbee, A.P., Gulley, M.R., and Cunningham, M.R. (1990) 'Support seeking in close personal relationships,' *Journal of Social and Personal Relationships* 7.

Barbee, A.P. and Lowe, G. (1990) 'Effects of attributions on interactive coping strategies among male friends,' paper presented at the Southeastern Psychological Association, Atlanta, GA, April.

Barden, R.C., Garber, J., Lieman, B., Ford, M.E., and Masters, J.C. (1985) 'Factors governing the effective remediation of negative affect and its cognitive and behavioral consequences,' *Journal of Personality and Social Psychology* 49: 1040–53.

Barrera, M. (1981) 'Social support in the adjustment of pregnant adolescents: assessment issues,' in B.H. Gottlieb (ed.) *Social networks and social support*. Beverly Hills, CA: Sage. pp. 161–96.

Barrera, M., Jr. (1986) 'Distinctions between social support concepts, measures, and models,' *American Journal of Community Psychology* 14: 413–45.

Barrera, M., Sandler, I.N., and Ramsay, T.B. (1981) 'Preliminary development of a scale of social support: studies on college students,' *American Journal of Community Psychology* 9: 435–47.

Barusch, A.S. (1988) 'Problems of coping strategies of elderly spouse caregivers,' *The Gerontologist* 28: 677–85.

Batson, C.D., O'Quin, K., Fultz, J., and Vanderplas, M. (1983) 'Influence of self-

reported distress and empathy on egoistic versus altruistic motivation to help,' *Journal of Personality and Social Psychology* 45: 706–18.

Bavelas, J.B. (1985) 'A situational theory of disqualification: using language to "leave the field",' in J.P. Forgas (ed.) *Language and social situations*. New York: Springer-Verlag. pp. 189–211.

Baxter, L.A. (1987) 'Symbols of relationship identity in relationship cultures,' *Journal of Social and Personal Relationships* 4: 261–80.

Baxter, L.A. (1988) 'A dialectical perspective on communication strategies in relationship development,' in S.W. Duck (ed.) *Handbook of personal relationships: theory, research, and interventions*. London: John Wiley. pp. 257–73.

Baxter, L.A. (1989) 'Dialectical contradictions in relationship development,' paper presented at the annual convention of the Western Speech Communication Association, Spokane, Washington.

Baxter, L.A. and Wilmot, W. (1984) 'Secret tests: social strategies for acquiring information about the state of the relationship,' *Human Communication Research* 11: 171–201.

Belle, D. (1982a) 'The stress of caring: women as providers of social support,' in L. Goldberger and S. Bresnitz (eds) *Handbook of stress: theoretical and clinical aspects*. New York: Free Press. pp. 496–505.

Belle, D. (ed.) (1982b) *Lives in stress: women and depression*. Beverly Hills, CA: Sage.

Belle, D. (1983) 'The impact of poverty on social networks and support,' *Women and Health* 9: 89–103.

Berg, J.H. (1984) 'The development of friendship between roommates,' *Journal of Personality and Social Psychology* 46: 346–56.

Berg, J.H. and Clark, M.S. (1986) 'Social exchange and the decision to pursue close friendship,' in V.J. Derlega and B. Winstead (eds) *Friendship and social interaction*. New York: Springer-Verlag. pp. 101–28.

Berg, J.H. and McQuinn, R.D. (1986) 'Attraction and exchange in continuing and non-continuing dating relationships,' *Journal of Personality and Social Psychology* 50: 942–52.

Berg, J.H. and McQuinn, R.D. (1989) 'Loneliness and aspects of social support networks,' *Journal of Social and Personal Relationships* 6: 359–71.

Berg, J.H. and Peplau, L.A. (1982) 'Loneliness: the relationship of self-disclosure and androgyny,' *Personality and Social Psychology Bulletin* 8: 624–30.

Berg, J.H. and Piner, K.E. (1989) 'Social networks, social support, and loneliness,' unpublished manuscript, University of Mississippi.

Berger, C.R. (1988) 'Uncertainty and information exchange in developing relationships,' in S.W. Duck (ed.) *Handbook of personal relationships: theory, research and interventions*. New York: Wiley.

Berkman, L.F. and Syme, S.L. (1979) 'Social networks, host resistance and mortality: a nine year follow-up of Alameda County residents,' *American Journal of Epidemiology* 109: 186–204.

Berkowitz, A. and Perkins, H.W. (1984) 'Stress among farm women: work and family as interacting systems,' *Journal of Marriage and the Family* 46: 161–5.

Berkowitz, A. and Perkins, H.W. (1988) 'Personality characteristics of children of alcoholics,' *Journal of Consulting and Clinical Psychology* 56: 206–9.

Bernstein, B. (1975) *Class, codes, and control: theoretical studies toward a sociology of language* (rev. edn). New York: Schoken Books.

Billings, A.G. and Moos, R.H. (1984) 'Coping, stress and social resources among

adults with unipolar depression,' *Journal of Personality and Social Psychology* 46: 877–91.

Billings, A.G., Cronkite, R.C., and Moos, R.H. (1983) 'Social-environmental factors in unipolar depression: comparisons of depressed patients and nondepressed controls,' *Journal of Abnormal Psychology* 92: 119–33.

Blazer, D.G. (1982) 'Social support and mortality in an elderly community population,' *American Journal of Epidemiology* 115: 685–94.

Blumstein, P. and Kollock, P. (1988) 'Personal relationships,' *Annual Review of Sociology* 14: 467–90.

Bochner, A.P. (1984) 'The functions of human communication in interpersonal bonding,' in C. Arnold and J. Bowers (eds) *Handbook of rhetorical and communication theory*. Boston: Allyn & Bacon. pp. 544–621.

Bolger, N., DeLongis, A., Kessler, R.C., and Wethington, E. (1989) 'The contagion of stress across multiple roles,' *Journal of Marriage and the Family* 51: 175–83.

Bolton, W. and Oatley, K. (1987) 'A longitudinal study of social support and depression in unemployed men,' *Psychological Medicine* 17: 453–60.

Borys, S. and Perlman, D. (1985) 'Gender differences in loneliness,' *Personality and Social Psychology Bulletin* 11: 63–74.

Brand, S. and Hirsch, B.J. (1989) 'Social networks and the well-being of working women: contextual variation across work shift schedules and stages of the family life cycle,' unpublished manuscript.

Brand, S., Brand, J.F., and Rowland, K. (1989) 'Shiftwork and well-being: the moderating role of dimensions of the work environment,' unpublished manuscript.

Brennan, T. and Auslander, N. (1979) *Adolescent loneliness: an exploratory study of social and psychological predispositions and theory* (Vol. 1). Boulder, CO: Behavioral Institute.

Brickman, P., Kidder, L.H., Coates, D., Rabinowitz, V., Cohn, E., and Karuza, J. (1983) 'The dilemmas of helping: making aid fair and effective,' in J.D. Fisher, A. Nadler, and B.M. DePaulo (eds) *New directions in helping*, Vol. 1. New York: Academic Press. pp. 17–49.

Brickman, P., Rabinowitz, V.C., Karuza, J., Coates, D., Cohn, E., and Kidder, L. (1982) 'Models of helping and coping,' *American Psychologist* 37: 368–84.

Brody, E. (1981) 'Women in the middle and family help to older people,' *The Gerontologist* 21: 471–80.

Brody, E.M. (1985) 'Parent care as a normative family stress,' *The Gerontologist* 25: 19–29.

Bronfenbrenner, U. (1979) *The ecology of human development*. Cambridge, MA: Harvard University Press.

Brookings, J.B. and Bolton, B. (1988) 'Confirmatory factor analysis of the Interpersonal Support Evaluation List,' *American Journal of Community Psychology* 16: 137–47.

Brown, G. and Harris, T. (1978) *Social origins of depression: a study of psychiatric disorder in women*. New York: Free Press.

Brown, G.W., Bhrolchain, M., and Harris, T. (1975) 'Social class and psychiatric disturbance in an urban population,' *Sociology* 9: 225–54.

Bruhn, J.G. and Philips, B.U. (1984) 'Measuring social support: a synthesis of current approaches,' *Journal of Behavioral Medicine* 7: 151–69.

Burgoon, J.K., Parrott, R., Le Poire, B.A., Kelley, D.L., Walther, J.B., and Perry, D. (1989) 'Maintaining and restoring privacy through communication in different types of relationships,' *Journal of Social and Personal Relationships* 6: 131–57.

Burleson, B.R. (1982) 'The development of comforting communication skills in childhood and adolescence,' *Child Development* 53: 1578–88.

Burleson, B.R. (1984a) 'Age, social-cognitive development, and the use of comforting strategies,' *Communication Monographs* 51: 140–53.

Burleson, B.R. (1984b) 'Comforting communication,' in H.E. Sypher and J.L. Applegate (eds) *Communication by children and adults: social cognitive and strategic processes*. Beverly Hills, CA: Sage. pp. 63–104.

Burleson, B.R. (1985) 'The production of comforting messages: social-cognitive foundations,' *Journal of Language and Social Psychology* 4: 253–73.

Burleson, B.R. (1986) 'Communication skills and childhood peer relationships: an overview,' in M.L. McLaughlin (ed.) *Communication Yearbook*, vol. 9. Beverly Hills, CA: Sage. pp. 143–80.

Burleson, B.R. (1987) 'Cognitive complexity,' in J.C. McCroskey and J.A. Daly (eds) *Personality and interpersonal communication*. Newbury Park, CA: Sage. pp. 305–49.

Burleson, B.R. (in press) 'Comforting messages: features, functions, and outcomes,' in J.A. Daly and J.M. Wiemann (eds) *Communicating strategically: strategies in interpersonal communication*. Hillsdale, NJ: Erlbaum.

Burleson, B.R. and Samter, W. (1985a) 'Consistencies in theoretical and naive evaluations of comforting messages,' *Communication Monographs* 52: 103–23.

Burleson, B.R. and Samter, W. (1985b) 'Individual differences in the perception of comforting messages: an exploratory investigation,' *Central States Speech Journal* 36: 39–50.

Burleson, B.R. and Samter, W. (1988) 'Effects of cognitive complexity on the perceived importance of communication skills in friends,' paper presented at the International Communication Association convention, New Orleans, May.

Burleson, B.R. and Waltman, P.A. (1987) 'Popular, rejected, and supportive preadolescents: social-cognitive and communicative characteristics,' in M.L. McLaughlin (ed.) *Communication yearbook*, vol. 10. Newbury Park, CA: Sage. pp. 533–52.

Burleson, B.R., Applegate, J.L., and Delia, J.G. (1990) 'Effects of maternal communication on children's cognitive, communicative, and social competencies,' paper presented to Annual Convention of International Commnication Association, Dublin.

Burleson, B.R., Werking, K.J., Samter, W., and Holloway, R. (1988) 'Person-centered communication and friendship in young adults: which skills matter most?,' paper presented at the Speech Communication Association convention, New Orleans, November.

Burleson, B.R., Applegate, J.L., Burke, J.A., Clark, R.A., Delia, J.G., and Kline, S.L. (1986) 'Communicative correlates of peer acceptance in childhood,' *Communication Education* 35: 349–61.

Burnett, R. (1986) 'Conceptualisation of personal relationships', unpublished D.Phil. thesis, Oxford University.

Burt, R.S. (1980) 'Models of network structure,' *Annual Review of Sociology* 6: 79–141.

Cacioppo, J.T. and Petty, R.E. (1983) 'Social psychological procedures for cognitive response assessment: the thought-listing technique,' in T.V. Merluzzi, C.R. Glass, and M. Genest (eds) *Cognitive assessment*. New York: Guilford. pp. 309–42.

Cancian, F.M. (1987) *Love in America*. Cambridge: Cambridge University Press.

Caplan, R.D. (1976) 'Social-psychological dynamics in shift work,' in P.G. Rentos and R.D. Shepard (eds) *Shift work and health*. Washington, DC: National Institute for Occupational Safety and Health. pp. 198–210.

Carlson, M. and Miller, N. (1987) 'Explanation of the relation between negative mood and helping,' *Psychological Bulletin* 102: 91–108.

Carlson, M., Charlin, V. and Miller, N. (1988) 'Positive mood and helping behavior: a test of six hypotheses,' *Journal of Personality and Social Psychology* 55: 211–27.

Carpentier, J. and Cazamian, P. (1977) *Night work*. Geneva: International Labor Organization.

Carver, C.S., Scheier, M.F. and Weintraub, J.K. (1989) 'Assessing coping strategies: a theoretically based approach,' *Journal of Personality and Social Psychology* 56: 267–83.

Cate, R.M. and Lloyd, S.A. (1988) 'Courtship,' in S.W. Duck (ed.) *Handbook of personal relationships*. New York: John Wiley.

Chesler, M.A. and Barbarin, O.A. (1984) 'Dilemmas of providing help in a crisis: the role of friends with parents with cancer,' *Journal of Social Issues* 41: 47–63.

Cialdini, R.B. and Kenrick, D.T. (1976) 'Altruism as hedonism: a social development perspective on the relationship of negative mood state and helping,' *Journal of Personality and Social Psychology* 34: 907–14.

Cicirelli, V.G. (1983) 'Personal strains and negative feelings in adult children's relationships with elderly parents,' *Journal of Academic Psychology Bulletin* 5: 31–6.

Clark, M.S. (1983) 'Some implications of close social bonds for help-seeking,' in J.D. Fisher, A. Nadler, and B.M. DePaulo (eds) *New directions in helping, Vol. 1: Recipients' reaction to aid*. New York: Praeger. pp. 205–27.

Clark, M.S. and Mills, J. (1979) 'Interpersonal attraction in exchange and communal relationships,' *Journal of Personality and Social Psychology* 37: 12–24.

Clark, M.S. and Reis, H.T. (1988) 'Interpersonal processes in close relationships,' *Annual Review of Psychology* 39: 609–72.

Clark, M.S., Miller, J. and Powell, M.E. (1986) 'Keeping track of needs in communal and exchange relationship,' *Journal of Personality and Social Psychology* 51: 333–8.

Clark, M.S., Ouellette, R., Powell, M.C. and Milberg, S. (1987) 'Recipient's mood, relationship type, and helping,' *Journal of Personality and Social Psychology* 53: 94–103.

Clark, N.M. and Rakowski, W. (1983) 'Family caregivers of older adults: improving helping skills,' *The Gerontologist* 23: 637–42.

Clausen, J.A. (1986) *The life course*. Englewood Cliffs, NJ: Prentice-Hall.

Coates, D., Wortman, C.B., and Abbey, A. (1979) 'Reactions to victims,' in I.H. Frieze, D. Bartal, and J.S. Carroll (eds) *New approaches to social problems*. San Francisco: Jossey-Bass.

Cobb, S. (1976) 'Social support as a moderator of life stress,' *Psychosomatic Medicine* 38: 300–14.

Cohen, J. and Cohen, P. (1975) *Applied multiple regression/correlation analysis for the behavioral sciences*. New York: Lawrence Erlbaum Associates.

Cohen, S. and Hoberman, H. (1983) 'Positive events and social support as buffers of life change stress,' *Journal of Applied Social Psychology* 13: 99–125.

Cohen, S. and McKay, G. (1984) 'Social support, stress and the buffering hypothesis: a theoretical analysis,' in A. Baum, J.E. Singer, and S.E. Taylor (eds) *Handbook of psychology and health*, Vol. 4. Hillsdale: LEA. pp. 253–67.

Cohen, S. and Syme, S.L. (1985) 'Issues in the study and application of social support,' in S. Cohen and S.L. Syme (eds) *Social support and health*. Orlando: Academic Press. pp. 3–22.

Cohen, S. and Wills, T.A. (1985) 'Stress, social support, and the buffering hypothesis,' *Psychological Bulletin* 98: 310–57.

Cohen, S., Mermelstein, R., Kamarck, T., and Hoberman, H.N. (1985) 'Measuring the functional components of social support,' in I. Sarason and B. Sarason (eds) *Social support: theory, research and applications*. Dordrecht, The Netherlands: Martinus Nijhoff. pp. 73–94.

Constable, J.F. and Russell, D. (1986) 'The effect of social support and the work environment upon burnout among nurses,' *Journal of Human Stress* 12: 20–6.

Corty, E. and Young, R.D. (1980) 'Social contact and loneliness in a University population,' paper presented at the meeting of the Midwestern Psychological Association.

Costanza, R.S., Derlega, V.J., and Winstead, B.A. (1988) 'Positive and negative forms of social support: effects of conversational topics on coping with stress among same-sex friends,' *Journal of Experimental Social Psychology* 24: 182–93.

Cowen, E. (1982) 'Help is where you find it,' *American Psychologist* 37: 385–95.

Coyne, J.C. (1976a) 'Depression and the response of others,' *Journal of Abnormal Psychology* 85: 186–93.

Coyne, J.C. (1976b) 'Toward an interactional description of depression,' *Psychiatry* 39: 28–40.

Coyne, J.C. and DeLongis, A. (1986) 'Going beyond social support: the role of social relationships in adaptation,' *Journal of Consulting and Clinical Psychology* 54: 454–60.

Coyne, J.C., Ellard, J.H., and Smith, D.A.F. (in press) 'Social support, interdependence, and the dilemmas of helping,' in B.R. Sarason, I.G. Sarason, and G.R. Pierce (eds) *Social support: an interactional view*. New York: Wiley.

Coyne, J.C., Wortman, C.B., and Lehman, D.R. (1988) 'The other side of social support: emotional over-involvement and miscarried helping,' in B.H. Gottlieb (ed.) *Marshalling social support: formats, processes and effects*. Newbury Park, CA: Sage. pp. 305–30.

Coyne, J.C., Kessler, R.C., Tal, M., Turnbull, J., Wortman, C.B., and Greden, J.F. (1987) 'Living with a depressed person,' *Journal of Consulting and Clinical Psychology* 55: 347–52.

Cozby, P.C. (1973) 'Self-disclosure: a literature review,' *Psychological Bulletin* 79: 73–91.

Cunningham, M.R. (1979) 'Weather, mood and helping behavior: quasi-experiments with the sunshine samaritan,' *Journal of Personality and Social Psychology* 37: 1947–56.

Cunningham, M.R. (1986) 'Levites and brother's keepers: sociobiological perspectives on altruistic behavior,' *Humboldt Journal of Social Relations* 13: 35–67.

Cunningham, M.R. (1988a) 'What do you do when you're happy or blue?: mood, expectancies and behavioral interest,' *Motivation and Emotion* 12: 309–31.

Cunningham, M.R. (1988b) 'Does happiness mean friendliness? The effects of mood and self-esteem on social interaction and self-disclosure,' *Personality and Social Psychology Bulletin* 14: 283–97.

Cunningham, M.R. and Barbee, A.P. (1987) 'Personal mood, social news events and decision-making about money,' paper presented at the annual convention of the American Psychological Association, New York, August.

Cunningham, M.R., Steinberg, J., and Grev, R. (1980) 'Wanting to and having to help: separate motivations for positive mood and guilt-induced helping,' *Journal of Personality and Social Psychology* 38: 181–92.

Cunningham, M.R., Shaffer, D.R., Barbee, A.P., Wolff, P., and Kelly, D. (1990) 'Separate processes in the relation of elation and depression to helping: social versus personal concerns,' *Journal of Experimental Social Psychology* 26: 13–33.

Cutrona, C.E. (1982) 'Transition to college: loneliness and the process of social adjustment,' in L.A. Peplau and D. Perlman (eds) *Loneliness: a sourcebook of current theory, research and therapy.* New York: Wiley. pp. 291–301.

Cutrona, C.E. (1984) 'Social support in the transition to parenthood,' *Journal of Abnormal Psychology* 93: 378–90.

Cutrona, C.E. (1986a) 'Objective determinants of perceived social support,' *Journal of Personality and Social Psychology* 50: 349–55.

Cutrona, C.E. (1986b) 'Behavioral manifestations of social support: a microanalytic investigation,' *Journal of Personality and Social Psychology* 51: 201–8.

Cutrona, C.E. and Russell, D.W. (1987) 'The provisions of social relationships and adaptation to stress,' in W.H. Jones and D. Perlman (eds) *Advances in personal relationships*, Vol. 1. Greenwich, CT: JAI Press. pp. 37–67.

Dant, T. (1988) 'Dependency and old age: theoretical accounts and practical understandings,' *Aging and Society* 8: 171–88.

Davis, K.E. and Todd, M.J. (1985) 'Assessing friendship: prototypes, paradigm cases, and relationship description,' in S.W. Duck and D. Perlman (eds) *Understanding personal relationships: an interdisciplinary approach.* London: Sage. pp. 17–38.

Deaux, K. (1976) *The behavior of women and men.* Belmont, CA: Brooks/Cole.

Delia, J.G., Burleson, B.R., and Kline, S.L. (1979) 'Person-centered parental communication and the development of social-cognitive and communicative abilities: a preliminary longitudinal analysis,' paper presented at the Central States Speech Association convention, St Louis, April.

DeLongis, A., Coyne, J.C., Dakof, G., Folkman, S., and Lazarus, R.S. (1982) 'Relation of daily hassles, uplifts, and major life events to health status,' *Health Psychology* 1: 119–36.

DePaulo, B.M. (1978) 'Accuracy in predicting situational variation in helpseekers' responses,' *Personality and Social Psychology Bulletin* 4: 330–3.

DePaulo, B.M. (1982) 'Social-psychological processes in informal help seeking,' in T.A. Wills (ed.) *Basic processes in helping relationships.* New York: Academic Press. pp. 255–79.

Derlega, V.J. and Margulis, S.T. (1982) 'Why loneliness occurs: the interrelationship of social-psychological and privacy concepts,' in L.A. Peplau and D. Perlman (eds) *Loneliness: a sourcebook of theory, research, and therapy.* New York: Wiley. pp. 152–65.

DiMatteo, M.R. and Hays, R. (1981) 'Social support and serious illness,' in B.H. Gottlieb (ed.) *Social networks and social support.* Newbury Park, CA: Sage. pp. 117–48.

Domhoff, G.W. (1970) *The higher circles: the governing class in America.* New York: Random House.

Dovodio, J.F. and Gaertner, S.L. (1983) 'Race, normative structure, and help-seeking', in B.M. DePaulo, A. Nadler, and J.D. Fisher (eds) *New directions in help-seeking: help seeking*, Vol. 2. New York: Academic Press, pp. 285–302.

Dressler, W.W. (1985) 'Extended family relationships, social support, and mental health in a southern black community,' *Journal of Health and Social Behavior* 26: 39–48.

Duck, S.W. (1982) 'A topography of relationship disengagement and dissolution,' in S.W. Duck (ed.) *Personal relationships 4: Dissolving personal relationships.* London: Academic Press.

Duck, S.W. (1984) 'A perspective on the repair of personal relationships: repair of what, when?,' in S.W. Duck (ed.) *Personal relationships 5: Repairing personal relationships.* London: Academic Press.

Duck, S.W. (1985) 'How to lose friends without influencing people,' in M.E. Roloff and G.R. Miller (eds) *Interpersonal processes: new directions in communication research.* Newbury Park, CA: Sage.

Duck, S.W. (1986) *Human relationships.* London: Sage.

Duck, S.W. (1988) *Relating to others.* Chicago: The Dorsey Press.

Duck, S.W. and Perlman, D. (1985) 'The thousand islands of personal relationships: a prescriptive analysis,' in S.W. Duck and D. Perlman (eds) *Understanding personal relationships research: an interdisciplinary approach.* London: Sage.

Duck, S.W. and Pond, K. (1989) 'Friends, Romans, Countrymen, lend me your retrospective data: rhetoric and reality in personal relationships,' in C. Hendrick (ed.) *Review of personality and social psychology, Vol. 10: Close relationships.* Newbury Park, CA: Sage.

Duck, S.W. and Rutt, D. (1989) 'The experience of everyday relational communications: are all communications created equal?,' paper to Annual Convention of Speech Communication Association, New Orleans, November.

Duck, S.W. and Sants, H.K.A. (1983) 'On the origins of the specious: are interpersonal relationships really interpersonal states?,' *Journal of Social and Clinical Psychology* 1: 27–41.

Duck, S.W., Pond, K., and Leatham, G. (in preparation) 'The eye of the beholder revisited: insider and outsider view of relational events,' manuscript in preparation.

Duck, S.W., Cortez, C.A., Hoy, M., and Strejc, H. (1989) 'Recalled parameters of successful and unsuccessful first dates as a function of loneliness,' paper to Annual Convention of Speech Communication Association, New Orleans, November.

Dunham, R.B. (1977) 'Shift work: a review and theoretical analysis,' *Academy of Management Review* 2: 624–34.

Dunkel-Schetter, C. (1984) 'Social support and cancer: findings based on patient interviews and their implications,' *Journal of Social Issues* 40 (4): 77–98.

Dunkel-Schetter, C. and Wortman, C.B. (1981) 'Dilemmas of social support: parallels between victimization and aging,' in S.B. Kiesler, J.N. Morgan, and V.K. Oppenheimer (eds) *Aging: social change.* New York: Academic Press.

Dunkel-Schetter, C. and Wortman, C.B. (1982) 'The interpersonal dynamics of cancer: problems in social relationships and their impact on the patient,' in H.S. Friedman and M.R. DiMatteo (eds) *Interpersonal issues in health care.* New York: Academic Press. pp. 69–100.

Dunkel-Schetter, C., Folkman, S., and Lazarus, R.S. (1987) 'Social support received in stressful situations,' *Journal of Personality and Social Psychology* 53: 71–80.

Dunn, J. (1988) 'Relations among relationships,' in S.W. Duck (ed.) *Handbook of personal relationships.* Chichester: Wiley. pp. 193–210.

Dunst, C.J., Trivette, C.M., and Cross, A.H. (1986) 'Mediating influences of social

support: personal, family and child outcomes,' *American Journal of Mental Deficiencies* 90: 403–17.

Eagly, A.H. and Crowley, M. (1986) 'Gender and helping behavior: a meta-analytic review of the social psychological literature,' *Psychological Bulletin* 100: 284–308.

Eckenrode, J. (1983) 'The mobilization of social supports: some individual constraints,' *American Journal of Community Psychology* 11: 509–28.

Eckenrode, J. (1984) 'Impact of chronic and acute stressors on daily reports of mood,' *Journal of Personality and Social Psychology* 46: 907–18.

Eckenrode, J. and Gore, S. (1981) 'Stressful life events and social supports: the significance of context,' in B. Gottlieb (ed.) *Social networks and social support.* Beverly Hills, CA: Sage. pp. 43–68.

Ell, K. (1984) 'Social networks, social support and health status: a review,' *Social Science Review* 58: 133–49.

Elliott, R. (1985) 'Helpful and nonhelpful events in brief counseling interviews: an empirical taxonomy,' *Journal of Counseling Psychology* 32: 307–22.

Eysenck, H.J. (1981) *A model for personality.* Berlin: Springer-Verlag.

Fiore, J., Becker, J., and Coppel, D.B. (1983) 'Social network interactions: a buffer or a stress?,' *American Journal of Community Psychology* 11: 423–39.

Fisher, G.A. and Tessler, R.C. (1986) 'Family bonding of the mentally ill: an analysis of family visits with residents of board and care homes,' *Journal of Health and Social Behavior* 27: 236–49.

Fisher, J.D., Nadler, A., and Whitcher-Alagna, S. (1982) 'Recipient reactions to aid,' *Psychological Bulletin* 91: 27–54.

Fisher, J.D., Goff, B., Nadler, A., and Chinsky, J.M. (1988) 'Social psychological influences on help-seeking and support from peers,' in B. Gottlieb (ed.) *Marshalling social support: formats, processes, and effects.* Beverly Hills, CA: Sage. pp. 267–304.

Fitzpatrick, M.A. (1988) *Between husbands and wives: communication in marriage.* Beverly Hills, CA: Sage.

Fitzpatrick, M.A., Fallis, S., and Vance, L. (1982) 'Multifunctional coding of conflict resolution strategies in marital dyads,' *Family Relations* 31: 61–70.

Flaherty, J.A. and Richman, J.A. (1986) 'Effects of childhood relationships on the adult's capacity to form social supports,' *American Journal of Psychiatry* 143: 851–5.

Folkman, S. and Lazarus, R.S. (1985) 'If it changes it must be a process: a study of emotion and coping during three stages of a college examination,' *Journal of Personality and Social Psychology* 48: 150–70.

Folkman, S., Lazarus, R.S., Gruen, R.J., and DeLongis, A. (1986) 'Appraisal, coping, health status and psychological symptoms,' *Journal of Personality and Social Psychology* 50: 571–9.

Franzoi, S.L. and Davis, M.H. (1985) 'Adolescent self-disclosure and loneliness: private self-consciousness and parental influences,' *Journal of Personality and Social Psychology* 48: 768–80.

Freeman, L. (1988) 'Computer programs and social network analysis,' *Connections* 11: 26–31.

Frost, P.J. and Jamal, M. (1979) 'Shift work, attitudes, and reported behavior: some associations between individual characteristics and hours of work and leisure,' *Journal of Applied Psychology* 64: 77–81.

Gadbois, C. (1980) 'Women on night shift: interdependence of sleep and off-the-job-activities,' in A. Reinberg, N. Vieux, and P. Andlauer (eds) *Night and shift work: biological and social aspects*. New York: Pergamon Press. pp. 223–7.

Gallagher, D.E. (1985) 'Intervention strategies to assist caregivers of frail elders: current research status and future research directions,' in C. Eisdorfer, M.P. Lawton, and G.L. Maddox (eds) *Annual review of gerontology and geriatrics*, Vol. 5. New York: Springer.

Gergen, K.J. and Gergen, M.M. (1983) 'Social constructions of helping relationships,' in J.D. Fisher, A. Nadler, and B.M. DePaulo (eds) *New directions in helping, Vol. 1: Recipients reaction to aid*. New York: Praeger. pp. 143–63.

Gerstel, N. (1988) 'Divorce and kin ties: the importance of gender,' *Journal of Marriage and the Family* 50: 209–19.

Gibson, L., Cunningham, M.R., and Barbee, A.P. (1990) 'Athletic coaches' pep-talk strategies,' paper presented to the American Psychological Association, Boston, MA, August.

Gilbert, L.A., Holohan, C.K., and Manning, L. (1981) 'Coping with conflict between professional and maternal roles,' *Family Relations* 30: 419–26.

Giles, H. (1989) 'Gosh you don't look it: the discourse of intergenerational acquainting,' paper presented at the 2nd Iowa Conference on Personal Relationships, Iowa City, Iowa.

Gimbert, M., Barberger-Gateau, J.C. and Galley, P. (1989) 'Evaluation of independence in elderly people: results of the Paquid Research Project (1989),' paper read at the XIV International Congress of Gerontology, Acapulco, Mexico, June.

Ginsburg, G.P. (1986) 'The structural analysis of primary relationships,' in R. Gilmour and S.W. Duck (eds) *The emerging field of personal relationships*. Hillsdale, NJ: Erlbaum. pp. 41–62.

Glidewell, J.C., Tucker, S., Todt, M., and Cox, S. (1982) 'Professional support systems – the teaching profession,' in A. Nadler, J.D. Fisher, and B.M. DePaulo (eds) *New directions in helping 3: Applied research in help-seeking and reactions to aid*. New York: Academic Press.

Goldberg, J.G. (ed.) (1981) *Psychotherapeutic treatment of cancer patients*. New York: Academic Press.

Goldenberg, S. (1987) *Thinking sociologically*. Belmont, CA: Wadsworth.

Goldfarb, A. (1969) 'The psychodynamics of dependency and the search for aid,' in R. Kalish (ed.) *The dependencies of old people*. University of Michigan, Institute of Gerontology.

Goldsmith, D. (1988) 'To talk or not to talk: the flow of information between romantic dyads and members of their communication networks.' Unpublished master's thesis, University of Washington, Seattle, Washington.

Gore, S. (1979) 'Does help-seeking increase psychological distress?,' *Journal of Health and Social Behavior* 20: 201–2.

Gore, S. (1985) 'Social support and styles of coping with stress,' in S. Cohen and L. Syme (eds) *Social support and health*. New York: Academic Press. pp. 263–78.

Gottlieb, B.H. (1978) 'The development and application of a classification scheme of informal helping behaviors,' *Canadian Journal of Science* 10: 105–16.

Gottlieb, B.H. (1981) *Social networks and social support*. Beverly Hills, CA: Sage.

Gottlieb, B.H. (1983) *Social support strategies: guidelines for mental health practice*. London: Sage.

Gottlieb, B.H. (1985) 'Social support and the study of personal relationships,' *Journal of Social and Personal Relationships* 2: 351–75

Gottlieb, B.H. (1987) *Marshalling social support: formats, processes, and effects*. Beverly Hills, CA: Sage.

Gottlieb, B.H. (1988) 'Support interventions: a typology and agenda for research,' in S.W. Duck (ed) *Handbook of Personal Relationships*. Wiley: Chichester.

Gottlieb, B.H. (1990) 'The contingent nature of social support,' in J. Eckenrode (ed.) *Social context of stress*. New York: Plenum.

Gottlieb, B.H. and Pancer, S.M. (1988) 'Social networks and the transition to parenthood,' in G.Y. Michaels and W.A. Goldberg (eds) *The transition to parenthood*. New York: Cambridge University Press.

Gottman, J.M. (1979) *Marital interaction: experimental investigations*. New York: Academic Press.

Gottman, J.M. and Levenson, R.W. (1985) 'A valid procedure for obtaining self-report of affect in marital interaction,' *Journal of Consulting and Clinical Psychology* 53: 151–60.

Gouaux, C. (1971) 'Induced affective states and interpersonal attraction,' *Journal of Personality and Social Psychology* 20: 37–43.

Gourash, N. (1978) 'Help-seeking: a review of the literature,' *American Journal of Community Psychology* 6: 413–23.

Gove, W.R. and Tudor, J.F. (1973) 'Adult sex roles and mental illness,' *American Journal of Sociology* 78: 812–35.

Gove, W.R., Hughes, M., and Style, C.B. (1983) 'Does marriage have positive effects on the psychological well-being of the individual?,' *Journal of Health and Social Behavior* 24: 122–31.

Granovetter, M.S. (1973) 'The strength of weak ties,' *American Journal of Sociology* 78: 1360–80.

Granovetter, M.S. (1982) 'The strength of weak ties: a network theory revisited,' in P.V. Marsden and N. Lin (eds) *Social structure and network analysis*. Newbury Park, CA: Sage. pp. 105–30.

Grant, I. (1985) 'The social environment and neurological disease,' *Advances in Psychosomatic Medicine* 13: 26–48.

Greenberg, J. and Pyszczynski, T. (1986) 'Persistent high self-focus after failure and low self-focus after success: the depressive self-focusing style,' *Journal of Personality and Social Psychology* 50: 1039–44.

Gross, A.E. and McMullen, P.A. (1983) 'Models of the help-seeking process' in B.M. DePaulo, A. Nadler, and J.D. Fisher (eds) *New directions in helping*, Vol 2. New York: Academic Press. pp. 47–70.

Gross, A.E., Wallston, B.S., and Piliavin, I. (1979) 'Reactance, attribution, equity, and the help recipient,' *Journal of Applied Social Psychology* 9: 297–313.

Hakkinen, S. (1980) 'Adaptability to shiftwork,' *Studia Laboris et Salutis* 4: 68–80.

Hall, A. and Wellman, B. (1985) 'Social networks and social support,' in S. Cohen and S.L. Syme (eds) *Social support and health*. New York: Academic Press.

Hammer, M. (1983) '"Core" and "extended" social networks in relation to health and illness,' *Social Science and Medicine* 17: 405–11.

Hansell, S. (1985) 'Adolescent friendship networks and distress in school,' *Social forces* 63: 698–715.

Hart, C.H., Ladd, G.W., and Burleson, B.R. (in press) 'Children's expectations of the outcomes of social strategies: relationships with sociometric status and maternal disciplinary styles,' *Child Development*.

Hauser, G.A. (1988) *Introduction to rhetorical theory*. Harper & Row: New York.

Haw, M. (1982) 'Women, work, and stress: a review and agenda for the future,' *Journal of Health and Social Behavior*, 23: 132–44.

Hays, R.B. (1984) 'The development and maintenance of friendship,' *Journal of Social and Personal Relationships* 1: 75–97.

Hays, R.B. (1985) 'A longitudinal study of friendship development,' *Journal of Personality and Social Psychology* 48: 909–24.

Hays, R.B. (1988) 'Friendship,' in S.W. Duck (ed.) *Handbook of personal relationships*. New York: John Wiley.

Hays, R.B. (1989) 'The day-to-day functioning of close versus casual friendships,' *Journal of Social and Personal Relationships* 6: 21–37.

Hays, R.B. and Oxley, D. (1986) 'Social network development and functioning during a life transition,' *Journal of Personality and Social Psychology* 50: 305–13.

Hazan, C. and Shaver, P. (1987) 'Romantic love conceptualized as an attachment process,' *Journal of Personality and Social Psychology* 52: 511–24.

Heitzmann, C.A. and Kaplan, R.M. (1988) 'Assessment of methods for measuring social support,' *Health Psychology* 7: 75–109.

Heller, K. (1989) 'The structure of supportive ties among the elderly,' paper to the Second Iowa Conference on Personal Relationships, Iowa City, May.

Heller, K. and Lakey, B. (1985) 'Perceived support and social interactions among friends and confidants,' in I.G. Sarason and B.R. Sarason (eds) *Social support: theory, research, and applications*. The Hague: Martinus Nijhoff, pp. 287–300.

Heller, K. and Swindle, R.W. (1983) 'Social networks, perceived support, and coping with stress,' in R.D. Felner, L.A. Jason, N. Moritsugu, and S.S. Farber (eds) *Preventive psychology: theory, research, and practice*. New York: Pergamon. pp. 87–103.

Heller, K., Price, R.H., and Hogg, J.R. (in press) 'The role of social support in community and clinical intervention,' in B.R. Sarason, I.G. Sarason, and G.R. Pierce (eds) *Social support: an interactional view*. New York: Wiley.

Henderson, S. (1974) 'Care-eliciting behavior in man,' *Journal of Nervous and Mental Disease* 159 (3): 172–81.

Henderson, S., Duncan-Jones, P., Byrne, D.G., and Scott, R. (1980) 'Measuring social relationships: the Interview Schedule for Social Interactions,' *Psychological Medicine* 10: 723–34.

Hinde, R.A. (1979) *Towards understanding relationships*. Academic Press: London.

Hirsch, B.J. (1979) 'Psychological dimensions of social networks: a multimethod analysis,' *American Journal of Community Psychology* 7: 263–77.

Hirsch, B.J. (1980) 'Natural support systems and coping with major life changes,' *American Journal of Community Psychology* 8: 159–72.

Hirsch, B.J. (1981) 'Social networks and the coping process,' in B. Gottlieb (ed.) *Social networks and social support*. Beverly Hills, CA: Sage. pp. 149–70.

Hirsch, B.J. and Rapkin, B.D. (1986a) 'Multiple roles, social networks, and women's well-being,' *Journal of Personality and Social Psychology* 51: 1237–47.

Hirsch, B.J. and Rapkin, B.D. (1986b) 'Social networks and adult social identities: profiles and correlates of support and rejection,' *American Journal of Community Psychology* 14: 395–410.

Hirsch, B.J. and Reischl, T.M. (1985) 'Social networks and developmental psychopathology: a comparison of adolescent children of a depressed, arthritic, or normal parent,' *Journal of Abnormal Psychology* 94: 272–81.

Hirsch, B.J., Engel-Levy, A., DuBois, D., and Hardesty, P. (in press) 'The role of

social environments in social support,' in B. Sarason, I. Sarason, and G. Pierce (eds) *Social support: an interactional view*. New York: Wiley.

Hobfoll, S.E. and London, P. (1986) 'The relationship of self-concept and social support to emotional distress among women during war,' *Journal of Social and Clinical Psychology* 4: 189–203.

Hobfoll, S.E. and Stokes, J.P. (1988) 'The process and mechanics of social support,' in S.W. Duck (ed.) *Handbook of personal relationships*. New York: John Wiley.

Hobfoll, S.E., Nadler, A., and Leiberman, J. (1986) 'Satisfaction with social support during crisis: intimacy and self-esteem as critical determinants,' *Journal of Personality and Social Psychology* 51: 296–304.

Hochschild, A. (1989) *The second shift: working parents and the revolution at home*. New York: Viking.

Hokanson, J.E., Loewenstein, D.A., Hedeen, C., and Howes, M.J. (1986) 'Dysphoric college students and roommates: a study of social behaviors over a three-month period,' *Personality and Social Psychological Bulletin* 12: 311–24.

Holahan, C.J. and Moos, R.H. (1986) 'Personality, coping and family resources in stress resistance: a longitudinal analysis,' *Journal of Personality and Social Psychology* 51: 389–95.

Holohan, C. and Gilbert, L. (1979a) 'Interrole conflict for working women: career versus jobs,' *Journal of Applied Psychology* 64: 86–90.

Holohan, C. and Gilbert, L. (1979b) 'Conflict between major life roles: women and men in dual career couples,' *Human Relations* 32: 419–26.

Homel, R., Burns, A., and Goodnow, J. (1987) 'Parental social networks and child development,' *Journal of Social and Personal Relationships* 4: 159–77.

Hooyman, N.R. and Lustbader, W. (1986) *Taking care: supporting older people and their families*. New York: The Free Press.

Hopper, R., Knapp, M.L., and Scott, L. (1981) 'Couples' personal idioms: exploring intimate talk,' *Journal of Communication* 31: 23–33.

Horl, J. and Rosenmeyer, L. (1989) 'Help is not enough – toward a theory of assistance,' paper read at the XIV International Congress of Gerontology, Acapulco, Mexico.

Horowitz, A. (1985) 'Family caregiving to the frail elderly,' in C. Eisdorfer, M.P. Lawton, and G.L. Maddox (eds) *Annual review of gerontology and geriatrics*, Vol. 5. New York: Springer.

House, J.S. (1981) *Work stress and social support*. Reading, MA: Addison Wesley.

House, J.S. and Kahn, R.L. (1985) 'Measures and concepts of social support,' in S. Cohen and L. Syme (eds) *Social support and health*. New York: Academic Press. pp. 83–108.

House, J.S., Umberson, D., and Landis, K.R. (1988) 'Structures and processes of social support,' *Annual review of sociology* 14: 293–318.

Howes, J.S., Hokanson, J.E. and Loewenstein, D.A. (1985) 'Induction of depressive affect after prolonged exposure to a mildly depressed individual,' *Journal of Personality and Social Psychology* 49: 1110–13.

Howes, M.J. and Hokanson, J.E. (1979) 'Conversational and social responses to depressive interpersonal behavior,' *Journal of Abnormal Psychology* 88: 625–34.

Huston, T.L. and Levinger, G. (1978) 'Interpersonal attraction and relationships,' *Annual Review of Psychology* 29: 115–56.

Iannotti, R.J. (1981) 'Prosocial behavior, perspective taking, and empathy in preschool children: an evaluation of naturalistic and structured settings,' paper pres-

ented at the biennial meeting of the Society for Research in Child Development, Boston, April.

Ierodiakonou, C.S. (1988) 'Adolescents' mental health and the Greek family: preventive aspects,' *Journal of Adolescence* 11: 11–19.

Ingersoll-Dayton, B. and Antonucci, T.C. (1988) 'Reciprocal and nonreciprocal social support: contrasting sides of intimate relationships,' *Journal of Gerontology* 43: 565–73.

Isen, A.M. (1970) 'Success, failure, attention and reaction to others: the warm glow of success,' *Journal of Personality and Social Psychology* 15: 294–301.

Isen, A.M., Shalker, T., Clark, M. and Karp, L. (1978) 'Affect, accessibility of material in memory and behavior: a cognitive loop?,' *Journal of Personality and Social Psychology* 36: 1–12.

Israel, B.A. (1982) 'Social networks and health status: linking theory, research, and practice,' *Patient Counseling and Health Education* 4: 65–79.

Jacobson, D.E. (1986) 'Types and timing of social support,' *Journal of Health and Social Behavior* 27: 250–64.

Jamal, M. (1981) 'Shift work related to job attitudes, social participation and withdrawal behavior: a study of nurses and industrial workers,' *Personnel Psychology* 34: 535–47.

Jamal, M. and Jamal, S.M. (1982) 'Work and nonwork experiences of employees on fixed and rotating shifts: an empirical assessment,' *Journal of Vocational Behavior* 20: 282–93.

Jemmott, J.B., III and Magliore, K. (1988) 'Academic stress, social support, and secretory immunoglobin A,' *Journal of Personality and Social Psychology* 55: 803–10.

Johnson, C.L. and Catalano, D.J. (1983) 'A longitudinal study of family supports to impaired elderly,' *The Gerontologist* 23: 612–18.

Johnson, M.P. and Leslie, L. (1982) 'Involvement and network structure: a test of the dyadic withdrawal hypothesis,' *Social Psychology Quarterly* 45: 34–43.

Jones, W.H. (1981) 'Loneliness and social contact,' *Journal of Social Psychology* 113: 195–6.

Jones, W.H. (1985) 'The psychology of loneliness: some personality issues in the study of social support,' in I.G. Sarason and B.R. Sarason (eds) *Social support: theory, research, and applications.* The Hague: Martinus Nijhoff. pp. 223–40.

Jones, W.H. and Moore, T.L. (1987) 'Loneliness and social support,' *Journal of Social Behavior and Personality* 2: 145–56.

Jones, W.H., Freeman, J.E., and Goswick, R.A. (1981) 'The persistence of loneliness: self and other determinants,' *Journal of Personality* 49: 27–48.

Jones, W.H., Cavert, W., Snyder, R.L., and Bruce, T. (1985) 'Relational stress: an analysis of situations and events associated with loneliness,' in S.W. Duck and D. Perlman (eds) *Understanding personal relationships: an interdisciplinary approach.* London and Beverly Hills, CA: Sage. pp. 193–220.

Jourard, S.M. (1964) *The transparent self.* New York: Van Nostrand.

Kahn, J., Coyne, J.C., and Margolin, G. (1985) 'Depression and marital disagreement: the social construction of despair,' *Journal of Social and Personal Relationships* 2: 447–61.

Kanner, A.D., Coyne, J.C., Schaefer, C., and Lazarus, R.S. (1981) 'Comparison

of two modes of stress measurement: daily hassles and uplifts versus major life events,' *Journal of Behavioral Medicine* 4: 1–39.

Kanter, R.M. (1977) *Men and women of the corporation*. New York: Basic Books.

Kelley, H.H. (1979) *Personal relationships: their structure and processes*. New York: John Wiley.

Kelley, H.H. (1983) 'Love and commitment,' in H.H. Kelley and a cast of thousands *Close relationships*. Freeman: San Francisco.

Kelley, H.H. (1987) 'Toward a taxonomy of interpersonal conflict processes,' in S. Oskamp and S. Spacapan (eds) *Interpersonal processes*. Newbury Park, CA: Sage. pp. 122–47.

Kelley, H.H., Berscheid, E., Christensen, A., Harvey, J.H., Huston, T.L., Levinger, G., McClintock, E.M., Peplau, L.A., and Petersen, D.R. (1983) *Close relationships*. New York: W.H. Freeman.

Kenny, D.A. (1986) 'Measuring interpersonal processes: characteristics of dyads and groups,' in W.D. Crano and M.B. Brewer (eds) *Principles and methods of social research*. Boston: Allyn & Bacon.

Kessler, R.C. and McLeod, J.D. (1984) 'Sex differences in vulnerability to undesirable life events,' *American Sociological Review* 49: 620–31.

Kessler, R.C. and McLeod, J.D. (1985) 'The costs of sharing,' in I.G. Sarason and B.R. Sarason (eds) *Social support theory, research and application*. The Hague: Martinus Nijhof.

Kessler, R.C. and McRae, J.A. (1982) 'The effects of wives' employment on the mental health of married men and women,' *American Sociological Review* 47: 216–27.

Kessler, R.C., Price, R.H., and Wortman, C.B. (1985) 'Social factors in psychopathology: stress, social support, and coping processes,' *Annual Review of Psychology* 36: 531–72.

Kleinefelter, D.S. (1984) 'Aging, autonomy, and the value of life,' *Journal of Applied Gerontology* 3: 7–19.

Knoke, D. and Kuklinski, J.H. (1982) *Network analysis*. Beverly Hills, CA: Sage.

Koller, M., Haider, M., Kundi, M., Cervinka, R., Katschnig, H., and Kufferle, B. (1980) 'Possible relations of irregular working hours to psychiatric psychosomatic disorders,' in A. Reinberg, N. Vieux, and P. Andlauer (eds) *Night and shift work: biological and social aspects*. New York: Pergamon Press. pp. 465–72.

Kurdek, L.A. and Krile, C. (1982) 'A developmental analysis of the relation between peer acceptance and both interpersonal understanding and perceived social self-competence,' *Child Development* 53: 1485–91.

La Fromboise, T.D. and Bigfoot, D.S. (1988) 'Cultural and cognitive considerations in the prevention of American Indian adolescent suicide,' *Journal of Adolescence* 11: 139–53.

La Gaipa, J.J. (1977a) 'Testing a multi-dimensional approach to friendship,' in S.W. Duck (ed.) *Theory and practice in interpersonal attraction*. New York and London: Academic Press. pp. 249–70.

La Gaipa, J.J. (1977b) 'Interpersonal attraction and social exchange,' in S.W. Duck (ed.) *Theory and practice in interpersonal attraction*. New York and London: Academic Press. pp. 129–64.

La Gaipa, J.J. (1981a) 'The meaning of friendship in old age,' paper presented at Canadian Psychological Association, Toronto, May.

La Gaipa, J.J. (1981b) 'A systems approach to personal relationships,' in S.W.

Duck and R. Gilmour (eds) *Personal relationships 1: studying personal relationships*. London and New York: Academic Press. pp. 67–89.

La Gaipa, J.J. (1982) 'Rules and rituals in disengaging from relationships,' in S.W. Duck (ed.) *Personal relationships 4: Dissolving personal relationships*. London: Academic Press. pp. 189–210.

La Gaipa, J.J. (1984) 'A comparative analysis of friendship and kinship in crisis situations,' paper presented at the Second International Conference on Personal Relationships, Madison, WI, July.

La Gaipa, J.J. (1986a) 'Changes in caregiving within the extended family: a systems approach,' paper presented at the Third International Conference on Personal Relationships, Herzlia, Israel, July.

La Gaipa, J.J. (1986b) 'Friendship and dependency in the elderly,' paper presented at the annual convention of Canadian Association on Gerontology, Quebec City, November.

La Gaipa, J.J. (1987) 'Friendship expectations,' in R. Burnett, P. McGhee, and D. Clarke (eds) *Accounting for relationships*. London and New York: Methuen.

La Gaipa, J.J. (1989) 'Dormitory nightlife and psychosexual privacy,' paper presented at the Second Iowa Conference on Personal Relationships, Iowa City, May.

La Gaipa, J.J. and Friesen, N. (1984) 'Burnout in the informal, social network of cancer patients,' paper presented at the Second International Conference on Personal Relationships, Madison, WI, July.

La Gaipa, J.J. and Klein, H. (1984) 'An experimental study of advice giving,' paper presented at the Canadian Psychological Association, Ottawa, June.

La Gaipa, J.J. and Malott, O. (1989) 'What to do with mother, dear?,' paper presented at the Second Iowa Conference on Personal Relationships, Iowa, City, June.

La Gaipa, J.J. and Wood, D. (1981) 'Friendship in disturbed adolescents,' in S.W. Duck and R. Gilmour (eds) *Personal relationships 3: Personal relationships in disorder*. New York and London: Academic Press.

Lazarus, R.S. and Cohen, J.B. (1977) 'Environmental stress,' in I. Altman and J. Wohlwill (eds) *Human behavior and environment*, Vol. 2. New York: Plenum Press. pp. 89–127.

Lazarus, R.S. and Folkman, S. (1984) *Stress, appraisal, and coping*. New York: Springer.

Le Fevre, P. (1981) 'The paradox of prayer,' *Journal of Chicago Theological Seminary Register* 11: 13–20.

Leatham, G. and Duck, S.W. (1990) 'Conversations with friends and the dynamics of social support,' in S.W. Duck (with R. Silver) (eds) *Personal relationships and social support*. London: Sage. pp. 1–27.

Leavy, R.L. (1983) 'Social support and psychological disorder: a review,' *Journal of Community Psychology* 11 (January): 3–21.

Lee, E. (1988) 'Cultural factors in working with Souteast Asian refugee adolescents,' *Journal of Adolescence* 11: 167–79.

Lehman, D.R., Ellard, J.H., and Wortman, C.B. (1986) 'Social support for the bereaved: recipients' and providers' perspectives on what is helpful,' *Journal of Consulting and Clinical Psychology* 54: 438–46.

Leslie, L.A., Johnson, M.P., and Huston, T.L. (1986) 'Parental reactions to dating relationships: do they make a difference?,' *Journal of Marriage and the Family* 48: 57–66.

Lewin, E. and Damrell, J. (1978) 'Female identity and career pathways: post-

baccalaureate nurses ten years after,' *Sociology of Work and Occupations* 5: 31–54.

Lewis, R.A. (1973) 'Social reaction and the formation of dyads: an interactionist approach to mate selection,' *Sociometry* 36: 409–18.

Lewis, R.A. (1978) 'Emotional intimacy among men,' *Journal of Social Issues* 34: 108–21.

Lewis, S.N.C. and Cooper, C.L. (1987) 'Stress in two-earner couples and stage in the family life cycle,' *Journal of Occupational Psychology* 60: 289–303.

Lieberman, M.A. (1982) 'The effects of social support on responses to stress,' in L. Goldberger and S. Breznits (eds) *Handbook of stress: theoretical and clinical aspects*. New York: Free Press.

Lieberman, M.A. (1986) 'Social supports – the consequences of psychologizing: a commentary,' *Journal of Consulting and Clinical Psychology* 54: 461–5.

Lin, N. (1986) 'Modeling the effects of social support,' in N. Lin, A. Dean, and W. Ensel (eds) *Social supports, life events, and depression*. Orlando: Academic Press. pp. 173–212.

Lindemann, E. (1965) 'Symptomatology and management of acute grief,' in H.J. Parad (ed.) *Crisis intervention: selected readings*. New York: Family Service Association of America. pp. 7–21.

McCall, G.J. (1982) 'Becoming unrelated,' in S.W. Duck (ed.) *Personal relationships 4: Dissolving personal relationships*. London: Academic Press. pp. 211–31.

McCall, G.J. (1988) 'The organizational life cycle of relationships,' in S.W. Duck (ed.) *Handbook of personal relationships*. Chichester: Wiley. pp. 467–84.

McCall, G.J. and Simmons, J.L. (1978) *Identities and interactions*. Free Press, New York.

McCannell, K. (1988) 'Social networks and the transition to motherhood,' in R.M. Milardo (ed.) *Families and social networks*. Newbury Park, CA: Sage. pp. 83–106.

McCoy, C.L. and Masters, J.C. (1985) 'The development of children's strategies for the social control of emotion,' *Child Development* 56: 1214–22.

McCrae, R.R. (1984) 'Situational determinants of coping responses: loss, threat and challenge,' *Journal of Personality and Social Psychology* 46: 919–28.

Mace, N. and Rabins, P. (1981) *The 36-hour day*. Baltimore, MD: Johns Hopkins Press.

McLeroy, K.R., DeVellis, R., DeVellis, B., Kaplan, B., and Toole, J. (1984) 'Social support and physical recovery in stroke population,' *Journal of Social and Personal Relationships* 1: 395–413.

McMullen, P.A. and Gross, A.E. (1983) 'Sex differences, sex roles, and health-related help-seeking,' in B.M. DePaulo, A. Nadler, and J.D. Fisher (eds) *New directions in helping*, Vol. 2. New York: Academic Press. pp. 233–63.

McReynolds, P. and DeVoge, S. (1978) 'Use of improvisational techniques in assessment,' in P. McReynolds (ed.) *Advances in psychological assessment*, Vol. 1. San Francisco: Jossey-Bass. pp. 222–77.

Maddison, D. and Raphael, B. (1972) 'Normal bereavement as an illness requiring care: psychopharmacological approaches,' *Journal of Thanatology* 2: 785–98.

Maddison, D. and Walker, W.L. (1967) 'Factors affecting the outcome of conjugal bereavement,' *British Journal of Psychiatry* 113: 1057–67.

Main, M., Kaplan, N., and Cassidy, J. (1985) 'Security in infancy, childhood, and adulthood: a move to the level of representation,' *Monographs of the Society for Research in Child Development* 50: 66–104.

Malkinson, R. (1987) 'Helping and being helped: the support paradox,' *Death Studies* 11: 205–19.

Mallinckrodt, B. and Fretz, B.R. (in press) 'Social support and the impact of job loss on older professionals,' *Journal of Counseling Psychology*.

Mankowski, E.S. (1989) 'The effects of early experience on social perception: a new measurement paradigm,' unpublished manuscript, University of Washington, Department of Psychology, Seattle.

Martin, E. and Martin, J.M. (1978) *The black extended family*. Chicago: University of Chicago Press.

Masters, J.C. and Furman, W. (1976) 'Effects of affect inductions on expectancies for serendipitous positive events, success on task performance and beliefs in internal or external control of reinforcement,' *Developmental Psychology* 12: 176–9.

Metts, S. (1989) 'An exploratory investigation of deception in close relationships,' *Journal of Social and Personal Relationships* 6: 159–80.

Meyer, J.P. and Mulherin, A. (1980) 'From attribution to helping: an analysis of the mediating effects of affect and expectancy,' *Journal of Personality and Social Psychology* 39: 201–10.

Miell, D.E. (1987) 'Remembering relationships development: constructing a context for interactions,' in R. Burnett, P. McGee, and D. Clarke (eds) *Accounting for relationships*. Methuen: London.

Milardo, R.M. (1982) 'Friendship networks in developing relationships: converging and diverging social environments,' *Social Psychology Quarterly* 45: 163–71.

Milardo, R.M. (ed.) (1988) *Families and social networks*. Newbury Park, CA: Sage.

Milardo, R.M. and Lewis, R.A. (1985) 'Social networks, families, and mate selection: a transactional analysis,' in L. L'Abate (ed.) *Handbook of family psychology and therapy*, Vol. 1. Homewood, IL: Dorsey Press. pp. 258–83.

Milardo, R.M., Johnson, M.P., and Huston, T.L. (1983) 'Developing close relationships: changing patterns of interaction between pair members and social networks,' *Journal of Personality and Social Psychology* 44: 964–76.

Miller, L.C., Berg, J.H., and Archer, R.L. (1983) 'Who becomes intimate with whom? Two personality variables that affect self-disclosure,' paper presented at the annual meeting of the American Psychological Association, Montreal, Canada.

Mills, J. and Clark, M.S. (1986) 'Communications that should lead to perceived exploitation in communal and exchange relationships,' *Journal of Social and Clinical Psychology* 4: 225–34.

Montgomery, B.M. (1988) 'Quality communication in personal relationships,' in S.W. Duck (ed.) *Handbook of personal relationships*. New York: John Wiley.

Moos, R.H. and Mitchell, R.E. (1982) 'Social network resources and adaptation: a conceptual framework,' in T.A. Wills (ed.) *Basic processes in helping relationships*. New York: Academic Press.

Morgan, D.L. (1986) 'Personal relationships as an interface between social networks and social cognitions,' *Journal of Social and Personal Relationships* 3: 403–22.

Morgan, D.L. (1988) *Focus groups as qualitative research*. Beverly Hills, CA: Sage.

Morgan, D.L. (1989a) 'Adjustment to widowhood: do social networks really help?,' *The Gerontologist* 29: 101–7.

Morgan, D.L. (1989b) 'Social support for families of patients with Alzheimer's: a final report to the AARP Andrus Foundation.' Portland, OR: Institute on Aging.

Morgan, J.N. (1981) 'Child care when parents are employed,' in S. Hill, D.H. Hill,

and J.N. Morgan (eds) *Five thousand American families: patterns of economic progress*, Vol. 9. Ann Arbor: University of Michigan, Institute for Social Research. pp. 441–56.

Morse, S.J. (1983) 'The nature of the help-related interchange as a determinant of person's attitude toward other,' in J.D. Fisher, A. Nadler, and B.M. DePaulo (eds) *New directions in helping, Vol. 1: Recipients reaction to aid*. New York: Praeger, pp. 305–22.

Murawski, B.J., Penman, P., and Schmitt, M. (1978) 'Social support in health and illness: the concept and its measurement,' *Cancer Nursing* 4 (October): 365–71.

Nadler, A. (1983) 'Personal characteristics and help-seeking,' in B.M. DePaulo, A. Nadler, and J.D. Fisher (eds) *New directions in helping*, Vol. 2. New York: Academic Press, pp. 303–40.

Neimeyer, G.J. and Neimeyer, R.A. (1985) 'Relational trajectories: a personal construct contribution,' *Journal of Social and Personal Relationships* 2: 325–50.

Nock, S.L. and Kingston, P.W. (1984) 'The family work day,' *Journal of Marriage and the Family* 46: 333–43.

Noller, P. and Venardos, C. (1986) 'Communication awareness in married couples,' *Journal of Social and Personal Relationships* 3: 31–42.

Norris, F.J. and Murrell, S.A. (1984) 'Protective functions of resources related to life events, global stress and depression in older adults,' *Journal of Health and Social Behavior* 25: 424–37.

Norton, R. (1983) *Communicator style: theory, applications, and measures*. Newbury Park, CA: Sage.

Notarius, C.I. and Herrick, L.R. (1988) 'Listener response strategies to a distressed other,' *Journal of Social and Personal Relationships* 5: 97–108.

O'Brien, J.E. (1984) 'Network analysis of mid-life transitions: a hypothesis on phases of change in microstructures,' in W.A. Peterson and J. Quadagno (eds) *Social bonds in later life*. Beverly Hills, CA: Sage.

O'Bryant, S.L. (1989) 'Older widows and independent lifestyles,' paper read at the XIV International Conference on Gerontology, Acapulco, Mexico, June.

O'Connor, P. and Brown, G.W. (1984) 'Supportive relationships: Fact or fancy?,' *Journal of Social and Personal Relationships* 1: 159–75.

O'Keefe, B.J. and Delia, J.G. (1982) 'Impression formation and message production,' in M. Roloff and C. Berger (eds) *Social cognition and communication*. Beverly Hills, CA: Sage. pp. 33–72.

O'Keefe, B.J. and McCornack, S.A. (1987) 'Message design logic and message goal structure: effects on perceptions of message quality in regulative communication situations,' *Human Communication Research* 14: 68–92.

O'Keefe, B.J. and Shepherd, G.J. (1987) 'The pursuit of multiple objectives in face-to-face persuasive interactions: effects of construct differentiation on message organization,' *Communication Monographs* 54: 396–419.

Ory, M.G., Williams, R.F., Emr, M., Lebowitz, B., Rabins, P., Salloway, J.C., Sluss-Radbough, T., Wolff, E., and Zarit, S. (1985) 'Families, informal supports, and Alzheimer's Disease: current research and future agendas,' *Research on Aging* 7: 623–44.

Pagel, M.D., Erdly, W.W., and Becker, J. (1987) 'Social networks: we get by with

(and in spite of) a little help from our friends,' *Journal of Personality and Social Psychology* 53: 793–804.

Parkes, C.M. and Weiss, R.S. (1983) *Recovery from bereavement*. New York: Basic Books.

Parks, M.R. (1982) 'Ideology in interpersonal communication: off the couch and into the world,' in M. Burgoon (ed.) *Communication yearbook 5*. Beverly Hills, CA: Sage. pp. 79–108.

Parks, M.R. (1985) 'Interpersonal communication and the quest for personal competence,' in M.L. Knapp and G.R. Miller (eds) *Handbook of interpersonal communication*. Newbury Park, CA: Sage. pp. 171–204.

Parks, M.R. and Eggert, L.L. (in press) 'The role of social context in the dynamics of personal relationships,' in W.H. Jones and D. Perlman (eds) *Advances in personal relationships*, Vol 2. Greenwich, CT: JAI Press.

Pearlin, L.I. (1983) 'Role strains and personal stress,' in H.B. Kaplan (ed.) *Psychosocial stress: trends in theory and research*. New York: Academic Press.

Pearlin, L.I. (1985) 'Social structure and processes of social support,' in S. Cohen and L. Syme (eds) *Social support and health*. New York: Academic Press. pp. 43–60.

Pearlin, L.I. and McCall, M.E. (1990) 'Occupational stress and marital support: a description of microprocesses,' in J. Eckenrode and S. Gore (eds) *Stress between work and family*. New York: Plenum.

Pearlin, L.I. and Schooler, C. (1978) 'The structure of coping,' *Journal of Health and Social Behavior* 19: 2–21.

Pennybaker, J.W. and O'Heeron, R.C. (1984) 'Confiding in others and illness rate among spouses of suicide and accidental death victims,' *Journal of Abnormal Psychology* 93: 473–83.

Peplau, L.A., Gerson, A.C., and Spinner, B.C. (1978) 'Loneliness among senior citizens: an empirical report,' *Essence* 2: 239–48.

Perlman, D. and Duck, S.W. (eds) (1987) *Intimate relationships*. Beverly Hills, CA: Sage.

Perlman, D. and Peplau, L.A. (1981) 'Toward a social psychology of loneliness,' in S.W. Duck and R. Gilmour (eds) *Personal relationships 3: Personal relationships in disorder*. London: Academic Press. pp. 31–56.

Perlman, D. and Rook, K.S. (1987) 'Social support, social deficits, and the family: toward the enhancement of well-being,' in S. Oskamp (ed.) *Family processes and problems: social psychological aspects*, Vol. 7. Beverly Hills, CA: Sage. pp. 17–44.

Pettit, G.S., Dodge, K.A., and Brown, M.M. (1988) 'Early family experience, social problem solving patterns, and children's social competence,' *Child Development* 59: 107–20.

Pierce, G.R., Sarason, B.R., and Sarason, I.G. (1989) 'Quality of relationships and social support: empirical and conceptual distinctions,' paper presented at the annual meeting of the American Psychological Association, New Orleans, LA.

Pierce, G.R., Sarason, B.R., and Sarason, I.G. (1990) 'Integrating social-support perspectives: working models, personal relationships, and situational factors,' in S.W. Duck (with R. Silver) (eds) *Personal relationships and social support*. London: Sage. pp. 173–89.

Pierce, G.R., Sarason, I.G., and Sarason, B.R. (1988) 'Quality of relationships and social support as personality characteristics,' paper presented at the annual meeting of the American Psychological Association, Atlanta, GA.

Pignatiello, M.F., Camp, C.J., and Rasar, L.A. (1986) 'Musical mood induction:

an alternative to the Velten technique,' *Journal of Abnormal Psychology*, 95: 295–7.

Pillemer, K. (1985) 'The dangers of dependency: new findings on domestic violence against the elderly,' *Social Problems* 33: 146–58.

Pleban, R. and Tesser, A. (1981) 'The effect of relevance and quality of another's performance on interpersonal closeness,' *Social Psychology Quarterly* 44: 178–285.

Pleck, J.H. (1977) 'The work-family role system,' *Social Problems* 24: 27–41.

Pleck, J.H. and Staines, G.L. (1985) 'Work schedules and family life in two-earner couples,' *Journal of Family Issues* 6: 68–82.

Pleck, J.H., Staines, G.L., and Lang, L. (1978) 'Work and family life: first reports on work-family interference and workers' formal child care arrangements,' Quality of Employment Survey (1977), Working Paper No. 11. Cambridge, MA: Wellesley College Center for Research on Women.

Presser, H.B. (1982) 'Working women and child care,' in P.W. Berman and E.R. Ramey (eds) *Women: a developmental perspective*. NIH Publication No. 82–2298. US Department of Health and Human Services. pp. 237–49.

Presser, H.B. (1984) 'Job characteristics of spouses and their work shifts,' *Demography* 21: 575–89.

Presser, H.B. (1986) 'Shift work among American women and child care,' *Journal of Marriage and the Family* 48: 551–63.

Presser, H.B. and Cain, V. (1983) 'Shift work among dual earner couples with children,' *Science* 219: 876–9.

Procidano, M.E. and Heller, K. (1983) 'Measures of perceived support from friends and from family: three validation studies,' *American Journal of Community Psychology* 11: 1–24.

Rahim, M.A. (1983) 'A measure of styles of handling interpersonal conflict,' *Academy of Management Journal* 26: 368–76.

Rands, M. (1988) 'Changes in social networks following divorce and separation,' in R.M. Milardo (ed.) *Families and social networks*. Newbury Park, CA: Sage. pp. 127–46.

Ratcliff, K.S. and Bogdan, J. (1988) 'Unemployed women: when 'social support' is not supportive,' *Social Problems* 35: 54–63.

Raush, H.L., Barry, W.A., Hertel, R.K., and Swain, M.A. (1974) *Communication, conflict, and marriage*. San Francisco: Jossey-Bass.

Reis, H.T. and Shaver, P. (1988) 'Intimacy as an interpersonal process,' in S.W. Duck (ed.) *Handbook of personal relationships*. Chichester: Wiley. pp. 367–90.

Reis, H.T., Wheeler, L., Kernis, M.H., Spiegel, N., and Nezlek, J. (1983) 'On the specificity of the impact of social participation on physical and psychological health.' Unpublished MS, University of Rochester, NY.

Reisman, J.M. and Yamokoski, T. (1974) 'Psychotherapy and friendship: an analysis of the communications of friends,' *Journal of Counseling Psychology* 21: 269–73.

Renshaw, P.D. and Asher, S.R. (1982) 'Social competence and peer status: the distinction between goals and strategies,' in K.H. Rubin and H.D. Ross (eds) *Peer relationships and social skills in childhood*. New York: Springer-Verlag. pp. 375–95.

Repetti, R.L. (1989) 'The effects of daily workload on subsequent behavior during marital interaction: the roles of social withdrawal and social support,' *Journal of Personality and Social Psychology* 57: 651–9.

Richman, J. and Flaherty, J. (1985) 'Coping and depression,' *Journal of Nervous and Mental Diseases* 173: 590–95.

Riley, D. and Eckenrode, J. (1986) 'Social ties: subgroup differences in costs and benefits,' *Journal of Personality and Social Psychology* 51: 770–8.

Roberts, W. and Strayer, J. (1987) 'Parents' responses to the emotional distress of their children: relations with children's competence,' *Developmental Psychology* 23: 415–22.

Rodehoever, D. and Datan, N. (1986) 'The needy and the proud: cultural context and dilemmas of social services for the aged,' paper read at the 21st Congress of the International Association of Applied Psychology, Jerusalem, July.

Rogers, C.R. (1951) *Client-centered therapy: its current practice implication and theory.* Boston: Houghton-Mifflin.

Rogers, C.R. (1961) *On becoming a person.* Boston, MA: Houghton-Mifflin.

Roloff, M.E., Janiszewski, C.A., McGrath, M.A., Burns, C.S., and Manrai, L.A. (1988) 'Acquiring resources from intimates: when obligation substitutes for persuasion,' *Human Communication Research* 14: 364–96.

Rook, K.S. (1984) 'The negative side of social interaction: impact on psychological well-being,' *Journal of Personality and Social Psychology* 46: 1097–108.

Rook, K.S. (1985) 'The functions of social bonds: perspectives from research on social support, loneliness and social isolation,' in I.G. Sarason and B.R. Sarason (eds) *Social support: theory research and applications.* The Hague: Martinus Nijhoff. pp. 242–68.

Rook, K.S. (1987) 'Social support versus companionship. Effects on life stress, loneliness, and judgment by others,' *Journal of Personality and Social Psychology* 52: 145–54.

Rook, K.S. (1989) 'Strains in older adults' friendships,' in R.G. Adams and R. Blieszner (eds) *Older adult friendship: structure and process.* Newbury Park, CA: Sage.

Rook, K.S. and Dooley, P. (1985) 'Applying social support research: theoretical problems and future directions,' *Journal of Social Issues* 41 (1): 5–28.

Rook, K.S. and Pietromonaco, P. (1987) 'Close relationships: ties that heal or ties that bind,' in D. Perlman and W. Jones (eds) *Advances in personal relationships,* Vol. 1. JAI Press: Greenwich, CT. pp. 1–35.

Rosen, S. (1983) 'Perceived inadequacy and help-seeking,' in B.M. DePaulo, A. Nadler, and J.D. Fisher (eds) *New directions in helping,* Vol. 2. New York: Academic Press. pp. 73–107.

Rosow, I. (1974) *Socialization to old age.* Berkeley, CA: University of California Press.

Ross, C.E., Mirowsky, J., and Huber, J. (1983) 'Dividing work, sharing work, and in-between: marriage patterns and depression,' *American Sociological Review* 48: 809–23.

Roth, S. and Cohen, L.J. (1986) 'Approach, avoidance, and coping with stress,' *American Psychologist* 41: 813–19.

Rubenstein, C. and Shaver, P. (1980) 'Loneliness in two northeastern cities,' in J. Hartog, J.R. Audy, and Y.A. Cohen (eds) *The anatomy of loneliness.* New York: International Universities Press. pp. 319–37.

Rusbult, C.E., Zembrodt, I.M., and Gunn, L.K. (1982) 'Exit, voice, loyalty and neglect: response to dissatisfaction in romantic involvements,' *Journal of Personality and Social Psychology* 43: 1230–42.

Russell, D. and Cutrona, C.E. (1984) 'The provisions of social relationships and

adaptation to stress, paper presented at the annual meetings of the American Psychological Association, Toronto, Canada, August.

Russell, D., Altmaier, E., and Van Velzen, D. (1987) 'Job-related stress, social support, and burnout among classroom teachers,' *Journal of Applied Psychology* 72: 269–74.

Russell, D., Peplau, L.A., and Ferguson, M.L. (1978) 'Developing a measure of loneliness,' *Journal of Personality Assessment* 42: 290–4.

Russell, D., Cutrona, C.E., Rose, J., and Yurko, K. (1984) 'Social and emotional loneliness: an examination of Weiss typology of loneliness,' *Journal of Personality and Social Psychology* 6: 1313–321.

Sacco, W.P., Milana, S., and Dunn, V.K. (1985) 'Effects of depression level and length of acquaintanceship on reactions of others to a request for help,' *Journal of Personality and Social Psychology* 49: 1728–37.

Salovey, P. and Rodin, J. (1985) 'Cognitions about the self: connecting feeling states and social behavior,' in C. Hendrick (ed.) *Review of personality and social psychology*, Vol. 6, Beverly Hills, CA: Sage.

Salzinger, S., Kaplan, S., and Artemyeff, C. (1983) 'Mother's personal social networks and child maltreatment,' *Journal of Abnormal Psychology* 92: 68–76.

Samter, W. (1989) 'Communication skills predictive of friendship and acceptance in group living situations.' Doctoral dissertation, Purdue University, West Lafayette, IN.

Samter, W. and Burleson, B.R. (1984) 'Cognitive and motivational influences on spontaneous comforting behavior,' *Human Communication Research* 11: 231–60.

Samter, W., Burleson, B.R., and Basden-Murphy, L. (1989) 'Behavioral complexity is in the eye of the beholder: effects of cognitive complexity and message complexity on impressions of the source of comforting messages,' *Human Communication Research* 15: 612–29.

Samter, W., Burleson, B.R., and Murphy, L. (1987) 'Comforting conversations: effects of strategy type on evaluations of messages and message producers,' *Southern Speech Communication Journal* 52: 263–84.

Sandler, I.N. and Barrera, M. Jr. (1984) 'Toward a multimethod approach to assessing the effects of social support,' *American Journal of Community Psychology* 12: 37–52.

Sarason, B.R., Sarason, I.G., and Pierce, G.R. (eds) (in press) *Social support: an interactional view*. New York: Wiley.

Sarason, B.R., Sarason, I.G., Hacker, T.A., and Basham, R.B. (1985) 'Concomitants of social support: social skills, physical attractiveness and gender,' *Journal of Personality and Social Psychology* 49: 469–80.

Sarason, B.R., Shearin, E.N., Pierce, G.R., and Sarason, I.G. (1987) 'Interrelations of social support measures: theoretical and practical implications,' *Journal of Personality and Social Psychology* 52: 813–32.

Sarason, B.R., Pierce, B.R., Shearin, E.N., Waltz, J.A., Poppe, L., and Sarason, I.G. (1989) 'Perceived social support and working models of self and others,' manuscript submitted for publication.

Sarason, I.G. and Sarason, B.R. (1986) 'Experimentally provided social support,' *Journal of Personality and Social Psychology* 50: 1222–5.

Sarason, I.G., Sarason, B.R., and Pierce, G.R. (in press) 'Social support: the search for theory,' *Journal of Social and Clinical Psychology*.

Sarason, I.G., Sarason, B.R., and Shearin, E.N. (1986) 'Social support as an

individual difference variable: its stability, origins, and relational aspects,' *Journal of Personality and Social Psychology* 50: 845–55.

Sarason, I.G., Levine, H.M., Basham, R.B., and Sarason, B.R. (1983) 'Assessing social support: the Social Support Questionnaire,' *Journal of Personality and Social Psychology* 44: 127–39.

Sarason, I.G., Sarason, B.R., Shearin, E.N., and Pierce, G.R. (1987) 'A brief measure of social support: practical and theoretical implications,' *Journal of Social and Personal Relationships* 4: 497–510.

Schaefer, C., Coyne, J.D., and Lazarus, R.S. (1981) 'The health-related functions of social support,' *Journal of Behavioral Medicine* 4: 381–406.

Schilling, R.F. II (1987) 'Limitations of social support,' *Social Service Review* 61: 19–31.

Schultz, N.R. and Moore, D. (1986) 'The loneliness experience of college students: sex differences,' *Personality and Social Psychology Bulletin* 22: 111–20.

Schuster, T.L., Morgan, D.L., and Butler, E.W. (1986) 'Non-support in social networks,' paper presented to the Sunbelt VI Networks Conference, Santa Barbara, CA.

Schwarz, N., Strack, F., Mueller, G., and Chassein, B. (1988) 'The range of response alternatives may determine the meaning of the question: further evidence of informative functions of response alternatives,' *Social Cognition* 6: 107–17.

Seidel, J.V. (1988) *The Ethnograph, Version 3.0* [computer program]. Littleton, CO: Qualis Research Associates.

Serafica, F.C. (1982) 'Conceptions of friendship and interaction between friends: an organismic-developmental perspective,' in F.C. Serafica (ed.) *Social-cognitive development in context*. New York: Guilford. pp. 100–32.

Seward, M.L. and Gatz, T. (1989) 'Elders' psychological symptoms and family burden,' paper read at the XIV International Conference on Gerontology, Acapulco, Mexico, June.

Shaffer, D.R. (1986) 'Is mood-induced altruism a form of hedonism?,' *Humboldt Journal of Social Relations* 13: 195–216.

Shaffer, D.R. and Smith, J. (1985) 'Effects of preexisting moods on observers' reactions to helpful and nonhelpful models,' *Motivation and Emotion* 9: 101–22.

Shapiro, E.G. (1980) 'Is seeking help from a friend like seeking help from a stranger?,' *Social Psychology Quarterly* 43: 259–63.

Shaver, P. and Buhrmester, D. (1983) 'Loneliness, sex-role orientation and group life: a social needs perspective,' in P.E. Paulus (ed.) *Basic group processes*. New York: Springer Verlag. pp. 259–88.

Shaver, P., Furman, W., and Buhrmester, D. (1985) 'Transition to college: network changes, social skills, and loneliness,' in S.W. Duck and D. Perlman (eds) *Understanding personal relationships: an interdisciplinary approach*. London: Sage. pp. 193–220.

Shea, L., Thompson, L., and Blieszner, R. (1988) 'Resources in older adults' old and new friendships,' *Journal of Social and Personal Relationships* 5: 83–96.

Shinn, M., Lehmann, S., and Wong, N. (1984) 'Social interaction and social support,' *Journal of Social Issues* 40: 55–76.

Shumaker, S.A. and Brownell, A. (1984) 'Toward a theory of social support: closing conceptual gaps,' *Journal of Social Issues* 40: 11–36.

Silver, R.C., Wortman, C.B., and Crofton, C. (in press) 'The role of coping in support provision: the self-presentational dilemma of victims of life crisis,' in B.R.

Sarason, I.G. Sarason, and G.R. Pierce (eds) *Social support: an interactional view*. New York: Wiley.

Simmel, G. (1950) *The sociology of Georg Simmel* (Trans. Kurt Wolff). New York: Free Press.

Simons, R.L. (1984) 'Specificity and substitution in the social networks of the elderly,' *International Journal of Aging and Human Development* 18: 121–39.

Smith, M., Ribordy, S.C., and Marinakis, G. (1988) 'Psychological characteristics of college-age children of alcoholic fathers,' *Family Perspective* 21: 183–94.

Smith, R.T. (1979) 'Disability and the recovery process: role of social network,' in E.G. Jaco (ed.) *Patients, physicians and illness*. New York: Free Press.

Snyder, M. (1979) 'Self-monitoring processes,' in L. Berkowitz (ed.) *Advances in experimental social psychology* 30. New York: Academic Press. pp. 526–37.

Sokolovsky, J. and Cohen, C.I. (1981) 'Toward a resolution of methodological dilemmas in network mapping,' *Schizophrenia Bulletin* 7: 109–16.

Solano, C.H., Batten, P.G., and Parish, E.A. (1982) 'Loneliness and patterns of self-disclosure,' *Journal of Personality and Social Psychology* 43: 532–41.

Spanier, G.B. (1976) 'Measuring dyadic adjustment: new scales for assessing the quality of marriage and similar dyads,' *Journal of Marriage and the Family* 38: 15–28.

Specht, H. (1986) 'Social support, social networks, social exchange and social work practice,' *Journal of Social Service Review* 60: 218–40.

Spitzberg, B. and Canary, D.J. (1985) 'Loneliness and relationally competent communication,' *Journal of Social and Personal Relationships* 2: 387–402.

Spitzberg, B. and Cupach, W. (1985) *Interpersonal communication competence*. Newbury Park, CA: Sage.

Staines, G.L. and Pleck, J.H. (1983) *The impact of work schedules on the family*. Ann Arbor: Institute for Social Research.

Staines, G.L. and Pleck, J.H. (1984) 'Nonstandard work schedules and family life,' *Journal of Applied Psychology* 69: 515–23.

Staines, G.L. and Pleck, J.H. (1986) 'Work schedule flexibility and family life,' *Journal of Occupational Behavior* 7: 147–53.

Starker, J., Morgan, D.L., and March, S. (1989) 'The development of closeness in social networks: the experience of recent movers,' paper presented at the Second Iowa Conference on Personal Relationships, Iowa City, Iowa.

Stein, K.F. (1989) 'Dependency stress and elders' abusive behavior toward family caregivers,' paper read at the XIV International Conference on Gerontology, Acapulco, Mexico, June.

Steinmetz, S.K. (1983) 'Dependency, stress, and violence between middle-aged caregivers and their elderly parents,' in J.I. Kosber (ed.) *Abuse and maltreatment of the elderly: causes and interventions*. Greenwich, CT: JAI.

Stephens, J. (1976) *Loners, losers, and lovers: elderly tenants in a slum hotel*. Seattle and London: University of Washington Press.

Stephens, M.A.P., Kinney, J.M., Norris, V.K., and Ritchie, S.W. (1987) 'Social networks as assets and liabilities in recovery from stroke by geriatric patients,' *Psychology and Aging* 2: 125–9.

Stokes, J.P. (1983) 'Predicting satisfaction with social support from social network structure,' *American Journal of Community Psychology* 11: 141–52.

Stokes, J.P. (1985) 'The relation of social network and individual difference variables to loneliness,' *Journal of Personality and Social Psychology* 48: 981–90.

Stokes, J.P. (1987) 'The relation of loneliness and self-disclosure,' in V.J. Derlega

and J.H. Berg (eds) *Self-disclosure: theory, research, and therapy*. New York: Plenum. pp. 175–202.

Stokes, J.P. and Lewin, I. (1986) 'Gender differences in predicting loneliness from social support characteristics,' *Journal of Personality and Social Psychology* 51: 1069–74.

Stone, A.A. (1981) 'The association between perceptions of daily experiences and self- and spouse-rated mood,' *Journal of Research in Personality* 15: 510–22.

Stone, A.A. and Neale, J.M. (1984a) 'Effects of severe daily events on mood,' *Journal of Personality and Social Psychology* 46: 137–44.

Stone, A.A. and Neale, J.M. (1984b) 'New measures of daily coping: development and preliminary results,' *Journal of Personality and Social Psychology* 46: 892–906.

Strayer, F.F. (1981) 'The nature and organization of altruistic behavior among preschool children,' in J.P. Rushton and R.M. Sorrentino (eds) *Altruism and helping behavior: social, personality, and developmental perspectives*. Hillsdale, NJ: Erlbaum.

Sullivan, J.S. (1953) *The interpersonal theory of psychiatry*. New York: Norton.

Tardy, C.H. (1985) 'Social support measurement,' *American Journal of Community Psychology* 13: 187–202.

Tasto, D.L., Colligan, M.J., Skjei, E.W., and Polly, S.J. (1978) *Health consequences of shift work*. Washington, DC: National Institute for Occupational Safety and Health.

Tesch, S.A. (1983) 'Review of friendship development across the life span,' *Human Development* 26: 266–76.

Thoits, P.A. (1982) 'Conceptual, methodological, and theoretical problems in studying social support as a buffer against life stress,' *Journal of Health and Social Behavior* 23: 145–58.

Thoits, P.A. (1985) 'Social support and psychological well-being: theoretical possibilities,' in I.G. Sarason and B.R. Sarason (eds) *Social support: theory, research, and applications*. Dordrecht: Martinus Nijhoff. pp. 51–72.

Thoits, P.A. (1986) 'Social support and coping assistance,' *Journal of Consulting and Clinical Psychology* 54: 416–23.

Tobin, S. (1969) 'Institutional dependency in the aged,' in R. Kalish (ed.) *The dependencies of old people*. University of Michigan, Institute of Gerontology.

Tripathi, R.C., Caplan, R.D., and Naidu, R.K. (1986) 'Accepting advice: a modifier of social support's effect on well being,' *Journal of Social and Personal Relationships* 3: 213–28.

Unger, D. and Powell, D. (1980) 'Supporting families under stress: the role of social networks,' *Family Relations* 29: 566–74.

Vanfossen, B. (1981) 'Sex differences in the mental health effects of spouse support and equity,' *Journal of Health and Social Behavior* 22: 130–43.

Vaux, A. (1988) *Social support: theory, research, and intervention*. Praeger: New York.

Vaux, A. and Harrison, D. (1985) 'Support network characteristics associated with support satisfaction and perceived support,' *American Journal of Community Psychology* 13: 245–67.

Velten, E. (1968) 'A laboratory task for induction of mood states,' *Behavior Research and Therapy* 6: 473–82.

Ventura, J.N. (1986) 'Parent coping, a replication,' *Nursing Research* 35 (March/April): 77–80.

Verbrugge, L.M. (1983) 'Multiple roles and the physical health of women and men,' *Journal of Health and Social Behavior* 24: 16–30.

Verwoerdt, A. (1981) *Clinical geropsychiatry*. Baltimore, MD: Williams & Wilkins.

Vetel, A.A. and Papin, A. (1984) 'Safeguarding autonomy,' paper presented at the XIV International Conference on Gerontology, Acapulco, Mexico, June.

Wahler, R. (1980) 'The insular mother: her problems in parent–child treatment,' *Journal of Applied Behavioral Analysis* 13: 207–19.

Waldman, E. (1983) 'Labor force statistics from a family perspective,' *Monthly Labor Review* 106: 16–20.

Walster, E., Walster, W., and Berscheid, E. (1978) *Equity: theory and research*. New York: Aldine.

Wedderburn, A.A.I. (1967) 'Social factors in satisfaction with swiftly rotating shifts,' *Occupational Psychology* 41: 85–107.

Weiner, B. (1980) 'A cognitive (attribution)–emotion–action model of motivated behavior: an analysis of judgments of help giving,' *Journal of Personality and Social Psychology* 39: 186–200.

Weisman, A.D. (1979) *Coping with Cancer*. New York: McGraw-Hill.

Weiss, R.S. (1969) 'The fund of sociability,' *Transaction/Society* 6: 36–43.

Weiss, R.S. (1973) *Loneliness: the experience of emotional and social isolation*. Cambridge, MA: MIT Press.

Weiss, R.S. (1974) 'The provisions of social relationships,' in Z. Rubin (ed.) *Doing unto others*. Englewood Cliffs, NJ: Prentice-Hall. pp. 17–26.

Weiss, R.S. (1984) 'The provisions of social relationships,' in Z. Rubin (ed.) *Doing unto others: joining, molding, conforming, helping*. Englewood Cliffs, NJ: Prentice-Hall Spectrum.

Weiss, R.S. (1990) 'Bringing work stress home,' in J. Eckenrode and S. Gore (eds) *Stress between work and family*. New York: Plenum.

Weitzman, E.D. (1976) 'Circadian rhythms,' in P.G. Rentos and R.D. Shepard (eds) *Shift work and health*. Washington, DC: National Institute for Occupational Safety and Health. pp. 51–6.

Wellman, B. (1985) 'Domestic work, paid work and net work,' in S.W. Duck and D. Perlman (eds) *Understanding Personal Relationships*. London: Sage. pp. 159–92.

Wellman, B., Mosher, P., Rottenberg, C., and Espinosa, V. (1987) 'Different strokes from different folks: which ties provide which forms of social support.' Working paper No. 457, Institute of Urban and Regional Development, University of California, Berkeley.

Wentowski, G.J. (1981) 'Reciprocity and the coping strategies of older people: cultural dimensions of network building,' *Gerontologist* 21: 600–9.

Werking, K.J., Samter, W., and Burleson, B.R. (1989) 'Gender differences in the perceived importance of communication skills in same-sex friends: two studies,' unpublished manuscript, Department of Communication, Purdue University, West Lafayette, IN.

Werner, H. (1957) 'The concept of development from a comparative and organismic point of view,' in D.B. Harris (ed.) *The concept of development*. Minneapolis: University of Minnesota Press. pp. 125–46.

Wethington, E. and Kessler, R.C. (1986) 'Perceived support, received support, and

adjustment to stressful life events,' *Journal of Health and Social Behavior* 27: 78–89.

Wethington, E., McLeod, J.D., and Kessler, R.C. (1987) 'The importance of life events for explaining sex differences in psychological distress,' in R.C. Barnett, L. Biener, and G.K. Baruch (eds) *Gender and stress*. New York: Free Press. pp. 144–56.

Wheaton, B. (1985) 'Models for the stress-buffering functions of coping resources,' *Journal of Health and Social Behavior* 26: 352–64.

Wheeler, L. and Nezlek, J. (1977) 'Sex difference in social participation,' *Journal of Personality and Social Psychology* 35: 742–54.

Wheeler, L., Reis, H.T., and Nezlek, J. (1983) 'Loneliness, social interaction, and sex roles,' *Journal of Personality and Social Psychology* 45: 943–53.

Williams, J.G. and Solano, C.H. (1983) 'The social reality of feeling lonely: friendship and reciprocation,' *Personality and Social Psychology* 9: 237–42.

Wills, T.A. (1983) 'Social comparison in coping and help-seeking,' in B.M. DePaulo, A. Nadler, and J.D. Fisher (eds) *New directions in helping 2: Help seeking*. New York: Academic Press, pp. 109–41.

Wilson, W.J. (1987) *The truly disadvantaged*. Chicago: University of Chicago Press.

Winstead, B.A. (1986) 'Sex differences in same-sex friendships,' in V.J. Derlega and B.A. Winstead (eds) *Friendship and social interaction*. New York: Springer-Verlag. pp. 81–100.

Winstead, B.A. and Derlega, V.J. (1985) 'Benefits of same-sex friendships in a stressful situation,' *Journal of Social and Clinical Psychology* 3: 378–84.

Winstead, B.A. and Derlega, V.J. (in press) 'An experimental approach to studying social interaction and coping with stress among friends,' in W.H. Jones and D. Perlman (eds) *Advances in personal relationships*. Greenwich, CT: JAI Press.

Winstead, B.A., Derlega, V.J., Lewis, R.J., and Margulis, S.T. (1988) 'Understanding the therapeutic relationship as a personal relationship,' *Journal of Social and Personal Relationships* 5: 109–25.

Wiseman, J.P. (1986) 'Friendship: bonds and binds in a voluntary relationship,' *Journal of Social and Personal Relationships* 3: 191–211.

Wittenberg, M.T. and Reis, H.T. (1986) 'Loneliness, social skills, and social perceptions,' *Personality and Social Psychology Bulletin* 12: 121–30.

Wortman, C.B. (1983) 'Coping with victimization: conclusions and implications for future research,' *Journal of Social Issues* 39 (2): 195–221.

Wortman, C.B. and Dunkel-Schetter, C. (1979) 'Interpersonal relationships and cancer: a theoretical analysis,' *Journal of Social Issues* 35 (1): 120–55.

Wortman, C.B. and Dunkel-Schetter, C. (1987) 'Conceptual and methodological issues in the study of social support,' in A. Baum and J.E. Singer (eds) *Handbook of psychology and health: Vol. 5. Stress*. Hillsdale, NJ: Erlbaum. pp. 63–108.

Wortman, C.B. and Silver, R.C. (1989) 'The myths of coping with loss,' *Journal of Consulting and Clinical Psychology* 57: 359–57.

Yatomi, N., Niina, Y.I. and Honoma, A. (1989) 'Stress in family caregivers caring demented aged,' paper read at the XIV International Conference on Gerontology, Acapulco, Mexico, June.

Zimmermann, S. (1989) 'Comforting communication in the hospice interdisciplinary team,' paper presented at the International Communication Association convention, San Francisco, May.

Author Index

Abramson, L. J., 53, 216
Acitelli, L. K., 7, 216
Acock, A. C., 11, 13, 216
Adams, R. G., 194, 216
Adelman, M. B., 13, 18, 19, 20, 74, 75, 77, 104, 105, 115, 193, 216
Adler, A., 162, 216
Akiyami, H., 126, 216
Albee, G. W., 2, 216
Albo, B. D., 141, 216
Albrecht, T. L., 13, 18, 19, 20, 74, 75, 77, 104, 105, 115, 193, 216
Alloy, L. B., 53, 216
Altman, I., 107, 120, 216
Andrisani, P., 161, 216
Antaki, C., 5, 216
Antonucci, T. C., 96, 126, 129, 188, 189, 216, 217, 230
Applegate, J. L., 69, 70, 217
Asher, C. C., 16, 217
Asher, S. R., 79, 237
Auslander, N., 145, 219

Baltes, P. B., 199, 217
Barbarin, O. A., 106, 124, 221
Barbee, A. P., xii, 54, 55, 56, 57, 58, 59, 60, 61, 63, 217, 223
Barrera, M., Jr., 1, 38, 87, 88, 89, 90, 98, 175, 217, 239
Barusch, A. S., 127, 217
Batson, C. D., 49, 56, 62, 217
Bavelas, J. B., 108, 116, 218
Baxter, L. A., 4, 107, 108, 116, 120, 127, 218
Belle, D., 101, 160, 218
Berg, J. H., 124, 141, 142, 144, 145, 148, 149, 150, 151, 154, 155, 156, 218
Berger, C. R., 4, 128, 143, 147, 218
Berkman, L. F., 13, 218
Berkowitz, A., 161, 218

Bernstein, B., 70, 218
Bigfoot, D. S., 130, 231
Billings, A. G., 90, 101, 218
Blazer, D. G., 30, 175, 219
Blieszner, R., 194, 240
Blumstein, P., 190, 219
Bochner, A. P., 107, 219
Bogdan, J., 127, 237
Bolger, N., 93, 219
Bolton, B., 177, 180, 181, 219
Bolton, W., 178, 219
Borys, S., 149, 219
Brand, J. F., 170, 171, 219
Brand, S., 165, 168, 170, 171, 219
Brennan, T., 145, 219
Brickman, P., 49, 97, 139, 219
Brody, E. M., 100, 133, 136, 211, 219
Bronfenbrenner, U., 169, 170, 219
Brookings, J. B., 177, 180, 181, 219
Brown, G. W., 17, 129, 219, 235
Brownell, A., 98, 240
Bruhn, J. G., 11, 219
Buhrmester, D., 148, 150, 240
Burgoon, J. K., 123, 219
Burleson, B. R., 1, 68, 69, 70, 77, 78, 79, 80, 82, 103, 118, 120, 147, 220
Burnett, R., 7, 220
Burt, R. S., 193, 220

Cacioppo, J. T., 45, 220
Cain, V., 163, 237
Canary, D. J., 18, 241
Cancian, F. M., 95, 220
Caplan, R. D., 169, 221
Carlson, M., 49, 53, 221
Carpentier, J., 164, 221
Catalano, D. J., 134, 230
Cate, R. M., 49, 221
Cazamian, P., 164, 221
Chesler, M. A., 106, 124, 221
Cialdini, R. B., 54, 221

Cicirelli, V. G., 133, 221
Clark, M. S., 17, 49, 55, 92, 106, 127, 142, 144, 189, 199, 218, 221, 234
Clark, N. M., 132, 221
Coates, D., 97, 221
Cobb, S., 66, 177, 221
Cohen, C. I., 193, 241
Cohen, J., 167, 221
Cohen, J. B., 72, 232
Cohen, L. J., 51, 238
Cohen, P., 167, 221
Cohen, S., 12, 49, 86, 88, 90, 97, 141, 177, 178, 180, 221, 222
Constable, J. F., 177, 222
Cooper, C. L., 163, 164, 233
Corty, E., 145, 222
Costanza, R. S., 52, 222
Cowen, E., 18, 222
Coyne, J. C., 54, 88, 94, 98, 175, 179, 202, 222
Cozby, P. C., 86, 222
Cronkite, R. C., 90, 101, 219
Crowley, M., 49, 225
Cunningham, M. R., 53, 54, 56, 57, 59, 61, 62, 217, 222
Cupach, W., 9, 18, 241
Cutrona, C. E., xi, 1, 28, 30, 36, 64, 66, 74, 87, 141, 142, 145, 150, 152, 173, 177, 180, 181, 223

Damrell, J., 161, 233
Dant, T., 123, 223
Datan, N., 137, 238
Davis, K. E., 75, 223
Davis, M. H., 145, 225
Deaux, K., 154, 223
Delia, J. G., 69, 108, 116, 223, 235
DeLongis, A., 73, 88, 93, 219, 222, 223
DePaulo, B. M., 16, 106, 223
Derlega, V. J., 52, 105, 147, 223, 244
DeVoge, S., 44, 233
DiMatteo, M. R., 106, 223
Domhoff, G. W., 141, 223
Dooley, P., 2, 238
Dovidio, J. F., 107, 223
Dressler, W. W., 129, 224
Duck, S. W., x, 2, 4, 5, 6, 8, 9, 12, 14, 18, 20, 21, 23, 28, 29, 124, 127, 128, 184, 198, 199, 200, 224, 236
Dunham, R. B., 167, 169, 224

Dunkel-Schetter, C., 94, 104, 106, 107, 125, 180, 194, 196, 224, 244
Dunn, J., 199, 224
Dunst, C. J., 13, 224

Eagly, A. H., 49, 225
Eckenrode, J., 1, 12, 33, 73, 89, 91, 102, 225, 237
Eggert, L. L., 104, 120, 236
Ell, K., 16, 225
Elliott, R., 70, 74, 225
Eysenck, H. J., 49, 225

Fiore, J., 105, 175, 204, 225
Fisher, G. A., 135, 225
Fisher, J. D., 66, 92, 93, 178, 225
Fitzpatrick, M. A., 34, 128, 225
Flaherty, J., 137, 237
Folkman, S., 9, 12, 49, 50, 51, 62, 84, 225, 232
Franzoi, S. L., 145, 223
Freeman, L., 193, 225
Fretz, B. R., 178, 234
Freud, Sigmund, 123
Friesen, N., 132, 133, 232
Frost, P. J., 162, 167, 225
Furman, W., 53, 234

Gadbois, C., 163, 226
Gaertner, S. L., 107, 223
Gallagher, D. E., 203, 226
Gatz, T., 133, 240
Gergen, K. J., 2, 226
Gergen, M. M., 2, 226
Gerstel, N., 130, 226
Gibson, L., 64, 226
Gilbert, L. A., 161, 162, 163, 226, 229
Giles, H., 49, 226
Gimbert, M., 137, 226
Ginsburg, G. P., 199, 200, 226
Glidewell, J. C., 19, 41, 92, 107, 226
Goldberg, J. G., 13, 226
Goldenberg, S., 193, 226
Goldfarb, A., 123, 226
Goldsmith, D., 104, 106, 108, 226
Gore, S., 83, 88, 89, 101, 225, 226
Gottlieb, B. H., 1, 2, 3, 9, 10, 41, 50, 83, 87, 175, 194, 195, 196, 199, 200, 201, 226, 227
Gottman, J. M., 6, 32, 34, 44, 227

Gouaux, C., 53, 227
Gourash, N., 30, 227
Gove, W. R., 94, 100, 126, 227
Granovetter, M. S., 99, 193, 227
Grant, I., 13, 227
Greenberg, J., 54, 227
Gross, A. E., 84, 85, 92, 93, 227, 233
Gulley, M. R., 55, 56, 61, 217

Hall, A., 96, 227
Hammer, M., 193, 227
Hansell, S., 126, 227
Harris, T., 17, 219
Harrison, D., 175, 242
Hart, C. H., 81, 227
Hauser, G. A., 3, 227
Haw, M., 160, 228
Hays, R., 106, 223
Hays, R. B., 49, 143, 144, 160, 189, 194, 228
Hazan, C., 49, 94, 184, 228
Heitzmann, C. A., 187, 228
Heller, K., x, 1, 13, 30, 33, 83, 145, 180, 181, 188, 228, 237
Henderson, S., 95, 180, 228
Herrick, L. R., 72, 74, 81, 235
Hinde, R. A., 20, 228
Hirsch, B. J., 1, 161, 165, 166, 168, 171, 197, 201, 219, 228, 229
Hoberman, H., 49, 90, 221
Hobfoll, S. E., x, 1, 8, 9, 11, 12, 13, 15, 126, 127, 130, 182, 194, 229
Hochschild, A., 99–100, 229
Hokanson, J. E., 54, 229
Holohan, C., 161, 163, 229
Homel, R., 174, 229
Hooyman, N. R., 134, 229
Hopper, R., 4, 229
Horl, J., 135, 229
Horowitz, A., 203, 229
House, J. S., 78, 99, 161, 190, 195, 196, 229
Howes, M. J., 54, 229
Hurlbert, J. S., 11, 13, 216
Huston, T. L., 199, 229

Iannotti, R. J., 72, 229
Ierodiakonou, C. S., 130, 230
Ingersoll-Dayton, B., 129, 230
Isen, A. M., 53, 200

Israel, B. A., 96, 193, 217, 230

Jackson, J. S., 189, 217
Jacobson, D. E., 83, 86, 97, 198, 230
Jamal, M., 162, 167, 225, 230
Jemmott, J. B., III, 30, 230
Johnson, C. L., 134, 230
Johnson, M. P., 197, 201, 230
Jones, W. H., 64, 145, 146, 151, 153, 154, 155, 156, 157, 230
Jourard, S. M., 86, 230

Kahn, J., 54, 230
Kanner, A. D., 73, 230
Kanter, R. M., 100, 231
Kaplan, R. M., 187, 228
Kelley, H. H., xi, 14, 30, 32, 33, 34, 44, 120, 192, 198, 199, 231
Kelly, George, 29
Kenny, D. A., 63, 231
Kenrick, D. T., 54, 221
Kessler, R. C., 30, 66, 90, 93, 98, 99, 126, 161, 176, 219, 231, 244
Kingston, P. W., 163, 235
Klein, H., 125, 232
Klinefelter, D. S., 136, 231
Knoke, D., 193, 231
Koller, M., 167, 231
Kollock, P., 190, 219
Krile, C., 79, 231
Kuklinkski, J. H., 193, 231
Kurdek, L. A., 79, 231

La Fromboise, T. D., 130, 131
La Gaipa, J. J., 122, 124, 125, 128, 129, 132, 133, 134, 135, 200, 231, 232
Lakey, B., 145, 228
Lazarus, R. S., 9, 12, 49, 50, 51, 72, 84, 225, 232
Le Fevre, P., 123, 232
Leatham, G., xi, 30, 88, 95, 102, 103, 173, 176, 178, 232
Leavy, R. L., 16, 232
Lee, E., 130, 232
Lehman, D. R., 20, 50, 60, 61, 70, 73, 90, 179, 202, 232
Leslie, L., 197, 201, 230, 232
Levenson, R. W., 44, 227
Lewin, E., 161, 232
Lewin, I., 150, 242

Lewis, R. A., 75, 104, 120, 233, 234
Lewis, S. N. C., 163, 164, 233
Lieberman, M. A., 17, 88, 233
Lin, N., 89, 233
Lindemann, E., 68, 233
Lloyd, S. A., 49, 221
London, P., 12, 13, 126, 229
Lustbader, W., 134, 229

Mace, N., 204, 233
Maddison, D., 196, 233
Magliore, K., 30, 230
Main, M., 184, 233
Malkinson, R., 127, 234
Mallinckrodt, B., 178, 234
Malott, O., 133, 232
Mankowski, E. S., 182, 183, 186, 234
Margulis, S. T., 147, 223
Martin, E., 129, 234
Martin, J. M., 129, 234
Marx, Karl, 123
Masters, J. C., 49, 53, 55, 233, 234
McCall, G. J., 128, 199, 200, 233
McCall, M. E., 84, 85, 87, 95, 236
McCannell, K., 195, 233
McCornack, S. A., 67, 235
McCoy, C. L., 49, 55, 233
McCrae, R. R., 49, 55, 233
McLeod, J. D., 98, 99, 126, 231
McLeroy, K. R., 137, 233
McMullen, P. A., 84, 85, 93, 227, 233
McQuinn, R. D., 141, 149, 150
McRae, J. A., 161, 231
McReynolds, P., 44, 233
Metts, S., 128, 234
Miell, D. E., 7, 234
Milardo, R. M., 11, 13, 104, 120, 121, 201, 234
Miller, L. C., 154, 155, 234
Miller, N., 49, 53, 221
Mills, J., 127, 234
Mitchell, R. E., 93, 234
Montgomery, B. M., 4, 234
Moore, D., 149, 240
Moore, G., 141, 216
Moore, T. L., 154, 230
Moos, R. H., 90, 93, 101, 219, 234
Morgan, D. L., xiv, 88, 103, 128, 173, 176, 193, 195, 197, 200, 201, 202, 205, 207, 209, 234

Morgan, J. N., 163, 234
Morse, S. J., 17, 235
Murawski, B. J., 11, 235
Murrell, S. A., 10, 235

Nadler, A., 92, 235
Neale, J. M., 49, 50, 242
Neimeyer, G. J., 198, 199, 235
Neimeyer, R. A. 198, 199, 235
Nezlek, J., 28, 244
Nock, S. L. 163, 235
Noller, P., 6, 235
Norris, F. J., 10, 235
Norton, R., 235
Notarius, C. I., 72, 74, 81, 235

O'Brien, J. E., 198, 235
O'Bryant, S. L., 138, 235
O'Connor, P., 129, 235
O'Heeron, R. C., 52, 236
O'Keefe, B. J., 67, 108, 116, 120, 235
Oatley, K., 178, 219
Ory, M. G., 203, 235
Oxley, D., 194, 228

Pagel, M. D., 125, 182, 235
Pancer, S. M., 195, 227
Papin, A., 139, 243
Parkes, C. M., 98, 236
Parks, M. R., 75, 77, 104, 108, 115, 120, 216, 236
Pearlin, L. I., 83, 84, 85, 87, 90, 96, 101, 236
Pennebaker, J. W., 52, 236
Peplau, L. A., 18, 144, 145, 148, 218, 236
Perkins, H. W., 161, 218
Perlman, D., 18, 93, 144, 149, 199, 200, 219, 224, 236
Pettit, G. S., 81, 236
Petty, R. E., 45, 220
Pierce, G. R., xiv, 1, 41, 119, 182, 193, 236
Pietromonaco, P., 106, 196, 209, 238
Pignatiello, M. F., 56, 236
Pillemer, K., 134, 237
Piner, K. E., 124, 150, 151, 154, 155, 156, 218
Pleban, R., 60, 237
Pleck, J. H., 162, 163, 164, 166, 167, 168, 171, 237, 241

Pond, K., 4, 8, 224
Powell, D., 100, 242
Presser, H. B., 160, 161, 163, 164, 237
Procidano, M. E., 30, 33, 180, 181, 237
Proust, Marcel, 8
Pyasczynski, T., 54, 227

Rabins, P., 204, 233
Rahim, M. A., 49, 237
Rakowski, W., 132, 221
Rands, M., 195, 201, 237
Rapkin, B. D., 1, 161, 165, 166, 228
Ratcliff, K. S., 127, 237
Raush, H. L., 32, 43, 237
Reis, H. T., x, 28, 148, 199, 221, 237, 244
Reisman, J. M., 74, 237
Renshaw, P. D., 79, 237
Repetti, R. L., 93, 237
Richman, J., 137, 238
Riley, D., 12, 91, 102, 238
Roberts, W., 80, 238
Rodehoever, D., 137, 238
Rogers, C. R., 43, 70, 125, 236
Roll, Y., 162, 216
Roloff, M. E., 117, 120, 238
Rook, K. S., 2, 66, 73, 93, 105, 106, 125, 140, 141, 142, 146, 147, 151, 152, 175, 196, 209, 236, 238
Rosen, S., 92, 107, 238
Rosenmeyr, L., 135, 229
Rosow, I., 211, 238
Ross, C. E., 161, 238
Roth, S., 51, 238
Rowland, K., 170, 171, 219
Rubenstein, C., 18, 146, 238
Russell, D. W., 36, 141, 142, 145, 177, 180, 181, 222, 223, 238, 239
Rutt, D., 5, 6, 23, 28, 224

Sacco, W. P., 49, 54, 56, 239
Salzinger, S., 13, 239
Samter, W., 69, 70, 72, 77, 78, 79, 80, 120, 220, 239
Sandler, I. N., 1, 38, 87, 90, 175, 217, 239
Sants, H. K. A., x, 6, 14, 128, 184, 199, 224
Sarason, B. R., 41, 64, 145, 174, 176,

177, 180, 181, 182, 186, 187, 195, 197, 239
Sarason, I. G., 10, 30, 33, 44, 52, 64, 157, 180, 181, 182, 186, 239, 241
Schaefer, C., 13, 240
Schaie, K. W., 199, 217
Schilling, R. F., 11, 139, 240
Schooler, C., 90, 101, 236
Schultz, N. R., 149, 240
Schuster, T. L., 194, 240
Schwarz, N., 10, 240
Serafica, F. C., 75, 240
Seward, M. L., 133, 240
Shaffer, D. R., 49, 53, 54
Shapiro, E. G., 117, 240
Shapiro, M., 61, 216
Shaver, P., 18, 49, 94, 146, 148, 150, 184, 194, 199, 228, 237, 238, 240
Shea, L., 194, 240
Shepherd, G. J., 120, 235
Shinn, M., 83, 138, 240
Shumaker, S. A., 98, 240
Siedel, J. V., 205, 240
Silver, R. C., 105, 106, 107, 175, 179, 180, 240, 244
Simmel, G., 8, 241
Simmons, J. L., 128, 233
Simons, R. L., 126, 241
Smith, R. T., 13, 241
Snyder, M., 49, 241
Sokolovsky, J., 193, 241
Solano, C. H., 145, 241, 244
Spanier, G. B., 36, 241
Specht, H., 133, 241
Spitzberg, B., 9, 18, 241
Staines, G. L., 162, 163, 164, 166, 167, 168, 171, 237, 241
Starker, J., 194, 241
Stein, K. F., 137, 241
Steinmetz, S. K., 136, 137, 241
Stephens, J., 131, 241
Stephens, M. A. P., 175, 241
Stokes, J. P., x, 1, 8, 9, 11, 13, 15, 147, 150, 174, 194, 202, 229, 241
Stone, A. A., 49, 50, 73, 242
Strayer, F. F., 72, 242
Strayer, J., 80, 238
Swindle, R. W., 13, 83, 228
Syme, S. L., 12, 13, 141, 218, 222

Tardy, C. H., 11, 87, 242
Tasto, D. L., 162, 165, 167, 168, 169, 242
Taylor, D., 120, 216
Tesch, S. A., 75, 242
Tesser, A., 60, 237
Tessler, R. C., 135, 225
Thoits, P. A., 19, 50, 74, 98, 100, 106, 242
Tobin, S., 123, 242
Todd, M. J., 75, 223
Tripathi, R. C., 129, 242
Tudor, J. F., 100, 227

Unger, D., 100, 242

Vanfossen, B., 160, 242
Vaux, A., 9, 83, 84, 88, 97, 175, 242
Velten, E., 56, 59, 242
Venardos, C., 6, 235
Ventura, J. N., 13, 243
Verbrugge, L. M., 100, 243
Verwoerdt, A., 136, 243
Vetel, A. A., 139, 243
Viscusi, D., 53, 216

Wahler, R., 100, 243
Waldman, E., 164, 243
Walker, W. L., 196, 233
Walster, E., 97, 243

Wedderburn, A. A. I., 167, 243
Weiner, B., 49, 55, 61, 62, 243
Weisman, A. D., 135, 243
Weiss, R. S., 87, 92, 98, 142, 147, 148, 153, 177, 236, 243
Weitzman, E. D., 163, 243
Wellman, B., 13, 96, 194, 227, 243
Wentowski, G. J., 18, 243
Werking, K. J., 77, 243
Werner, H., 70, 243
Wethington, E., 30, 90, 93, 99, 176, 219, 243
Wheaton, B., 88, 89, 90, 244
Wheeler, L., 28, 153, 154, 155, 156, 244
Williams, J. G., 145, 244
Wills, T. A., 85, 86, 88, 97, 106, 107, 177, 178, 222
Wilmot, W., 127, 218
Wilson, W. J., 101, 244
Winstead, B. A., 49, 52, 77, 105, 244
Wiseman, J. P., 125, 244
Wittenberg, M. T., 148, 244
Wortman, C. B., 94, 106, 107, 125, 179, 180, 196, 224, 244

Yamokoski, T., 74, 237
Yatomi, N., 133, 244
Young, R. D., 145, 222

Zimmermann, S., 77, 244

Subject Index

Advice, 19, 20, 40, 86, 116, 118, 125, 129, 139, 147
AIDS, 92
Alcoholism, 130
Altruism, 47, 54
Alzheimer's Disease, 135, 203–212
Attachment, 31, 49, 94, 143, 144, 147, 152
Attribution, 47, 49, 53, 55, 56, 61, 62, 85, 96, 182
Autonomy, 123, 130, 137, 138, 139

Behavioral observation, 58f
Bereavement, 21, 33, 50, 61, 73, 86, 92, 98, 128, 173, 179, 194, 195, 202
Burnout, 97, 117

Cancer, 124, 125, 132, 179
Caregivers, *see* Caregiving; *see also* Burnout, Alzheimer's Disease
Caregiving, 132, 133, 134, 135, 136, 138, 191, 203, 204, 205, 206, 207, 208, 209, 210, 211, 212
Cheering up, 46ff, 59f, 61f
Chronic stress, 97, 134; *see also* Coping with stress, Life stress, War stress
Co-workers, 14, 49, 77, 78, 159, 160, 161, 162, 166, 167, 169, 170, 171
Comforting, 66ff, 70
Communal relationships, 17, 18, 19, 55, 92
Communication and support, 3, 5, 9, 16, 20, 38, 67, 68, 69, 77, 79, 105, 108, 117, 118, 119, 121, 136, 142
Communicative Functions Questionnaire (CFQ) 75, 76, 77, 79, 80
Communication skills, 9, 68, 70
Confiding, 129
Conversation and support, 3, 4, 5, 6, 12, 14, 19, 21, 22, 23, 28, 29, 59,

75, 78, 147; *see also* Communication and support
Coping strategies, 52, 104ff
Coping with stress, 2, 15, 22, 49, 50, 51, 52, 55, 56, 58, 60, 62, 63, 64, 81, 83, 84, 86, 87, 90, 96, 97, 98, 132, 173, 177, 185, 187; *see also* Interactive coping, Transactions of social support

Daily hassles, 5, 73
Dependency, 123, 138
Depression, 9, 49, 50, 52, 53, 54, 55, 57, 68, 73, 74, 81, 90, 98, 100, 130, 132; *see also* Postpartum depression
Diary methods, 5, 103
Disability, 13
Disease, 13
Distress, 68, 71, 72, 99, 120
Divorce, 21, 98, 194, 195
Dyadic relationships, 8, 20, 44, 54, 176, 185, 187

Elderly people, *see* Older adults
Equity theory, 129
Exchange relationships, 17, 18, 19, 55

Friendship, 1, 2, 5, 16, 17, 30, 47, 49, 52, 54, 55, 57, 58, 59, 60, 61, 64, 66, 67, 72, 74, 75, 77, 95, 104, 122, 125, 126, 132, 134, 135, 140, 142, 143, 144, 146, 147, 148, 151, 153, 156, 161, 162, 169, 197, 201

Grief, 33

Help-seeking, 6f, 8, 11, 17–20, 84, 85, 87, 89, 91, 101

Illness, 50, 104, 135

Immune function, 30
Impression management, 112, 113
Interactive coping, 47, 49, 56, 61; see
    also Coping, Transactions of social
    support
    Emotional and cognitive aspects of,
    53f
Interdependence, 122, 137
Interpersonal conflict, 175, 183, 198,
    199
Interpersonal Support Evaluation List
    (ISEL), 177, 180, 183
Intimacy, 7, 14, 92, 108, 120, 140, 142,
    143, 148, 149, 153, 154, 194, 199,
    200
Inventory of Socially Supportive
    Behavior (ISSB), 87, 90
Iowa Communication Record, 5, 23–29

Language, 4
    Functions of language in social
    support, 13–14, 19, 22
Leisure, 147
Life stress, 2, 3, 8, 9, 10, 11, 12, 18, 21,
    28, 32, 35, 37, 44, 52, 71, 72, 74,
    82, 83, 86, 88, 89, 90, 92, 95, 96,
    98, 99, 102, 173, 196, 199; see also
    Chronic stress
Loneliness, 18, 64, 80, 144, 146, 147,
    148, 149, 150, 151, 152, 153, 154,
    155, 156, 157, 158
Love, 95

Marital conflict, 31, 34
Marital distress, 21, 44
Marital satisfaction, 38, 161
Marriage, 14
Mental health, 30
Mood, 49, 54, 55, 56
Mortality, 30
Myocardial infarction, 179

Nonverbal behavior, 41, 43, 108, 110

Older adults, 10, 124, 131, 134, 135,
    136, 137, 138
Openers, 155
Organizations
    Religious, 100
    Work, 100

Personality, 33, 41, 49, 58, 63, 91, 119,
    129, 157, 186, 188
Postpartum depression, 177; see also
    Depression
Pregnancy, teenage, 92
Pressure cooker effect, 12
Privacy, 124
Psychotherapy, 70

Quality of relationships, 66, 68, 81

Rehabilitation, 13
Relationship dissolution, 198
Rhetorical theory, 3
Rochester Interaction Record (RIR),
    28, see also Iowa Communication
    Record
Role conflict, 163, 165, 168, 170, 172
Romantic couples, 56f
Rumination, 54

Self-disclosure, 5, 9, 54, 86, 91, 106,
    110, 111, 112, 113, 114, 115, 116,
    117, 118, 143, 148, 149, 150, 153,
    155, 157
Self-esteem, 31, 33, 54, 64, 85, 92, 93,
    97, 127, 130, 178
Social comparison, 85
Social Network List (SNL), 174
Social networks, 11, 12, 16, 20, 73, 87,
    91, 96, 97, 98, 100, 101, 120, 121,
    124, 132, 141, 142, 144, 145, 147,
    153, 174, 185, 186, 190, 192, 193,
    197, 200, 201, 214
    Density of, 16, 141, 150, 174
Social Provisions Scale (SPS), 36, 42,
    177, 178, 180, 183
Social Support Questionnaire (SSQ),
    181, 183
Social support,
    Dilemmas of, 106f
    Mobilizing, 83ff, 87, 91, 96; see also
        Comforting, Cheering up,
        Interactive coping, Transactions of
        social support
    Seeking, 104f
Strangers, 43, 143
Stress, see Chronic stress, Daily hassles,
    Life stress, War stress
Stroke patients, 137

Sympathy, 19, 57
Systems approach, 122

Thought listing technique, 45
Transactions of social support, 1, 3, 6ff,
    11, 13–14, 15ff, 20, 31, 32, 47ff

Ventilation, 19, 21

War stress, 13
Weak ties, 18, 99, 193
Widowhood, *see* Bereavement